PR

HOME MENDING MADE EASY

By

MARY BROOKS PICKEN

With Illustrations by

C. FLORENCE VALENTINE

and

PATRICIA LINGANE ROWE

1946

ODHAMS PRESS LTD., LONG ACRE, W.C.2

British Library Cataloguing-in-Publication Data
A catalogue record for this book is available from the
British Library

Sewing

Sewing is the craft of fastening or attaching objects using stitches made with a needle and thread. Sewing is one of the oldest of the textile arts, arising in the Palaeolithic era. Before the invention of spinning yarn or weaving fabric, archaeologists believe Stone Age people across Europe and Asia sewed fur and skin clothing using bone, antler or ivory needles and 'thread' made of various animal body parts including sinew, catgut, and veins. 'Needlework' is a broad term for all the handicrafts of decorative sewing and textile arts, encompassing anything that uses a needle for construction. The definition may expand to include related textile crafts such as a crochet hook (using a type of needle with a hook at one end used to draw thread through knotted loops) or tatting shuttles (which facilitate tatting by holding a length of wound thread and guiding it through loops to make the requisite knots).

Although usually associated with clothing and household linens, sewing is used in a variety of crafts and industries, including shoemaking, upholstery, sail-making, bookbinding and the manufacturing of some kinds of sporting goods. Sewing is the fundamental process underlying a variety of textile arts and crafts, including embroidery, tapestry, quilting, appliqué and patchwork. Sewers working on a simple pattern need only a few sewing tools: measuring tape, needle, thread, cloth, and sewing shears. More complex patterns done on a sewing machine may only need a few more simple tools to get the job done, but there are an ever-growing variety of helpful sewing aids available, such as presser foot attachments for sewing ruffles, or hem repair glue. Sewing machines are now made for a broad range of specialised sewing purposes, such as quilting machines, computerized machines for embroidery, and various sergers for finishing raw edges of fabric.

During the Middle Ages, Europeans who could afford it employed seamstresses and tailors. Sewing for the most part was a woman's occupation, and most sewing before the nineteenth century was for practical purposes. Clothing was an expensive investment for most people, and women had an important role in extending the longevity of items of clothing. Clothing that was faded would be turned inside-out so that it could continue to be worn, and sometimes had to be taken apart and reassembled in order to suit this purpose. Once clothing became so worn or torn that it could no longer be used, it would be further taken apart and made into quilts, or other coverings. The many steps involved in making clothing from scratch (weaving, pattern making, cutting, alterations, and so forth) meant that women often bartered their expertise in a particular skill with one another. Decorative needlework such as embroidery was a valued skill, and young women with the time and means would practise to build their skill in this area. From the Middle Ages to the seventeenth century, sewing tools such as needles, pins and pincushions were included in the trousseaus of many European brides.

The Industrial Revolution (1760-1840) shifted the production of textiles from the household to the mills. The world's first sewing machine was patented in 1790 by Thomas Saint, and by the early 1840s, other early sewing machines began to appear. Barthélemy Thimonnier introduced a simple sewing machine in 1841 to produce military uniforms for France's army; but shortly afterward, a mob of tailors broke into Thimonnier's shop and threw the machines out of the windows, believing the machines would put them out of work! By the 1850s, Isaac Singer developed the first sewing machines that could operate quickly and accurately - surpassing the productivity of a seamstress or tailor sewing by hand.

While much clothing was still produced at home by female members of the family, more and more ready-made clothes for the middle classes were being produced with sewing machines. Textile sweatshops full of poorly paid sewing machine operators grew into entire business districts in large cities like London and New York City. To further support the industry, piece work was done for little money by women living in slums. Needlework was one of the few occupations considered acceptable for women, but it did not pay a living wage. Women doing piece work from home often worked fourteen hour days to earn enough to support themselves, sometimes by renting sewing machines that they could not afford to buy. Contrastingly, it was also during this period that well-respected tailors became associated with high-end clothing.

In London, their status grew out of the dandy trend of the early nineteenth century, when new tailor shops were established around Savile Row. These shops acquired a reputation for sewing high-quality handmade clothing in the style of the latest British fashions, as well as more classic styles. The boutique culture of Carnaby Street was absorbed by Savile Row tailors during the late twentieth century, ensuring the continued flourishing of Savile Row's businesses. Sewing underwent further developments during the twentieth century; and as sewing machines became more affordable to the working class, demand for sewing patterns grew. People had become accustomed to seeing the latest fashions in periodicals during the late nineteenth and early twentieth century, increasing demand for sewing patterns yet more. American tailor and manufacturer Ebenezer Butterick met the demand with paper patterns that could be traced and used by home sewers. The patterns, sold in small packets, became wildly popular, and several pattern companies soon established themselves. Women's magazines also carried sewing patterns, and continued to do so for much of the twentieth century.

This practice declined during the last decades of the twentieth century, when ready-made clothing became a necessity as women (and men) joined the paid workforce, working longer hours in larger numbers, leaving them with less time to sew, if indeed they had an interest. Today, the low price of ready-made clothing in shops means that home sewing is confined largely to hobbyists in Western countries. It can be a thoroughly enjoyable means of creative expression however, incorporating designs from the very simplest pieces, to complex works of engineering. We hope that the current reader is inspired by this book to try some sewing of their own! Enjoy.

A well-stocked work box; a good light and
a comfortable chair make mending hours
a pleasure and garments take new life

PREFACE

PRACTICAL HOME MENDING MADE EASY really combines two books. The first is strictly mending, which means darning, reinforcing, re-sewing, repairing fabric. Whether or not you have ever sewn before, if you master the essential stitches, seams and finishes given here, you should be able to *mend* any type of garment. Then, once you have mastered fabric mending completely, you are ready for another whole book — the pages of refashioning and re-furbishing. With the ideas presented there you should be able to rejuvenate any garment in your wardrobe by eliminating worn or out-of-fashion parts, adding appropriate and practical material to what you have, combining two old garments to make one new outfit, and using tissue-paper patterns to advantage in refashioning your wardrobe.

If you are a business girl with hardly time to repair that broken shoulder strap or straighten that drooping hem, this book will show you how to use odd moments for your repairing and still do a job you needn't be ashamed of.

If you are a little girl just learning to handle needle and thread, you can be a life-saver to a busy mother by learning to mend by the easy ways shown in this book. And, who knows, maybe the bright ideas you put into perking up your pet party dress will make you a famous designer some day.

If you are a big girl with a new husband's shirts to take care of, you'll find the answers to some baffling questions right here, and your alertness to his material needs is sure to make a real hit with him.

If you are a favourite grandma with the responsibility for taking care of play clothes, renewing little knee parts, sewing on buttons and patching sleeping suits, doubtless a few of the new wrinkles presented here will speed your work.

If you're a veteran housekeeper, you already know how many, many jobs of mending turn up every day, and you'll welcome the varied time-saving repair tips in these pages.

If you are a wife with a husband with heavy work clothes to mend, this is the place for you to find how to stitch in new wear and strength with every patch and darn and how to make last year's dress like new for this.

If you are a teacher with the problem of teaching fabric repair and conservation, this book will prove a boon because the subject is covered from A to Z and is arranged for easy use in classrooms, as well as for quick reference.

A mere man? Yes—the book is for you, too. You needn't master all the information in it, but if you concentrate on a few essential pages and become expert in button sewing, patching and darning—and you can—you will have the admiration of all your girl and women friends, and be as independent as you please.

PRACTICAL HOME MENDING MADE EASY is for you—and you—and you.

You furnish the raw materials from your torn towels, split sheets, and shirts, worn woollens, and still-good-but-out-of-style dresses. Then your raw materials and your efforts, plus this book and the salvage secrets it supplies, will add up to new life for your valuable but vanishing wardrobe, new clothes for you and your family, and money in your pocket.

CONTENTS

V

vii

viii

THE
MENDING BASKET

*Needles of all kinds and sizes, including crewel and
  darning needles.*
Cotton in all colours and thicknesses.
Good quality pins (in two sizes).
A fine steel crochet hook.
Bias binding, tapes and edgings.
Black and white tacking thread, darning and linen threads.
Coloured silks, and buttonhole threads.
Wool for socks and jumpers.
Ribbons and laces for lingerie.
Elastic in all widths.
Linen, bone and pearl buttons in various sizes.
A thimble that is comfy to wear.
A medium sized pair of scissors and a tiny pair.
Ruler and a tape measure.
Tracing wheel, chalk and darning egg.
Snap fasteners, hooks and eyes, and zippers.
Mending tape and scraps for patching.

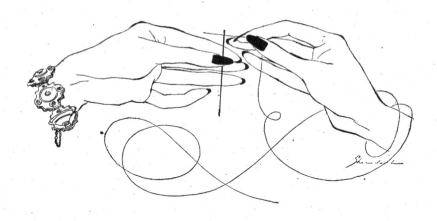

MEND FOR PLEASURE AND ECONOMY

WHEN FABRIC was very precious—woven as it was on hand looms, about one quarter yard a day—it was prized so highly that as it was worn or used, every thin place was watched and mended or rewoven at once. Throughout the ages, mending has kept woman's hands busy while her sweetheart has read aloud or spoken words of love to her. Even a half-century ago, mending was considered an art to be proud of when beautifully accomplished.

Mending embraces both reinforcing and patching. Patching should be necessary only if a fabric is torn beyond the possibility of mending otherwise, or if reinforcing has been unavoidably delayed too long. Thin places in fabric should be reinforced rather than patched. This means that one must watch for thin places and add reinforcement to the wrong side of the garment, or supporting stitches, when possible, so that the thin places will not become holes and thus require patches. Never mend or patch fabric that is too tender to hold your stitches.

An old adage is, " A patch beside a patch is neighbourly; a patch upon a patch, beggarly." When you patch, always use a piece of fabric of a weight and strength sufficient to last through the remaining life of the garment itself. Never use a fabric that will wear out before the garment does and thus have to "patch a patch." Every person —girl, boy, woman, man—should learn to mend fabric, because there are times when such mending is necessary for everybody.

It is an interesting thing to observe that, as a rule, the poorer people are, the less they mend and, consequently, the less they have, while the better circumstances of a family, the more mending you will find is done. Everything is kept in immediate repair. Nothing is allowed to go beyond that needed "stitch in time." Therefore, the life of clothes, the life of household linens, the life of all fabrics, is prolonged, and articles do not need so much replacement.

Pride in mending—the urge to do it—appreciation of it—are things to cultivate. It will bring much pleasure, save many a shilling, and give a certain satisfaction that nothing else quite equals.

Mend in time; patch to a purpose; reinforce for strength and take care with all.

TO MEND, YOU NEED—

To Proceed Slowly. Notice the thin place, or the tear, or the lost button the night before—not when you are dressing hurriedly in the morning. Mending cannot be rushed; rather, you need to proceed slowly. It can be very enjoyable if you take time to do it without a sense of hurried urgency. You can be proud of the ability to prolong the life of something you have enjoyed owning and wearing. It isn't worth doing at all if you resent the time it takes, for when you have mended hurriedly, you have not mended well.

If you have a favourite radio programme, plan your mending for that time. You will enjoy the programme more, accomplish something with your hands while you are listening, and be able to relax and mend at leisure, thus benefiting in several ways

Materials for Mending. Every woman should have an attractive box or work basket for things that need mending, all ready for deliberate stitches. It is surprising how much one can do if the work is prepared with matching thread, needles of the right sizes—all the necessary equipment—when an opportunity presents itself.

If you are a lap mender, buy for yourself a small, light-weight breadboard. One that costs only a few pence will do. Keep this with your sewing equipment.

Pins and Needles. Have a box of good quality pins and two or three papers of needles in an assortment of sizes—fine ones, numbers eight to ten—fine to large, eight to three—as well as a package of assorted sizes of crewel and darning needles. You'll need a fine steel crochet hook for picking up a thread, for working round corners, for pulling a thread through.

Threads and Yarn. When you buy a dress or suit, buy a spool of thread and a short roll of seam binding of the same colour and have these at hand for repair work. Don't have to hunt for them so that often, in desperation, you use the wrong thread to make emergency stitches that will show and thus rebuke you continually. Sometimes it is well to buy a box of small spools of assorted colours.

Buy darning threads in colours to match your stockings. Have an assortment of fine and coarse white thread, numbers one hundred, eighty, sixty, forty and twenty-four; a spool of mercerized thread in white, black and whatever colours you wear—grey, navy, brown, red, green; and a spool of each colour in silk. For wool socks and sweaters have appropriate yarns for mending.

For lingerie mending, have threads, ribbons, elastic, georgette in the right colours for your lingerie. Laces need to be bought for special mending jobs, but save each little scrap to appliqué over a tear or thin spot.

For mending for men—have buttonhole twist in colours to match suits. Have strong cotton thread and carpet thread for sewing buttons on overcoats. Have fine wool yarn at hand for mending thin places in suits and wool socks and, by all means, have darning cottons to match socks. If your husband wears tailor-made clothes, ask the tailor to give you some of the scraps of the suit and lining that you can use for mending.

Mending Essentials. Have a thimble that is comfortable to wear, a medium-sized pair of scissors and a tiny pair just to snip threads. Have a darning form or egg and an embroidery hoop for machine darning. You will also find it handy to have a 6-in. ruler, a longer ruler, an accurate tape measure, a tracing wheel, and chalk for accuracy in your work. Keep at hand some scraps of net and chiffon and a light-weight fabric for reinforcements. Save scraps from garments that are made or altered to use when a piece of mending material is required.

Notions. Pieces of seaming ribbon (binding), bias binding, braids, edgings, twilled tapes—all the fabric notions that make mending easy—also buttons, hooks and eyes, snap fasteners, zippers, elastic and all the other things that your mending requires. Keep all of these in a drawer in your very nice chest or work basket so that you don't have to hunt for them, perhaps annoy others and frequently, thereby, lose the urge to mend. That urge is something to capture, like a moment of bliss. Take advantage of it when it comes, and you will always have your mending done. Foster your own pride in the mending you do. There is a justifiable smugness about "stitches in time."

Dress Shields. Buy dress shields when your garments are new and thus protect them from the beginning. Launder shields frequently and change them often. Changing shields is far easier than reclaiming a dress stained by perspiration.

IN ADDITION TO MENDING with needle and thread, and applying patches, reinforcements, or reinforcing stitches, modern science has given us many new mending methods. Now we have also liquid thread, rubber cement, household cement, adhesive tape, all of which can be used for mending.

Mending Liquid. There is available a liquid glue that is very practical in many instances. One brand is called Liquid Thread. It is best to see, if possible, a demonstration of this type of mending liquid at your local store and follow instructions given with the purchase. This is good for putting up hems in very firm fabrics, for repairing the hem in men's trousers, for putting patches on firm fabrics. Read the directions carefully and if this method of mending appeals to you, learn to be expert in doing it. Practise using it on a scrap of material until you know how to use it perfectly.

Mending Tape. There is a mending tape that has the mending liquid applied to it and this you simply press over the hole or on the hem. Here again, see a demonstration, if possible, read the instruction booklet and know how to apply the tape correctly to get the results you want.

Rubber Tissue. There is a type of rubber tissue which you usually can buy in strips that you can press into the hems of trousers or skirts to hold them in place. Follow instructions that come with the product so that you get the best possible results.

To Press As You Sew or Mend. To sew well you need to be as loyal to your ironing board, iron and press cloths as you are to the sewing machine, sharp scissors and shears. Good sewing and good mending cannot be done without pressing throughout the process. Seams and edges generally require pressing before they are mended, and any new seam should be pressed before it joins another.

Throughout this book we ask you to press and iron. Learn the difference between pressing and ironing, and make it a habit to use the method that your fabric requires. See the section *Let's Clean It*, page 132, for directions.

How to Keep Materials for Patching and Mending. To have materials conveniently at hand for darning and mending is important. Not only threads, but scraps for patching should be in order so that time will not be wasted.

The form such order takes depends on the space available and the work to be done. The usual mixed collection of materials in a scrap bag may be satisfactory if there is only a little mending, but sorted scraps are a boon to mending.

Labelled boxes on the top shelves in the linen closet have answered one woman's problem for keeping different kinds of scraps separate and easily available. Wool, Coloured Cottons, White Goods, Lace, Miscellaneous, Findings, are the labels.

A similar plan is to make drawstring bags in different sizes. Perhaps eight, varying in size from 8 ins. by 12 ins. to 16 ins. by 27 ins. Sew a scrap of wool on one, a scrap of coloured cotton on another, a bit of lace on a third and so on. Bags take up less room than boxes and may be stuffed to hold more. Keep them in a large scrap bag, or better still, in a chest, a section of a window seat or in a deep drawer.

To Save Fabrics. Some materials and laces are likely to turn yellow or tarnish unless precautions are taken. Wrap white lace or fine white fabrics in blue tissue paper, or in old muslin dipped in strong blueing. Cover metallic fabrics with black tissue paper.

Miscellaneous Scraps. Save scraps of *canvas* to mend awnings and to make chair cushions, soles for house slippers, children's book covers and aprons for gardening. Pieces of American cloth can be used in practically the same way as canvas, and in addition, will make washable toys, place mats, or belts for children's clothes.

Rip old felt hats, particularly coloured ones, for trimmings for other hats, to make purses, mend bedroom slippers, to make appliqué patches for knit garments, novel lapel and hat pins, and for soft buttons for infants' sweaters. Use felt scraps, too, for table mats, or glue them to the bottoms of tiles, boxes and lamp bases to protect tables.

To obtain larger pieces of felt from an old hat, soak or wash it in warm water. This will usually remove the dressing and permit the hat to be flattened out and pressed smooth.

Scraps of *kid* and *leather* from old purses and gloves and chair seats should be kept for mending or palming gloves, for binding the edges of boys' jacket pockets, making novelties, to lengthen a belt, or cover buttons.

Save old bathroom curtains and make aprons, bibs and place mats. Line a bathing suit bag or a toilet bag.

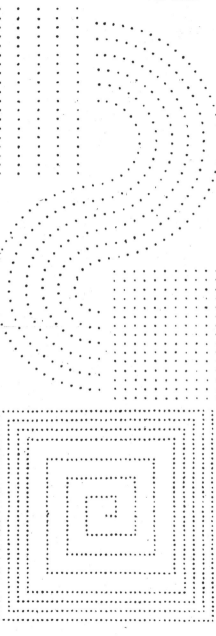

YOUR SEWING MACHINE

THE MODERN SEWING MACHINE is a marvel of ingenuity and convenience. Be sure that you get the most in performance from your machine by giving it the care it deserves and by understanding all its parts and attachments. If you have not been using all its attachments or if you don't know how to care for it, sit down for an hour with the instruction book that the manufacturer provided with your machine and learn the names and function of all the parts and try out each one of the attachments. In the long run it will save your time and improve your work to do this. If you have any difficulty, go to the local sewing-machine shop and get the help of the instructors. They are there to serve you and you will find them most co-operative.

Learn to stitch straight, using a side of the presser foot to guide you. Practise on paper, stitching straight parallel rows, circles and curves, square turns at corners. Pivot on the needle at corners, lifting the presser foot to do so. When you can do these things perfectly, your work will reward you by its neat and professional finish.

How to Sit at the Machine. Have a chair or stool of a comfortable height. For your spine's sake sit straight on it and reasonably far back. Draw the chair up close enough to the machine so that you needn't reach out too far or lean over to see what you are doing. Sit with your nose directly in line with the needle bar and be sure you have good light to work by. In this way you should be able to do your work efficiently and without fatigue.

Making the Machine Ready. Keep your machine oiled and clean. Before beginning stitching, wipe the head and the table with a clean piece of cheesecloth so that your fabric will not be soiled by oil or dust. After doing a big job of sewing, always clean the machine of fluff, then oil it. Leave a scrap of fabric under the presser foot to catch any oil that might drip down. Before beginning to sew next time stitch on this piece of fabric to make sure that any surplus oil is out, before beginning your sewing.

Be sure that the presser foot is securely fastened in place and properly adjusted. If it is not, your needle may break or the thread may be cut repeatedly.

Use needles of the right size for the work in hand. If you are working on large or heavy pieces, set a card table by the machine to hold the fabric and relieve the pull on the needle. Blunt needles should be replaced at once, as they also may break the thread, cause skipped stitches or puckered fabric.

Threading the Machine. Thread the machine with the same thread top and bottom, using one shade darker than the fabric or, if you are using a print, match the thread to the background. Drop the needle down just far enough to pick up the bobbin thread, bring it up, and draw both top and bottom threads out and back under the presser foot ready to stitch.

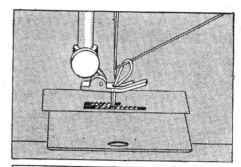

It is equally important to use thread that is correct for the fabric as well as to have a needle that is suitable in size for the thread and fabric you are using. A thread that is too fine or too coarse will also cause the thread to break or the fabric to pucker.

Test the stitch on a scrap of fabric before you begin, to see that the length is correct, the tension right, the needle secure, so that there will not be interruptions as you work. If you need to adjust the tension, follow the directions in your machine instruction book. Having tensions incorrectly adjusted may cause the thread to break either at the needle or at the bobbin or may pucker the stitching, so check this before starting to work. Test tensions by pulling both needle and bobbin threads together. If they do not pull evenly, adjust the one that seems to be too tight or too loose.

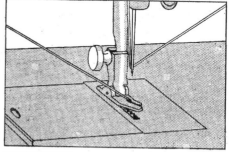

Be sure that you have your machine threaded correctly. If you experience difficulty with the thread breaking, don't immediately jump to the conclusion that the tension is wrong. Frequently, inexperienced workers try to adjust the tension when the trouble is really caused by not having the machine threaded correctly. Consult your instruction book if you are not sure.

Basting by Machine. This saves time on wash garments with long seams. Hold the two thicknesses flat and smooth and use your machine's longest stitch. Loosen the top tension to start.

To Terminate Machine Stitching. Pivot and turn or reverse your stitching and stitch back for a distance of a half-dozen stitches, or pull the top thread end through to the wrong side and tie it to the bobbin thread. When terminating your stitching, lift the thread lever up to its highest point. Then use the little cutting blade on your machine for your threads. This ensures leaving a length of thread that will not pull out of the machine needle when you begin stitching again.

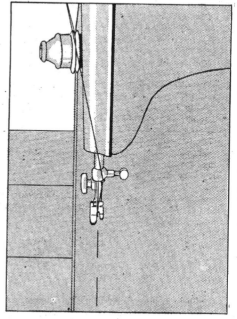

KNOW YOUR FABRIC

THE FIVE FIBRES that we have to work with in fabrics are—cotton, rayon, linen, silk and wool. Each has its own peculiar characteristics. If we take the trouble to know these, just as we know the prejudices, peculiarities, likes and dislikes of people, we will be able to get along with them better.

. All fabrics have certain things in common; for example, most of them are better when cut on the thread with regard to the way they are woven, their definite warp and woof, or lengthwise and widthwise threads. If we cut with the grain, a garment will fit better, keep shape longer and be more comfortable. Cottons, rayons and silks usually will tear easily. Silk taffeta will tear across the width but not on the lengthwise of the material. Linens and woollens should have a thread pulled and be cut on the thread, either on the widthwise or the lengthwise grain of the material.

Cottons and rayons may be pinned and do not always require basting, but woollens should always be basted. This is because there is a give that occurs even under the presser foot so that the top edge crowds ahead and tightens if it is not basted. Closely woven silk must always be basted, because one edge might slip and cause puckered seams. Any one who is not thoroughly experienced in handling fabrics should pin and then baste all seams and all edges so that the thicknesses of material go together perfectly and the joining seam is as inconspicuous as possible. Never begrudge the time spent in basting. You get your reward over and over again in the appearance of the finished garment.

Cotton and linen are vegetable fibres; silk and wool are animal fibres; and rayon is a man-made fibre from vegetable material. The vegetable fibres can stand the most heat in washing and pressing; animal fibres, a little less; and the man-made fibre, very little heat. Remember this as you work.

Cottons, linens and woollens require constant moisture in pressing; silks and rayons, very little, if any. Sometimes just a pressing cloth or tissue paper between them and the iron is all that is necessary. Avoid hot irons on silks and rayons. Never press woollens without a moist cloth between the iron and the fabric. Press all fabric, when possible, from the wrong side so as to keep the right side looking new.

Cottons and linens have a natural affinity and woollens, silks and rayons make harmonious unions, but rarely do you use silk and cotton together or linen and wool. True, these fibres are often woven together satisfactorily, but rarely are they combined together in a garment.

However, organdie can be combined with silk or velvet readily. Linen lace is often used on velvet. Cotton eyelet embroidery is often combined with silk or rayon in a dress. Crisp, sheer cotton fabrics and lace may be used with silk or rayon, even with linen, in a completely satisfactory way. There are certain traditions about the use of fabrics that the man-made fibre—rayon—has broken down in many instances. Rayon, for example, is now made to emulate wool and is used with wool. Much rayon is used to give body to silk where weighting was formerly used.

If you know the different characteristics of the fibres and what your fabric consists of—whether it is twenty per cent rayon and eighty per cent wool, or forty per cent cotton and sixty per cent rayon—and if you know how to treat all fibres, then you will know how to handle any fabric satisfactorily.

There are old rules that are just as good today as the day they were made. For example, in making garments, press—don't iron. Always press one seam before it joins another.

Blend your seam edges together so that they are of an equal length—one no tighter than the other. Be generous in your seam widths—never skimpy.

Never stitch a seam tightly. Adjust the length of the stitch on your machine to the thickness of your fabric so that it is of an easy length—not so short as to be tight nor so long as to make an open seam. Test your stitch on a scrap of the fabric before you make a seam and then you will be sure to have it the correct length.

Cut, pin, baste, and stitch with care—with respect for the fabric and pride for the article you are making.

How to Tell the Fibre of Your Fabric. If you are in doubt as to what the fabric is; if, perhaps, you've had it since long before the days of specific labelling, there are several simple tests you can make to distinguish between cotton, rayon, linen, silk and wool. It is difficult to tell just by looking at the fabric in these days of mixed fibres—cotton finished as linen, rayons like wool, and so on. You'll be able to see the difference best if you try the following tests first on scraps of fabric you are sure of—a pure silk, pure wool, etc. Then when you see how they react to the tests, try other scraps of fabric you aren't sure of.

The Burning Test. Cut a scrap from the fabric you want to test and touch a match to it. Pure silk burns rapidly and steadily with a characteristic odour (since it is an animal fibre) of burning hair. It is almost completely consumed except for a few tiny globules like those left when hair is burned. If the silk is weighted, it burns slowly and curls at the edges of the burn and leaves a slight gritty ash. Rayon burns with an odour of burning paper. It burns with a quick flame, but the fabric is consumed more slowly than silk and a residue of carbon ash is left. The acetate type seems to melt rather than burn and leaves a hard globule. Cotton also smells like burning paper, but the flame sputters and smothers. The burning is slower than with rayon, and the flame seems to be held in the charred and smouldering fabric ends. Wool, like silk, burns with a burnt-hair odour, so that you can distinguish it from rough-finished rayon or cotton. Linen burns more quickly than cotton.

Caustic Soda Test. To determine whether a wool fabric has any cotton in it, drop some caustic soda on a scrap. The wool will be completely dissolved, and any cotton present will be left.

Water Test. You can tell whether silk has been sized by washing or dropping water on a scrap of it. The water will leave a spot where it has dropped, or, if you wash the whole piece, the sizing will come out and cloud the water. Rayon, when wet, has an unmistakable feel—rather gummy. The fibres are weak when wet and it dries slowly, whereas silk dries quickly. The acetate rayons absorb very little water and feel dry almost as soon as they are out of the water.

To tell linen from cotton, drop a drop of water on the fabric. Cotton will hold the drop of water intact for a moment before it spreads slowly. On linen, the drop spreads and is quickly absorbed.

Oil or Glycerine Test. This also helps you to distinguish linen from cotton. Oil or glycerine dropped on linen makes a spot that is translucent when held up to the light. On cotton, the spot remains opaque.

Ink Test. This helps to tell whether the fabric is pure linen or a mixture of cotton and linen. Drop ink on a scrap and watch it spread. If it spreads quickly and evenly, the fabric is all linen. If it spreads further on some threads than on others adjoining, there is probably cotton in the fabric.

Thumbnail Test. Rayon can sometimes be identified by rubbing a scrap of the fabric with the thumbnail or a coin. The smoothness of rayon fibres may allow the threads to slip or separate under this test more easily than other fibres.

Ravel Test. Ravel a thread of the fabric to compare with one you are sure of. Cotton fibres are short and may be a bit fuzzy. Linen fibres are longer, more lustrous and have a woody quality. Both rayon and silk have a lustre that shows up against wool, and cotton, as compared with wool, lacks spring and the strong hairy feel of wool. Rayon yarns, besides having a lustre, feel cool and slippery in comparison with other fibres.

Whiteness. White rayon remains permanently white, while other white fabrics yellow in time unless cared for continually. If an old blouse, for instance, hasn't yellowed after years of disuse, it is rayon.

New Fibres. In addition to fabrics currently available, others are being introduced as new fibres are made practical for textiles. Still others are now in the experimental stage and show interesting promise.

Since textiles are in this state of change, it is not possible to give definite rules for handling all of them. There are entirely new yards in some materials, often a blending of several kinds of fibres in one yarn, and new finishes and weaves to cope with. Until textiles become more stable, informative labels are more important than ever and should be followed for handling all fabrics.

★   ★   ★

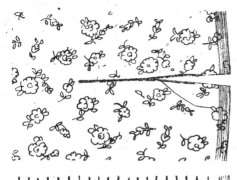

KNOW HOW TO

IN ORDER TO USE fabric successfully, you must understand its construction and its qualities. Some fabrics are light and delicate, some heavy and bulky, some frail or loosely woven and likely to ravel, others firm and strong. You need to know, in considering refashioning or adding new material to what you have, whether the fabric you are handling will drape, gather, hold a pleat, or tailor attractively.

Fabric Grain. It is well worth knowing about this. A loom is threaded for weaving with the warp or lengthwise threads. The woof or crosswise threads are carried by the shuttle back and forth over and under the warp threads. This back and forth weaving provides a finish on each edge called the selvedge which, because of the turn, is often drawn a little more tightly than the rest of the fabric.

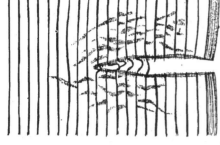

To Cut or Tear Fabric. First clip the selvedge. Some fabrics tear readily, and it is wise to tear when you can. Any fabric such as percale, in which the warp and woof threads are of the same or even weight and strength, may be torn rather than cut. After clipping the selvedge, hold firmly at each side of the clipped place and tear quickly. This will break the fabric threads without pulling them. Do not, however, attempt to tear a corded fabric. Note what happens as the strong threads resist breaking.

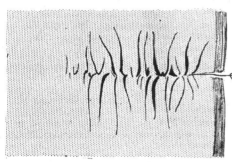

To cut a true line, pull out a thread and cut on this thread line. To do this, clip the selvedge; with a pin, pick up one crosswise thread and, holding it with your thumb and forefinger, pull it gently while you ease the fabric along with the other hand. The thread may break several times in the process of pulling it out, but pick it up again with the pin and continue pulling until you complete the line. Then cut on this line, proceeding slowly. For best results, work on a flat surface.

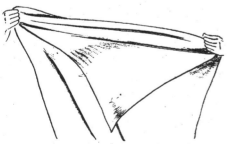

Straightening Fabric. Though fabric is woven straight, the processes through which it goes to be printed, finished, and rolled often pull it out of line. In such a case, straighten your fabric before cutting. To do this, take the piece you have torn or cut on a thread, grasp the edges at opposite sides, and stretch the fabric diagonally, pulling back and forth. Do this along the entire length of the piece. If it is still not straight, take it to the ironing board, bring the two crosswise sides together and press, working towards the part

HANDLE FABRIC

that is out of line.   This takes a little time, but it pays dividends in the long run, for fabric that is not straight when cut will not make satisfactory garments, however good the sewing.

Cutting on the Bias. You often need to use facings, bindings, and band trimmings cut on the bias; that is, on the true diagonal of the fabric grain. To get this true bias, first straighten the fabric. Turn back one corner so that the selvedge or lengthwise edge of the corner lies exactly on the line of a widthwise thread of the under part.   Crease the fold where the corner turns back, thus marking a true bias. Measure from this crease the width you want your bias strip to be, and mark the width at three or four places with chalk   Draw a line through these marks, using chalk and a ruler.   Repeat the procedure for the next strip, using the chalk line as the base. and so on until you have enough bias strips marked. Then cut on the marked lines.

To Join Bias Pieces. Always join bias ends on the true lengthwise or widthwise grain. Lay the right sides together and make the seam so that, when it is pressed open, the grain in the two pieces will be the same. We show several types of bias joinings here to illustrate how the ends are placed. This is important, for pieces that do not match in grain will not be satisfactory.

Mark a Bias Tube to Save Piecing. When a long strip of bias must be made from small pieces of fabric, mark the bias lines and join the two edges of the fabric to form a tube, as shown. Slip one marked line down until one width of bias extends beyond each end of the tube; then stitch the edges together, being sure that the marked bias lines meet at the seam.   Start cutting on the marked line at one end and cut along continuously until the entire tube has been cut into one long strip.

Ready-made Bias Binding. Join such binding on the lengthwise grain of the fabric. Never stitch it straight across.   If you find you have to join pieces of binding in the process of applying it. stop a few inches from the end of your piece, stitch on another length, making a diagonal seam, snip off surplus ends, press the seam and the joining edge, and continue with your binding.

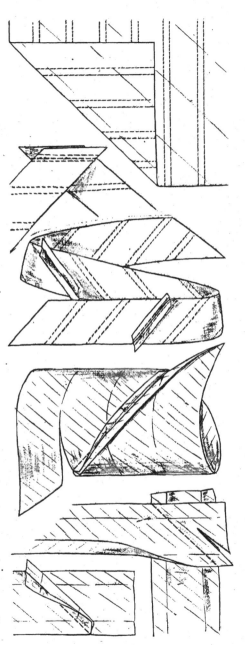

ESSENTIALS OF SEWING

Hand-Sewing. Use a thread from 20 ins. to 30 ins. long in your needle. The 30 ins. length is best, if it is to be doubled. Begin with a small knot in one end of the thread. Wind the thread around the tip of the forefinger and cross it, as shown; then with the thumb, roll the crossed end over the loop, and pull from the needle end to tighten the knot.

Hold the fabric in both hands for sewing and use both—one to smooth the fabric ahead of the needle, the other to handle the needle. Work on a table when possible, to protect the fabric, relieve your hands of weight and make for quicker work.

Begin with a knot for basting, gathering and shirring. Otherwise begin and end your stitching line with tiny back-stitches on the wrong side. Avoid knots that show or finishing-off stitches that will mar the uniformity of the line.

The drawings show stitches worked from right to left. Left-handed persons should, of course, work in the opposite direction. To see how this would look, hold the illustration in front of a pocket mirror, which will show the drawing in reverse as it would be done left-handed.

Threading Needle with Woollen Yarn. Two ways are shown here to thread a needle with a woollen thread without trying to put a fuzzy yarn end into the eye. In **A** the method is to catch the wool thread in a loop of ordinary sewing cotton and draw it through the eye. **B** shows the beginning of the second way. Turn back the yarn end and tighten the loop with the needle as shown, grasping the loop close to the needle with the fingernails. This flattens the loop so that it may be pressed through the eye as in **C**. The yarn ends do not separate when threaded this way.

Preparing for Seams. To make nice seams, always cut your fabric true so that your seams will be of an even width. Bring the two thicknesses of fabric exactly together, smoothing them together crosswise rather than lengthwise, so that the seam is smooth and even its full length. Coax the edge of the top piece lightly into place with the fingers as shown. Place the fabric flat on a table for pinning and basting. If you are new to handling fabric, always baste before stitching. If you are experienced, you may pin and stitch.

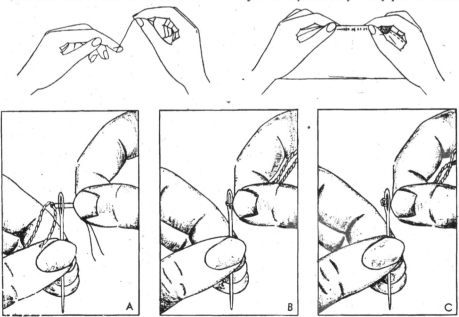

A   B   C

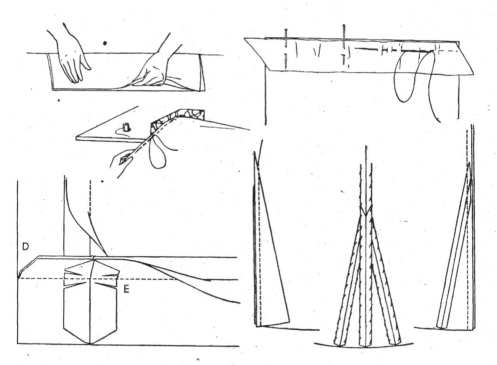

Use pins generously, placing them crosswise on the seam. In pinning, basting, and stitching seams, begin at the top of each seam—at the neck for a shoulder seam, at the underarm for the side seam of a blouse, and at the waistline for all skirt seams. Cut pattern notches carefully, and always put them together neatly in making a seam. When sewing firm fabrics, it is often convenient to pin one end to a covered brick or weight, so that the edge will be held evenly.

Joining Bias to Straight Edge. When a bias or even slightly bias edge is joined to a straight edge as in skirts, sleeves and godets, lay the bias edge on top and pin it to the straight edge. Then even-baste, easing in the fulness all along the seam so that there is no strain or stretch on the bias edge. Stitch and press the seam so that the joining appears as smooth as if the grain were the same on both sides.

Never cut off the end of a seam if one appears longer than the other. If you cut a garment correctly according to the pattern, all edges should come out even. The long edge should be eased in.

When you sew or stitch, use good thread that is right in colour and weight for the fabric.

Machine-stitch seams when possible. Use a stitch as short as practical for your purpose. Guide your work under the presser foot easily so that the seam will not tighten. If the fabric is an open weave, or soft, it may have a tendency to be delayed by the feed plate of the machine. With all such fabrics, place paper underneath the fabric and stitch through both the fabric and paper to insure a perfect stitching line. The needle usually will cut the paper so that it is a simple matter to pull it away.

Seams That Meet. Stitch the seam, remove basting, and press before joining the seam edge to another. Clip away surplus ends and corners as in **D**. In such a joining, clip seam edges above and below the stitching line, as in **E**, to give ease in the seam. Seams should give form, strength and weight to a garment; but should not appear bulky or break the flow of a line.

Piecing a Gored Skirt. Join small gores on a lengthwise thread. Make a straight even seam— and have the small piece long enough to extend beyond the seam line of skirt gore. Press seams open. Piecing seams is an art, one to learn and practise so that it will always be done to perfection.

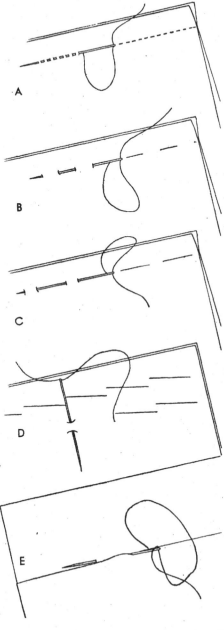

ESSENTIAL

A. Running-Stitch. This is perhaps the most elementary stitch in sewing. With your needle, pick up a tiny bit of the fabric, and continue putting the needle in and out until you have from three to six stitches on the needle. Pull the needle through. Repeat this throughout the length of the seam or darn. Practise to make the stitching line even and the stitches uniform. This is the basic stitch of darning, which is simply the weaving of running-stitches back and forth. Rows of running-stitches are placed up and down over a tear or weak spot, and then at right angles across it, the second set weaving over and under the first, as though duplicating the fabric threads.

B. Even-Basting. Basting is placing temporary stitches to hold fabric in place until permanent stitching is done. Even-basting is nothing more than long running-stitches. Put the needle in and out through the fabric, taking several stitches before pulling it through. Make the stitches $\frac{1}{4}$ in. long. A long needle is best for basting.

C. Uneven-Basting. This is a slight variation of even-basting. Take a fairly short stitch through the fabric and a long stitch on top. The top stitch may be as much as $\frac{1}{2}$ in. to 1 in. long and the under stitch about $\frac{1}{4}$ in. The advantage of this stitch is its speed. Otherwise work exactly as for basting, taking several stitches at once before pulling the needle through.

D. Diagonal-Basting. This stitch holds a little more strongly than either of the other basting-stitches, and prevents slipping if you are working with slippery or heavy fabrics. Take short stitches towards you through the fabric, long diagonal stitches on top, as shown in the illustration. The short crosswise stitch is $\frac{1}{8}$ in. to $\frac{3}{4}$ in. long; the diagonal stitches may be up to 3 ins. or 4 ins. long.

E Slip-Basting. This basting-stitch is used when you have to work from the right side of the fabric, as when matching plaids, stripes or fabrics with a definite design. The pieces of the fabric are laid flat, one edge turned under and brought over the other edge until the stripes or designs match. Pin the edges together. In order not to disturb the matching design, insert the needle into the folded edge and then work it invisibly in and out through the two pieces of fabric, taking

STITCHES

several stitches before pulling it through. On the wrong side the stitch will look like even-basting.

F. Back-Stitch. On the right side, this resembles machine-stitching. It is the most secure of hand-stitches. Put the needle through the fabric; half the length of the stitch back from where you brought it out, put it through again bringing it out beyond the last place. This results in a stitch twice as long underneath as on top. The stitch on top should be from 1/16 in. to ⅛ in. All rows of hand-stitching that are to be per-manent should begin and end with a back-stitch for strength. It is more easily made with a short needle.

G. Herringbone-Stitch. As a finish for seam edges, or bulky edges on which a hem turn would be clumsy, the herringbone-stitch is handy. Work back and forth across the edges, taking a tiny horizontal stitch first on one side and then on the other, as shown in the illustration. The resulting pattern looks like a series of inter-locked x's.

H. Combination-Stitch. When you need more strength than you get from a running-stitch and more speed than you get with back-stitch, combine the two by taking one back-stitch and several run-ning-stitches before pulling your needle through.

I. Overcasting. For fabrics that ravel easily or are bulky, this makes a flat, strong seam finish. Put the needle through from the underside, and carry the thread over the edge on a slant, as shown. Take several stitches at once before pulling your needle through. Be careful not to pull the thread so tight as to pucker the edge. In firm fabrics, make the stitches ⅛ in deep and a little wider apart than they are deep. In fabrics that ravel easily, make your stitches deeper and closer together

J. Oversewing. This is a secure stitch for joining two finished edges together so that the pieces open out flat with a practically invisible seam. It is useful for joining two selvedge edges or ribbons, or applying lace or insertions. Baste first to prevent slipping of the edges or fulling on one edge. Put the needle through from the under side and take a tiny stitch towards you. Do this over and over, the stitches very

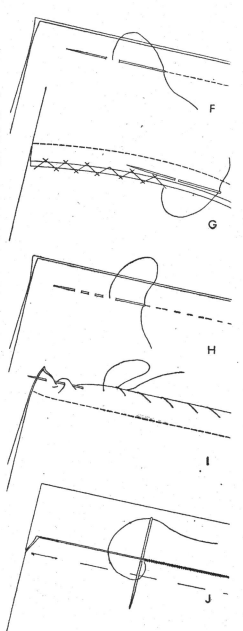

F

G

H

I

J

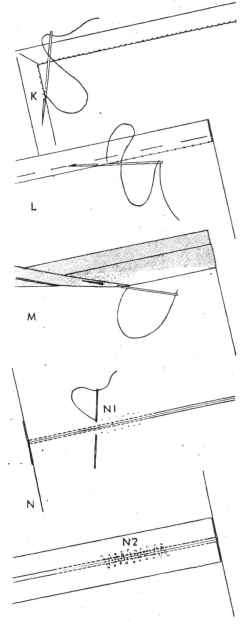

close together. The thread is carried over the edges as in overcasting, but much more finely and at much less of a slant

K. Hemming or Whipping. The most common way to hold a turned-under edge is to catch the needle through a few threads of the fabric and then through the creased edge of the hem, repeating this stitch the length of the hem. If the fabric is not too heavy, take two or three stitches at once before pulling the needle through. Practise doing this to get the stitches uniform and even in line.

L. Running-Hem. For table linens and stiff fabrics, this stitch is often preferred. Work towards yourself. With the needle, pick up a thread or two of the fabric; then put the needle under the hem and through to the wrong side. Continue doing this all along. The right side will look like a row of slanted stitches, the wrong side will have a series of tiny upright stitches. Also known as felling-stitch in men's tailoring

M. Slip-Stitch. This is a loose stitch concealed between two layers of fabric. Use it for a hem line when you do not need great strength and want the stitches to be invisible. Catch the needle in a thread of the fabric and then in the hem turn, keeping the stitches loose. Make them a little tighter if the fabric is quite heavy, to prevent pulling or sagging

N. Drawing-Stitch. This is useful for repairing broken stitches in a seam or for closing a straight cut or tear invisibly, where the fabric edges are not too firm. Work from the right side. Use a very fine needle and fine matching thread. Bring the needle from wrong side $\frac{1}{8}$ in. or $\frac{1}{4}$ in. from seam line. Insert point of needle very close to where it last came out as at **N1**. Hold the needle flat as if to split the fabric with the needle and take small running-stitches across the opening that only go through the wrong side of the fabric as at **N2**. Run the stitches diagonally across to the opposite side of the seam line. Continue to darn invisibly back and forth until the edges are joined together.

O. Fishbone-Stitch. This is a variation of the blanket-stitch that is ordinarily used in embroidery. This is made without the purled edge and is used to hold two edges together, as in the slash on page 48. Bring the needle through the two edges to be sewn together. Then take a diagonal stitch from one side towards yourself, as shown, bringing the needle out through the slit. Repeat on the other side of the line and continue alternating from side to side.

P. Rentering-Stitch. This is a stitch used by tailors to make a seam or piecing line inconspicuous. It is used chiefly on tweeds and other men's-wear fabrics. Double the fabric back from the seam on the right side and hold it firmly between thumb and forefinger. Using a fine thread of matching colour, stitch back and forth across the seam, placing the stitches as shown. Take a stitch across the seam through both of the doubled edges; then put the needle in close to where it came out and take another stitch across the seam, again picking up both doubled edges Always catch the fabric by just a single yarn and take the stitches as close to the seam as possible. The stitch should be small enough so that it is unseen. The stitches illustrated are greatly enlarged. Draw the thread tight. Scratch lightly over the seam with the needle to cover the stitching and then press.

Q. Stoating-Stitch. Used generally for repairing a cut or clean-edged tear in thick fabric such as felted fabrics or closely woven tweeds, this stitch is strong and concealed in the fabric so that it is invisible on the right side. Working from the wrong side, insert the needle into the thickness of the fabric, about 1/16 in. from the edge but not through to the right side. Run it through to the opposite side of the cut, keeping the needle in the centre of the fabric. Bring it out 1/16 in from the edge. Keep the needle straight and insert it again 1/16 in. from the first stitch so that the stitches seen on the wrong side will be slanted. Continue until cut is closed, drawing all stitches firmly.

R. Tailors' Tacks. These are used for marking pattern perforations or seam lines on two thicknesses of fabric where chalk marks or tracing wheel lines might not show or would be objectionable. They insure having both sides marked exactly alike. Lay the two layers of fabric flat and smooth with the pattern perforations, or pin marks, in the upper one. Use a double basting thread of a contrasting colour. Take a back-stitch in each perforation or on the seam line, leave a loose loop of thread and go on to the next perforation, or for 2 ins. or 3 ins., on the seam line. Take another back-stitch and continue. Clip the long stitches between the loops Pull the two thicknesses of fabric apart and clip the threads of the back-stitches as at **R1.**

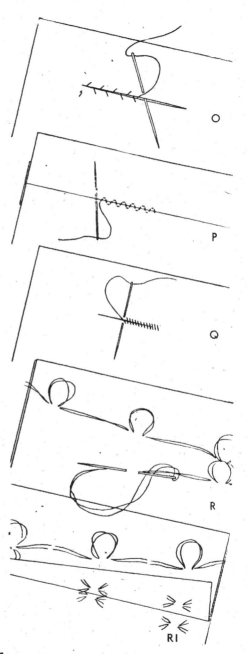

O

P

Q

R

R1

EMBROIDERY

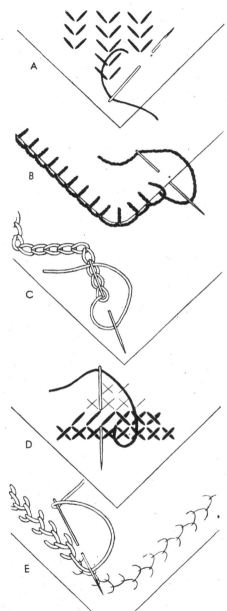

A. Arrowhead-Stitch. This is used for borders or for filling a surface. Begin by bringing the needle through from the wrong side. Then take a slanting stitch upward through the fabric, as shown. Insert the needle downward for the next stitch close to the middle hole and bring it out in line with the stitch, thus completing the arrowhead. Continue in this way until the row is finished. Then fasten your thread and begin over again at the top to make your next row of stitches.

B. Blanket-Stitch. This is a basic stitch from which many embroidery stitches and the buttonhole stitch developed. It is generally used on an edge, or along a line. Its main characteristic is the single purl, which is formed by bringing the needle out across the thread as shown. Take the stitches towards the edge, and hold the thread along the edge so that the needle crosses it when it is pulled through.

C. Chain-Stitch. Bring the needle through to the right side. Hold the thread with the thumb and take a stitch, as shown, so that the needle crosses the thread and forms a loop. Continue in this way until the chain is finished. This stitch is done with a firm twisted thread so that the loop is well formed. Practise to make the loops of equal size.

D. Cross-Stitch. Since the attractiveness of this stitch depends on its precision, many persons work it over canvas to make the stitches even. It can also be done on fabric by counting the fabric threads, or by use of a transfer pattern. The simplest way to get the effect of little squares is shown here. Work along a row, taking flat overcasting-stitches, then turn the work and make the stitches over the first row to complete the squares.

E. Feather-Stitch. This is the same idea as the blanket-stitch. Bring the needle out across the thread, but alternate from side to side of a line instead of working along an edge. A line may be marked by basting, creasing, or transferring a pattern to the fabric. A variation may be made by taking two or three stitches in downward line first at one side and then at the other. The effect may be varied by using different weights of thread, lengths of stitch, etc.

F. Lazy-Daisy. This is a variation of the chain-stitch, with the loops made longer and each one held down with a stitch at the end of the petal. Place the loops to form a flower as shown, bringing the needle out at the centre each time after completing a petal. To make leaves, use the same stitch, placing the loops along a stem.

STITCHES

G. Long-and-Short-Stitch. This is one of the simplest stitches used in embroidery for filling surfaces along stems, or outlining leaves, petals, etc. It is made by alternating long and short stitches side by side, as shown. A shaded effect in surface filling may be obtained by using colours that are close but not matching and placing the rows one against another.

H. Outline-Stitch. This stitch is worked backward. Take a short stitch toward yourself; then take the next one back from that, but put the needle through toward yourself. Continue this around the outline of your design. The effect is like that of a twisted cord laid along an outline. The same stitch may be used for filling in designs, as shown. Make the stitches ordinarily about ¼ in. long. The weight of floss used determines the effect of weight and solidity.

I. Surface Darning. Because of simplicity this is one of the most practical stitches to use as a filling stitch, especially when quite a large surface is to be covered. Use a long darning needle and rather coarse thread. Work the thread in and out of the fabric as for even or uneven-basting. Keep the stitches straight and evenly spaced. Almost any effect can be obtained by using stitches of different lengths and threads of varied colours. Coarse fabrics, or those with a definite weave or design are often used for this type of decoration. The design is formed by following the pattern of the fabric.

J. Smocking. This is a decorative stitching used to hold fulness in place, as at the yoke of a child's dress. There are several different stitches used for this, but the commonest stitch is the one illustrated, which forms a honeycomb or diamond pattern of the fulness. Use a transfer pattern to mark the fabric for stitching unless the fabric has dots or checks that can be used as a guide. Gather the fabric before the stitch is worked. Work from left to right. Knot your thread and bring the needle through to the right side, through the first dot in the second row. Take a short backward stitch over the dot, take another stitch over the second dot and draw the two together. Carry the thread on the right side up to the second dot on the first row, take stitches as before and draw the second and third dots together. Work in this way, alternating from row to row to the end. Turn the work round and go across as before, this time alternating between the second and third rows. Repeat for as many rows as are desired.

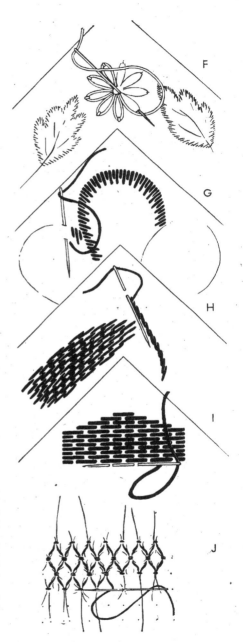

SEAMS AND HOW

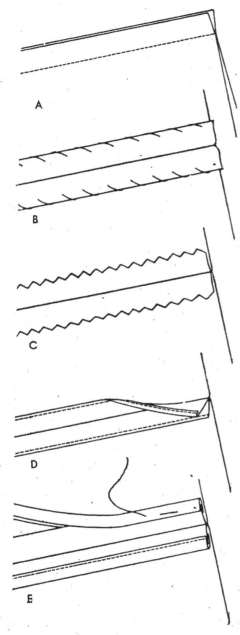

A. Plain Seam. Test your machine stitch on a scrap of fabric to determine the right length to hold your seam as you want it. Adjust the stitch so that it is neither too short nor too long for the texture of the fabric. Begin at the top and stitch down, keeping the work flat on the table of your machine. Never allow a seam to drag. Keep the weight of the fabric up, and feed easily and evenly under the presser foot. A plain seam is used more than any other. Practise stitching straight until you can do it perfectly. The manner of finishing raw edges varies greatly, but learn to do a plain seam perfectly and the good appearance of your sewing will reward you.

B. Overcast Seam. Garment seams, except in men's shirts and children's clothes, are usually pressed open and the seam edges clipped. If the material has a tendency to draw, or if it frays easily, overcast, as shown. Make the overcasting stitches as deep and close together as necessary to give a protected edge. In average fabrics, such as firm, light-weight woollens or crepes, the stitches may be made $\frac{1}{8}$ in. deep and $\frac{1}{4}$ in. apart. Take three to five stitches on your needle at once before you pull it through, thus speeding your work, and making it easier.

C. Pinked Seam. For fabrics that do not fray easily, such as taffeta and firm, light-weight crepes, and especially fabrics that are not washed, a pinked seam is a quick finish. This may be notched with the scissors or with pinking shears. If pinking shears are used, cut your garment with them rather than with plain scissors, and thus cut and finish your seams in one operation.

D. Clean-Stitched Seam. For quick finishing, and where a firm seam is desired, as for a light-weight crepe or semi-sheer cotton, turn each raw edge of the seam under, as shown, and stitch it on the machine with a long stitch, stretching the seam edge slightly so that it cannot possibly draw. In pressing such a seam, slip a strip of cardboard under each seam edge and press over this so that no seam line will show on the right side.

E. Bound Seam. In unlined jackets and coats, and in materials that fray easily but are likely to receive too much wear for overcasting, bind the seam edges. Before binding, make sure that the seam edge is not tight in any place; if it is, clip it at intervals so that the binding will not be too tight. Use a fairly long stitch, and be sure your binding is well over the edge of the seams so that it cannot pull away.

TO MAKE THEM

F. Self-Bound Seam. This is a very practical seam to use for children's clothes and other lightweight washable materials. Make a plain seam and cut away one side of the seam to within ¼ in. of the stitching line. Bring the other edge over, turn it under ¼ in., and stitch this down over the first stitching line. This is a self-bound seam— a sturdy, twice-stitched seam.

G. Top-Stitched Seam. This is practical for tailored skirts of firm wool or linen. Make a plain seam and finish the raw edges in the way best suited to the fabric. Press open, and stitch on the right side, as shown. The presser foot will guide your stitching; use either the narrow or the wide side for this.

H. Double-Stitched Seam. For soft materials, or those with an embroidered design, such as eyelet embroidery, where it would be difficult to make a French seam, the machine-stitched seam is entirely practical. To make this, first stitch on the seam line as for a plain seam. Then ¼ in. outside the first stitching line, make a second row of stitching. Then trim the fabric up close to the second row. If the material frays easily, do not trim away this extra seam width; overcast it, and use the two rows of stitching to give a firm, flat seam.

I. French Seam. This is a good seam to use in light-weight fabrics, such as lawn, organdie, and sheer muslin, or in any firm, sheer fabric. Bring the seam edges together on the right side and stitch ⅛ in. from the edge. Turn the garment wrong side out, and stitch a scant ¼ in. from the seam line, thus enclosing all the raw edges of the seam inside. Often it is desirable to trim the seam edge before the second row of stitching is put in, to make sure that no raw edges will show.

J. Imitation French Seam. Some feel that this is an easier seam to make than a French seam, but it gives much the same effect. Stitch on the seam line on the wrong side; then turn the raw edges in and stitch them together to give a firm, sturdy seam.

K. Lapped Seam. This seam is principally used for piecing interlinings of coats, etc., or where a flat concealed joining is necessary. Lap one edge over the other ⅜ in. to ½ in. and stitch down the centre of the overlap. This seam may also be used on heavy net and lace with a close all-over pattern. When used on these fabrics, the seam should be stitched on paper. All extra width is then trimmed off on either side of the seam. For a larger-patterned lace, allow more width in seams so that you can stitch round the lace motifs.

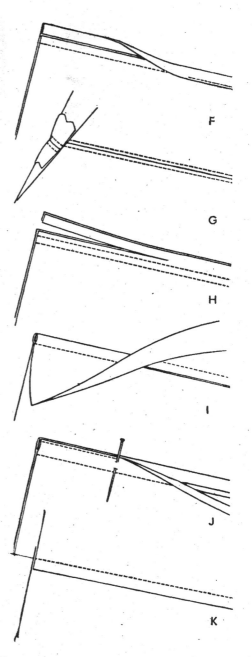

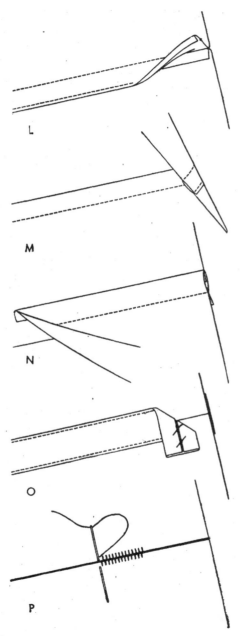

L. Flat Fell Seam. This seam is often used in tailored play clothes, men's shirts, and garments that receive hard wear and are washed often. To make it baste the seam on the right side of the garment. Stitch on the seam line. Trim one edge of the seam away to within ¼ in. of the stitching line. Turn the other edge in ⅛ in. and stitch it flat, as shown. If a wide flat fell is desired, have one edge of your first seam ¼ in. wide, and the other edge ⅝ in. wide. Then, instead of trimming away one edge, turn the other edge in ¼ in. for stitching down, so that you have a flat fell that is ½ in. wide.

M. Imitation Flat Fell Seam. This is the same as a flat fell except that it is made on the wrong side of the garment rather than the right and, consequently, there is only one row of stitching that shows on the right side.

N. Welt Seam. This is used in very firm fabrics, such as broadcloth and gabardine. Baste, stitch, and press open the seam. Cut one edge to within a scant ¼ in. of the stitching line. Press the wide seam over the narrow edge, and baste flat without turning the edge under. Press carefully from the right side; then stitch from the right side ½ in. in from the edge. This seam makes a firm, tailored finish with only one stitching line visible.

O. Strap Seam. In tailored garments it is often desirable to use a strap seam. In such a case, cut the strap on a true bias, bring the edges together, and overcast them, as shown. Press the strap. Make a plain seam in your garment and press it open; then stitch the strap over the seam. In broadcloth and firm woollens, where strap seams are frequently used, always cut the garment seam wider than usual so that the strap will lie perfectly flat. In some instances it is desirable to make a narrow seam on the right side of the garment, press it open, and then cover the seam with the strap.

P. Laced Seam. This seam is used for joining two edges together that do not overlap, as on the leather covering of a football. Put the needle straight in under the edge and through the fabric on one side of the opening. Bring out the needle; then insert it under the other side of the opening, as shown. Continue alternating stitches from side to side all along the seam. When placed close together, the stitches appear quite straight; when more widely spaced as on a football, they slant. The laced stitched seam is used for stocking patches. page 51—in mending gloves, page 112—and is good to use where seam allowances are lacking.

DARTS

DARTS ARE TAPERED TUCKS used to fit garments to the curves of the figure. They must be long and wide enough to lie smoothly without forming bulges. They are often used in groups of two, three, or five to distribute fulness evenly.

Often, in fitting a garment, you find that more fulness is required than is allowed in a pattern or in the original garment. Open the darts and pin in the proper fulness, baste and fit again before stitching them.

Position of darts, shown by dots in the illustrations, should be indicated on fabric with chalk or tailors' tacks. Bring the markings together, pin them in place, and baste. Always pin down from the top and up from the bottom alternately to make the dart smooth.

Hip, Shoulder and Underarm Darts. In stitching these, begin at the wide end and stitch to the point. On wash garments, turn at the point and stitch back along the outer edge of the dart. On wools, silks, linens and other heavier fabrics, stitch to the point, turn and stitch back for an inch over the first stitching. Then slash the dart and overcast the raw edges as shown.

Body Darts. Stitch first along the curved line. Then either stitch back on the straight edge or cut the dart open, clip the edges, so that they lie flat, and overcast.

Waistline Darts or Pleats. These are used to hold in fulness at the waistline. For the darts, stitch to the point and back along the outside edge. Press darts towards the centre-front or centre-back of the garment. In many cases, instead of stitching in darts, the fulness can be laid in pleats and held in place by stitching across the bottom.

Back-Neck Darts. These are often used in altering ready-made clothes to raise the shoulder line, give ease at the back or to fit the neckline. Two or more darts may be needed to distribute the fulness properly and get a correct fit. Pin up the fulness and then distribute it in as many darts as are required to make a smooth and well-fitting back.

Sleeve Darts. These are small darts used in groups of three, five, or seven, to hold elbow fulness and fit sleeves at the wrists. Fewer darts are needed in heavy fabrics, more in sheer. Make them slightly longer than one-fifth the elbow measurement; if this is 10 ins., make the darts $2\frac{1}{8}$ ins. long. For very slender arms, it may be necessary to use just a little gathering to hold the fulness rather than darts. In this case, ease the gathers in and press carefully.

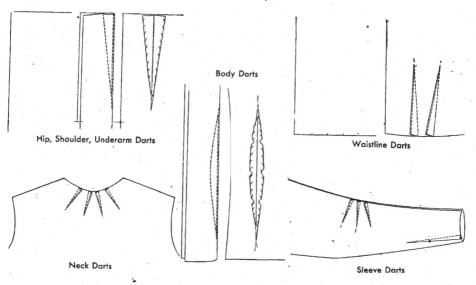

Hip, Shoulder, Underarm Darts

Body Darts

Waistline Darts

Neck Darts

Sleeve Darts

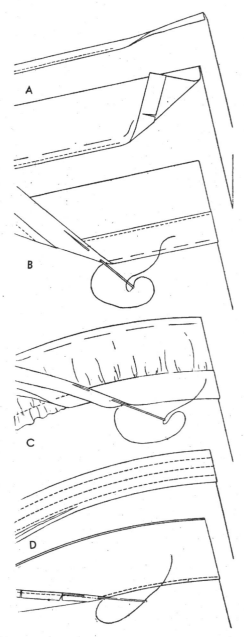

FINISHES FOR

A. Machine Hems. The width of these hems vary with the weight of the fabric. The narrowest ones may be done very quickly with the machine foot hemmer, if you have that attachment. Otherwise, for a narrow hem on the straight, turn the raw edge under about ⅛ in. Turn the hem to the depth you have planned, measuring and basting to be sure of a perfectly straight line. Stitch close to the crease. Pull the thread ends through to the wrong side and tie and clip them. Be sure to line up any seams that are crossed by the hem so that it will hang straight. Where the hem turns back in a seam, eliminate some of the bulk by cutting away surplus fabric in the hem seam. Illustrated here are both a narrow and a wide machine-stitched hem.

B. Seam-Binding Hem Finish. This is often used on fabric that is too thick to turn under, or for fabrics that fray or where the turned hem line might make a crease. This is also used on many ready-made garments. Stitch seam-binding to the raw edge of the hem. Sew the other edge of the binding to the garment with slip-stitches.

C. Hem on Curved Edge. Crease the hem turn and baste close to the fold. Then stitch along the top edge of the hem turn with a long machine-stitch. Draw up the bobbin thread, as shown, to ease in the fulness and distribute it evenly along the curve. To the slightly gathered edge, stitch a light-weight manufactured bias binding. Slip-stitch the other edge of the bias strip to the garment. If the curve is slight and the hem narrow, tiny pleats can be laid in the top of the hem

D. Hem on Flared or Circular Edge. Generally it is impractical to use a wide hem on a flared skirt, or on any circular edge. One method often used on skirts is to turn the edge and put in from three to five parallel rows of stitching along it, trimming the raw edge close to the top stitching line. If this top stitching is not desirable for the fabric you are using, cut a facing to fit the curve. Cut it either on a true bias or on the same line of the fabric as the circular edge or flare. Lay the right sides together and stitch along the edges. Then press the seam open and turn the facing under. Stitch the other edge of the facing and slip-stitch it to the garment

HEMS AND EDGES

E. Hem Over Pleat. To insure flat seam turns
and avoid bulk where a hem comes over a pleat,
clip that part of the seam that lies under the hem
and press it open. Then turn back the hem edge
and stitch it, as shown, before slip-stitching the
hem.

F. Slip-Stitched Hem. When you are not using
seam binding over a hem, and invisibility is more
important than strength, this hem is good. Turn
the hem and baste it. Then turn and stitch the raw
edge to give it body. Slip-stitch this edge to the
fabric with a fine needle and matching thread.
Make the stitches short enough to hold the weight
of the fabric without pulling down.

G. Half-Feather-Stitch Hem. This is a hem used
chiefly when the wrong side will not be seen at all,
as for a coat, the lining of which would cover the
hem line. Such stitching goes more quickly than
slip-stitching, and is excellent for fabrics with surface threads that can be caught up with the needle
without going all the way through. Work towards
yourself, catching a thread of the fabric and bringing the needle out through the hem across the
thread. It is really the same stitch as blanket-
stitch, except that it is spaced farther apart and is
used in a different way.

H. Pinked Edge. As a finish for some firm and
evenly woven fabrics, such as taffeta or glazed
chintz, a pinked edge is often favoured. Pinking
shears may be very satisfactorily used for this, or
you may have a sewing-machine pinker that is
practical. A scalloped and pinked edge is often used
on home furnishings. To make this, draw the
scallops on the fabric with pencil or chalk and then
cut with shears or pinker along the scalloped line.

I. Rolled Hem. This type of hem is for light-weight
fabrics. Be sure your fingers are immaculate and
dusted with French chalk so that the roll will be
dainty and fresh when you finish. Use a fine
needle and thread and place your stitches
sparingly. If the fabric is limp, put a row of
machine-stitching close to the edge. Then roll the
stitched edge to conceal the stitching and slip-
stitch the roll into position. Fabrics with a crisp
finish, such as organdie, hold their roll without the
row of machine-stitching.

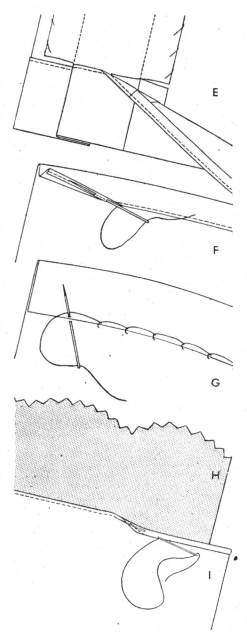

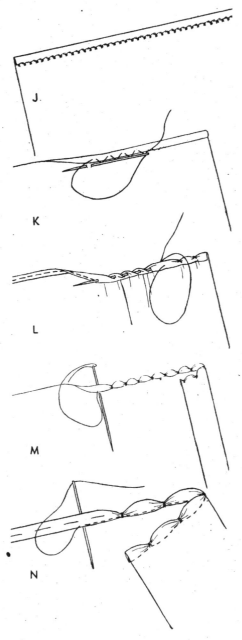

J. Turned Picot Edge. Have the edge hemstitched and cut the hemstitching through the centre to form a picot edge. Make a narrow turn-under, perhaps ⅛ in. or less, and catch the picot edge to the fabric with tiny stitches. The picot makes a durable and firm edge for flimsy fabrics such as georgette and chiffon.

K. Invisible Rolled Hem Line. This is a secure rolled hem for light-weight fabrics such as organdie. Roll the hem turn with the thumb and forefinger. Take a small slip-stitch in the fabric and then one in the roll. Take several stitches on the needle each time before pulling it through the fabric. This leaves no visible stitching line, looks attractive and launders fairly well if you straighten the hem as you iron it.

L. Overcast Shell Hem. This is attractive for lingerie edges, children's dresses, ruffles, neckwear, etc. Turn the edge back about ¼ in., and then turn it again. The width varies a little according to the fabric and the depth you want the shell to be. · Work from the wrong side, beginning with a back-stitch and continuing with overcasting. Use a double thread, and barely catch the hem turn with your stitches. Take several stitches on the needle at once before drawing the thread through. Be careful not to draw the thread so tight as to pucker the edge. The effect you want is the shaping of little shells along the edge. Practise on a scrap of fabric before setting to work on the garment. For sheer fabrics it is best to machine-stitch the first edge turn.

M. Lingerie Hem. This is a dainty finish for fine hand-made underclothing, infants' dresses, and lingerie touches for dresses. Roll the hem lightly as you sew, securing it at intervals of ⅛ in. to ⅜ in. with two straight stitches taken over the roll. This makes a series of little puffs along the edge. Conceal the stitch between puffs under the roll.

N. Shell Edge or Tuck. Crease your hem or tuck about ¼ in. deep. Run five or six fine running-stitches along the edge of the turn; then take a downward stitch, as for the lingerie hem, and a second one to secure it. Continue with another series of running-stitches and draw the edge down with the straight downward stitches again. Practise to make your shells of even width. For fine washable cotton or linen garments, blouses, baby things, and lingerie, this is attractive and practical.

O. Napery Hem. Chiefly used for table linen, this is a hem that looks almost exactly the same on both sides. Turn and crease the edge. Turn and crease again for a hem. Then fold the fabric back exactly in line against the hem and catch both creases with a small oversewing-stitch. Use strong thread. Press the hem.

P. Milliner's Fold. Turn the edge to the right side, making the turnback a little less than twice the width you want the finish to be. Then fold again to the same side, bringing the second turn just far enough over to cover the raw edge. You now have four thicknesses on the right side. Using an uneven-basting-stitch, sew from the wrong side through three of the thicknesses, as shown. This makes a nice finish with no stitching showing on the right side. The width of the fold depends on your fabrics—⅜ in. may be enough for light-weight fabrics, heavier or stiffer fabrics may need a ½ in. to ¾ in. turn. Appropriate for muslin, mourning crepe, all slightly stiffened non-washable fabrics.

Q. Tucked Hem. This is used when a very narrow hem is desirable, as on crisp, thin fabrics. The tuck is made a little narrower than the desired width of the finished edge—usually 1/16 in., ⅛ in. or ¼ in. It is made far enough from the edge so that it can be folded in to simulate a binding, as shown. If the tuck is a scant ⅛ in., make it ¼ in. from the edge for this effect. Use small even-basting-stitches to hold the hem in place.

R. Hand-Felled Binding. Stitch one edge of the binding to the right side of the fabric by machine. Then turn it over the edge and whip it down on the wrong side. This method of binding is good when there is too much thickness to use the machine binder or when you are binding large shallow scallops. Never stretch binding as you apply it; rather, ease it on. Always clip the seam edge of binding as it turns on a concave curve.

S. French Fold Binding. This is made with a true bias folded in half the narrow way. Stitch the raw edges of the bias to the right side of the fabric edge, using a ¼ in. seam. Trim the edges close to the stitching. Turn the folded edge of the binding over the seam edges and whip or slip-stitch it in place. The binding should be ⅛ in. to ¼ in. wide when finished. It should be pressed on the wrong side over a pad so that it will hold its roundness. Use on fine lingerie or georgette and chiffon.

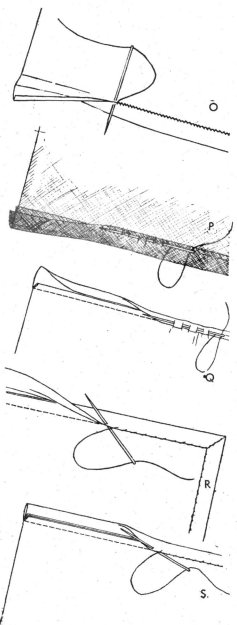

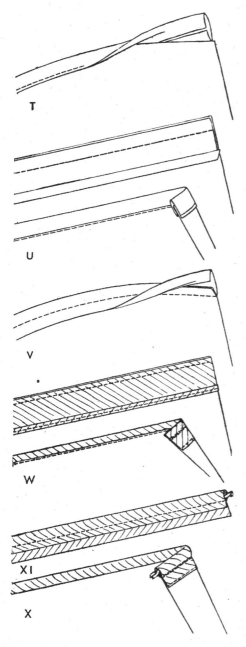

T. Machine Binding. The binder of your sewing machine will apply No. 5 ready-made bias binding with just one stitching and without preliminary basting. You can apply other widths of binding in the same way without the binder when you learn to hold it in place as easily and accurately as the binder does. Until you are expert at this, baste binding on before stitching, when sewing binding on a wash garment or when sewing a width narrower than 5. Turn edge and stitch it first. Bind over this and thus be sure your binding will not pull off.

U. Imitation French Binding. Stitch one edge of the true-bias piece to the right side of the garment. Make a $\frac{1}{4}$ in. turn-in on the other edge, as shown. Turn the bias to the wrong side so that the creased edge extends about $\frac{1}{8}$ in. beyond the line of stitching. Then on the right side stitch carefully along the line where the binding is joined to the fabric. Press the binding from the edge towards the centre of the fabric so that it conceals this second stitching line.

V. Centre-Stitched Binding. Stitch the right side of the true-bias strip to the wrong side of the garment. Press the seam up against the binding. Bring the other edge of the binding down to cover the stitching and crease the turn. Then press the fold down on the right side and stitch through the centre, as in the illustration. This is a little more decorative than a plain binding and very practical, especially on sheer fabric and taffeta.

W. Piped Edge. This is a finish, made by using a bias facing and allowing it to extend a little beyond the fabric edge. Make a scant $\frac{1}{8}$ in. turn on one edge of the facing and stitch it. The other edge is then stitched along the right side of the fabric edge, as shown. Turn the facing to the wrong side over the seam so that the seam edges serve as padding inside the piping. Stitch on the right side along the joining of fabric and facing.

X. Corded Edge. This is done in much the same way as a piped edge. To make cording, select cording of a size appropriate to the fabric and the purpose for which it is intended. Cover the cording with binding or fabric strips, as in XI. Do this either by hand or with the machine cording foot (*see page* 41). Then apply to edge to be finished. Cording can also be inserted into a seam line for an attractive finish.

GATHERS AND RUFFLES

A. Hand-Shirring. Using small running-stitches, make as many rows as are needed, spacing them evenly. To make the fulness even, draw up all the shirring threads at once to the desired position. To fasten each row, thread the needle with the thread end, carry it to the wrong side and take several back-stitches.

B. Machine-Shirring. Set the machine for a long stitch and use strong thread. Use the side of the presser-foot as a guide to space the rows of stitching evenly. Grasp all the bobbin threads at once and pull to distribute the fulness as desired, easing the gathers along as you pull. To fasten threads at the end of the row, pull the top thread to the wrong side and tie it to the bobbin thread.

Ruffles may be applied and finished in many ways. However, the points illustrated here are the ones most useful in remaking and repairing clothing and household articles.

Making Ruffles. Cut all crisp fabrics, such as lawn, taffeta and organdie, on the bias. Marquisette, voile and ninon, which are limp fabrics, should be torn crosswise of the fabric. Piece all crosswise ruffles on the straight, making narrow French seams. Clip off end of seam, as at **C**, so that it will go into your hemmer with ease. Piece all bias ruffles on the lengthwise of the fabric, as at **D**. Overcast raw edges.

E. Gathered Edge in French-Seam Turn. When applying a gathered edge to a straight edge, as in putting ruffles on wash clothes, lingerie, curtains, etc., this is practical. Draw up the gathering thread to the desired length. Stitch the gathered edge to the straight edge, turn the fabric over the seam edge as shown and stitch over the seam, thus concealing the raw edges within the fabric turn.

F and G. Applying Ruffle to Curve and Square Corner. The chief point about applying a ruffle to a curve is to have the ruffle twice as long as the curve and very full on a corner so that it will not cup when it is opened out.

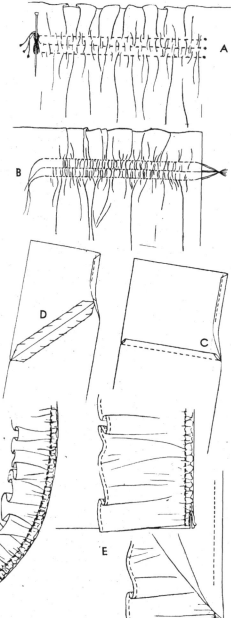

27

TUCKS

A. Hand-Run Tucks. These are often used on children's clothes for decoration and may be used to disguise piecing or mending. Crease on a fabric thread to insure straight lines and space the tucks evenly. Using fine thread and a long, thin needle, take tiny running-stitches along the tuck. Begin and end with back-stitches.

B. Oversewn Tucks. For decoration of children's clothes and lingerie, these are often used on a curved or above a scalloped edge. Mark the line the tuck is to follow and crease along the line. Oversew with embroidery thread. Two rows of oversewing may be used if desired—one placed over the other, from opposite directions, to give a cross-stitched effect.

C. Fulness Tucks. These are used in place of darts sometimes in fitting garments and often appear in yokes and sleeves. Measure off the desired width and spacing of tucks, and mark the appropriate line for their ending. They need not always end in a straight line, but they must end in some even design, such as the slanting line shown. They may be done by hand or machine.

D. Cluster Tucks. Like Fulness Tucks, these are sometimes used in fitting instead of darts, as around the waist or sleeves. They should be all the same length, but the width depends upon the amount of fulness to be taken up. If done by hand they should be finished with back-stitches; if by machine, the threads should be tied on the wrong side.

E. Nun Tucks. These are used, often in groups, on a curved edge. They may be used to conceal shortening or lengthening garments, especially children's clothes. Measure the width of the tucks and distance between. Put in the tucks by hand first to be sure they hang correctly, even if they are to be stitched by machine afterwards.

F. Graduated Tucks. These also can be used to disguise the lengthening or shortening of children's garments. Measure carefully the width and spacing of tucks so that pleasing proportions are achieved. Begin with the widest tuck and make each one that follows proportionately narrower. Often the space between tucks is the same as the wider tuck. These tucks are usually machine-stitched.

G. Cross Tucks. These are often seen at corners of collars, yokes and cuffs, but are especially useful in home furnishings. Use particular care in measuring and marking for these so that they will be perfectly even. Baste in the group that crosses at the corner to prevent their slipping out of line in stitching.

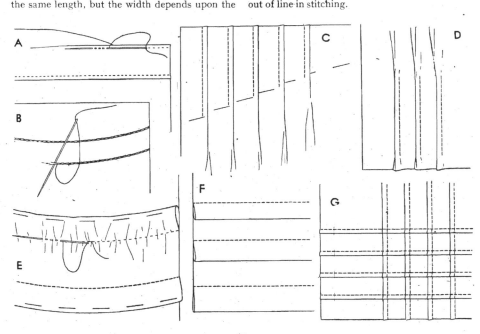

PLEATS

PLEATS ARE MADE in a great variety of styles. Those illustrated here are particularly useful for giving more fulness or freedom in remodelling garments. Other types are described in the instructions on your dress patterns.

Inverted Pleat on a Seam. Cut a piece of fabric twice the width of the pleat and baste and stitch it in place under the pleat as shown. Put the hem in at the lower edge. Baste the pleats down from the right side and press carefully. Mark the position for stitching to stay the top of the pleat and stitch this from the right side. The raw edges should be overcast together on the wrong side as shown.

Applied Inverted Pleat. This is satisfactory for giving needed ease in a too-narrow skirt. Place a piece of fabric on the right side of the garment with its centre line lying along the line where the pleat is to be. Stitch up and back over this line, leaving ⅜ in. between the stitching lines. Slash between the stitching lines as in **A**. Turn the piece of fabric to the wrong side and press carefully. Apply a second piece as in **B**. Cut it a little larger than the first piece and stitch the edges of the two pieces together. Oversew the upper edges to the garment, as shown, so that stitches will not show on the right side. The right side will appear as in **C**.

Stayed Pleats. To hold pleat edges sharp and true, certain types of skirts may be finished in this way. Stitch the pleats down over the hips. Then clip the bobbin thread, pull the body of the skirt out from under the presser foot, turn the spool back to rewind slack thread, and continue stitching the pleat edge to the bottom. Thread a needle with the thread ends and whip them in to secure the stitching.

Ready-Made Pleating. In many cities there are firms that do machine pleating. To prepare for having the pleating done, seam widths together and allow three times as much fabric as you require pleating. For example, for a skirt of a 39 ins. hip measure, use three widths of 39 ins. fabric. Seam widths together; put the hem in, but do not sew the last seam. This leaves fabric flat for pleating. When the work comes back, before removing pleating from the paper, stitch the pleats across the top to hold them in place.

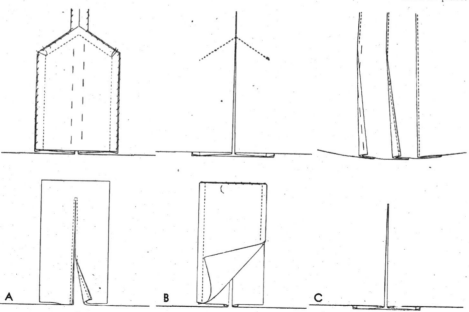

A   B   C

29

GODETS

A GODET IS A PIECE inserted along the bottom to give fulness. It may be used to good advantage to allow extra fulness in a narrow skirt or to break a long, plain line in a bedspread, etc. There are several different types of godets. The ones shown here are those most essential for repairing and remodelling garments.

Pointed Godet. Slash the edge of the garment on a fabric thread, making all slashes exactly the same depth. The inserted piece will be on the straight on one edge and bias on the other, so it must be carefully basted in so that it will hang properly. Begin at the top of the slash for each seam, allowing as little seam here as possible, and gradually widening the seam allowance towards the bottom. Clip off the tip end of the godet as shown. When the seam is pressed open, catch the very narrow top part with a few stitches to give strength. In making bedspreads,

it is well to make an additional row of stitching at the top of the godet to guard against strain.

Stayed Godet. When a godet is inserted in a seam or is in a position where strain may be put on the point, a staying piece may be applied as shown. This is cut in a point slightly wider than the godet top. The edges are turned in and the piece is whipped in place on the wrong side as shown. This serves to hold the fulness in place and reinforce the weak part of a pointed godet.

Round-Topped Godet in a Seam. To add fulness at the bottom of a skirt, this type of godet may be used. Open the seam and cut the rounded edge to the shape desired. Turn back a seam allowance on this curve, clipping it for ease, and baste. Apply the godet piece, baste, stitch. Complete skirt seam in the ordinary way.

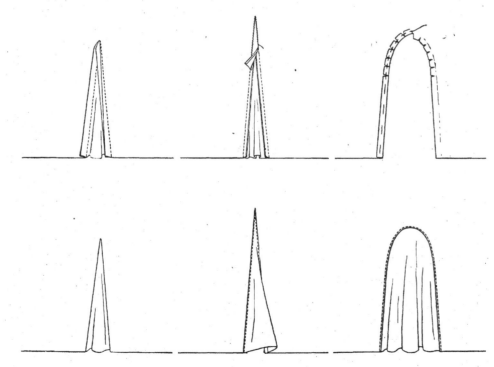

NECKLINE AND SLEEVE FINISHES

V-Neck Facing. Cut a true-bias strip, several inches longer than the neck opening and $\frac{1}{2}$ in. wider than the facing will be when finished. Lay the facing pieces on each side of the neck, right sides together. Baste and stitch the edges to within $\frac{1}{2}$ in. of the mitre, as in **A**. Mitre the facing at the point of the V and stitch the mitred seam, as at **B**. Cut away the extra fabric at the mitre; press the seam open; and finish the stitching along the V edges, as in **C**. Turn the facing to the wrong side; turn under the raw edges and stitch or slip-stitch the facing down, as in **D**

Square Neckline Mitre. Cut facing pieces to fit the corner. Pin and baste them in place, leaving a generous allowance at the mitre. Pin the pieces to form a true diagonal at the corner, as at **E**. Baste and stitch before cutting the corner away. Press the seam open, as at **F**. Stitch the neck edge and turn the facing to the wrong side. Baste, then stitch or slip-stitch it in position, as in **G**. This is also called Mitred Concave.

Tailored Corner. When a hem turns back along a square corner, as in a neck or yoke line, it is necessary to add a staying piece to secure it and prevent ravelling. Clip the corner diagonally to the desired depth of the hem, as in **H**. Crease the hem turn. Cut a piece of fabric for each corner, making it twice as wide as the hem and three times as long. Lay one of the long edges of the piece against the sides of the slash, with right sides of the fabric together, and stitch as in **I**. At the inside end of the slash, the seam just catches the fabric. If necessary, add a few back-stitches at that point to secure the seam. Smooth the corner back, and cut off the excess on the corner. Turn the raw edge under all along the entire hem turn, as in **J**, and baste close to the hem edge as shown. Then slip-stitch the corner in place. **K** shows how the neckline appears on the wrong side. No stitches should be visible on the right side.

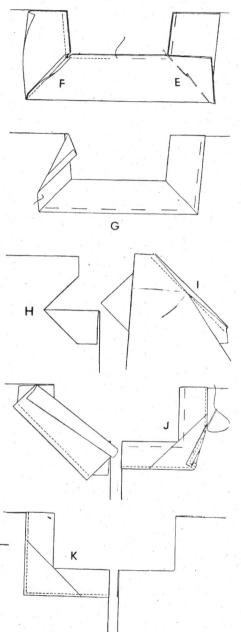

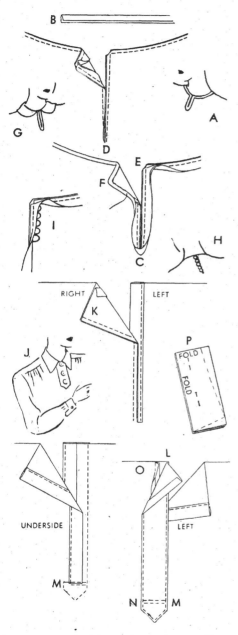

Bound Neck Opening. One of the simplest of neck finishes is that shown in **A**. To make it: Slash the opening down from the neck to the required depth. Cut a true bias strip three times as wide as the finished binding is to be. Fold this lengthwise ⅛ in. off the centre, as in **B**. Stitch this to the right side of the garment with the narrow side of the binding up. Beginning at one shoulder, stitch around the neck edge and along both sides of the opening. Stretch the binding slightly when turning the end of the slash, as in **C**, and make the seam narrow there, as in **D**. Clip off the corners as at **E**. Turn the edge of binding to wrong side and whip it down, as at **F**.

Peter Pan Collar. The bound opening may be used with a Peter Pan collar, as in **G**. Bind only the opening, in the same way as above, and apply the collar with a narrow bias facing.

Bound Back Opening. H shows the binding applied to a back opening, with loops added to hold the buttons. The loops are made of the bias also and are sewn in place when the binding is stitched on, as in **I**. The corners must be clipped to make a smooth flat turn.

Short Front Opening. Use this tab front as in **J**, on a collarless neckline. The matching cuff may be used on long or short sleeves.

Slash the neck to the required depth and measure the slash. Cut two strips on the straight of the fabric, one twice as wide as the widest part of the collar and the other half that width. For a 4 ins. collar, make one strip 4 ins. wide, the other 2 ins. The wide strip should be 2 ins. longer than the slash and the narrow one ½ in. longer. Pin the strips in place along the edges of the slash, beginning at the top and laying the right sides of the strips on the wrong side of the garment Stitch the narrow strip first on the left edge of the slash. Turn the other edge of this strip to the right side of the garment; turn the raw edge under ¼ in. and stitch it.

Stitch the wide strip to the right edge of the slash, as in **K**, and press the seams open. Turn the free edge of this strip under ½ in. and crease the turn. Bring this strip to the right side of the garment, as in **L**. Turn in the bottom, either square or in a point, cutting away surplus fabric Baste the folded edge of the tab. Then start at the top, at **L**, and stitch down to **M**, being guided by the edge of the presser foot to get the stitching straight and holding the edge away from the garment as you stitch. At **M**, pull the work out from under the presser foot and break the bobbin thread, leaving the top one unbroken. Smooth the tab over the under fabric. Wind the thread back on the spool to take up the slack and put the work back under the needle at **M**. Stitch around end to **N**, across to **M**, and back to **N** again, as shown on the wrong side drawing. Stitch up from **N** to **O**. To secure the bobbin thread broken off at **M**, thread it into a needle and take two back-stitches.

To make a collar as shown in **J**: Cut a lengthwise strip of fabric 7 ins. wide and 2 ins. longer than the neckline. Fold this through the centre lengthwise, then crosswise through the centre. Cut as indicated by dotted lines in **P**, beginning at the crosswise fold 1 in. from the edges and cutting diagonally to within 1 in. of the ends. Then cut from this point to the end of the other folded edges, as shown. Turn the piece wrong side out, fold it lengthwise through the centre and stitch across the short ends. Turn the collar right side out and apply it to the neck. Begin at the opening and work towards the centre-back. Then begin at the other end of the collar and work again towards the centre-back. Conceal the joining with a bias facing to cover the seam inside the collar.

Bias Sleeve Facing. Cut a bias strip the required length. Turn one edge under a scant $\frac{1}{8}$ in. and stitch. Pin the other edge to the right side of the sleeve, as in **A**, easing it in so that the outside stitched edge will lie perfectly flat. Stitch the facing on. Clip the seam edge to prevent drawing. Turn the facing to the wrong side and slip-stitch the edge to the sleeve. Bias is applied to a neckline in the same manner.

Sleeve Openings. For facing sleeves, seaming ribbon is excellent. Use matching ribbon of good quality. Stitch it $\frac{1}{4}$ in. from the seam edge on the right side; then turn to the wrong side. Mitre corners and whip the free edge down, as in **B**. Instead of ribbon, 1 in. wide bias strips of fabric may be used. Shaped facings, as shown in **C**, should be cut to fit, stitched to the right side, turned to the wrong, stitched in place on the top edge, and then slip-stitched flat to the sleeve.

Making Hem Cuff. Pin the underarm sleeve seams, stitch, and press open. At the bottom of sleeve, turn the edge up $\frac{1}{4}$ in. on the wrong side; then turn the hem up 2 ins. and stitch it, as in **D**. Turn the hem back $1\frac{3}{8}$ ins. on the right side, as in **E**. This gives you a cuff that is easy to make and can be turned down for quick ironing. Overcast the sleeve seam above the cuff. Rick rack makes a smart, sturdy trimming. Stitch the rick rack to the top of the turn-back cuff, as in **F**, holding the cuff free from the sleeve.

Making Band Cuff. Make a continuous placket as shown below. Then gather the sleeve end as in **G** and stitch the cuff over the gathering on the right side as in **H**. Then turn the cuff down and whip it in place on the wrong side as in **I**.

Continuous Placket. To make this placket, cut a $\frac{3}{4}$ in. bias strip twice as long as the opening. Stitch this in place on the right side of garment, taking a narrow seam and tapering the stitching at the turn as in **J**. Turn the binding piece under and whip it over the seam as in **K**.

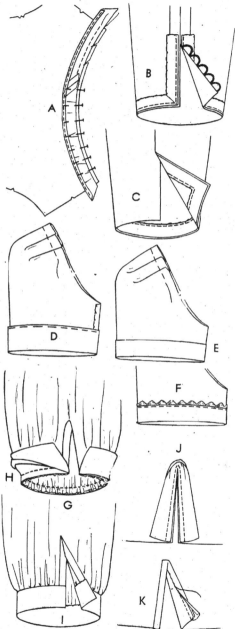

33

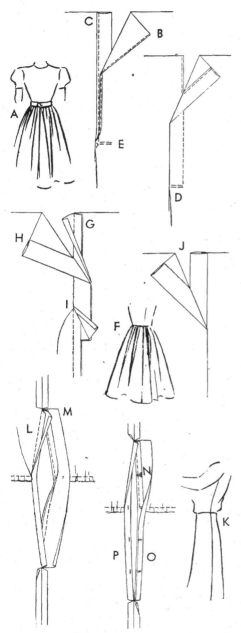

SKIRT AND DRESS PLACKETS

Peasant Placket. This simplest of all plackets is practical for any skirt with a gathered waistline. It is made in the centre-back, as in **A.** Cut the opening on a thread. Stitch a narrow hem for the underside, as at **B**, and a wider hem, ½ in. to 1 in. wide for the top side, as at **C.** The top hem should be stitched from the right side. Stitch twice across the end of the slash to hold it, as at **D.** Pull threads through to the wrong side and tie, as at **E.** If the placket is long, it may be well to use a snap or button half-way down to keep it closed.

Placket on a Seam. A placket is often most conveniently made on a side seam, as in **F.** Measure the length desired for the placket. Cut two facing strips of that length plus 1 in. for seams. One should be 1½ ins. wide; the other, 3 ins. wide. Stitch the narrower one in place, as at **G**; the wide one, as at **H.** Fell the free edges down, as in **I.** Fell or stitch the ends of the facing strips together at the bottom of the placket. **J** shows the finished placket.

Hook-and-Eye Dress Placket. Measure the length of the opening, as in **K**, and cut two bias facing strips 1¼ ins. wide and as long as the opening. Use one strip to bind the underside of the placket, as in **L.** On the top side of the placket, lay the other strip ⅛ in. from the seam edge, as at **M.** Stitch ¼ in. from the seam edge. Crease on the seam line, as shown. Sew the hooks on, as at **N.** Turn the raw edge of the facing under and fell it down over the hooks, covering all but the prongs, as at **O.** Work buttonhole eyes, as at **P.** Bring the two facing strips together at top and bottom of the opening, and stitch.

OTHER FINISHES

Mitred Hem. To have a true square corner, a hem must be mitred. This is done on household linens and on square collars, etc. Crease or press the hem turn along a fabric thread. Fold the corner as in **A**, and pin a true diagonal line as shown. Cut away the surplus fabric a seam's width above the pins. Remove pins and open the corner as in **B.** Turn the raw edges under, clipping the thickness away at the corners as shown. Fold the corner back in position and baste it in place as in **C.** Beginning with back-stitches at the outside corner, whip the diagonal edges together as shown. Finish the hem as desired.

Overlapping Corner. Coats and other garments that open down the front often have hems or facings along the opening that overlap the hem at the bottom and would create too much bulk there unless the thicknesses are thinned. To avoid this bulk, cut away the excess fabric as at **D**. Fold the front hem or facing to the right side and stitch its bottom edge to the bottom hem, as in **E**. Turn the front hem back in place and stitch or slip-stitch it down as in **F**.

Band Facing. Cut the facing strip so that the grain matches that in the edge it is to join. Pin and baste the facing in position. Stitch the edge to within 1 in. of the corner on each side, as at **G**. Mitre the corner, as shown, and stitch. Press the corner open and finish stitching the facing seams, pivoting as you turn the corner. Turn the facing to the other side and baste as in **H**. Top-stitch or slip-stitch the free edge down.

Fitted Facing on Curve. Cut the facing so that the grain runs the same way as that on the edge to be faced. Lay facing in place, right sides together, pin and stitch. Clip the seam around the curve, as at **I**. If the free edge of the facing is curved also, clip it before turning it under, as at **J**. Turn the facing to the wrong side, baste the outer edge, and slip-stitch the inner edge to the garment. Press carefully and remove bastings.

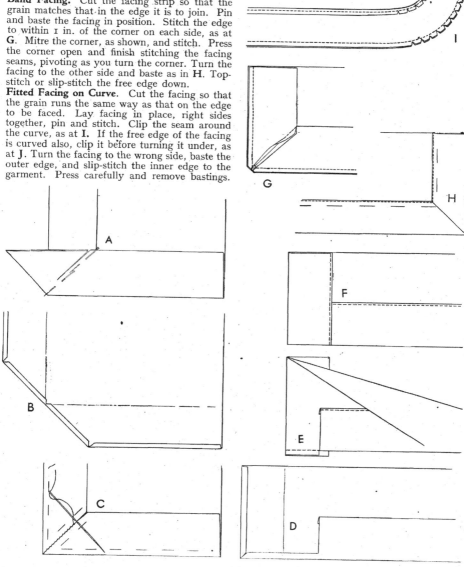

35

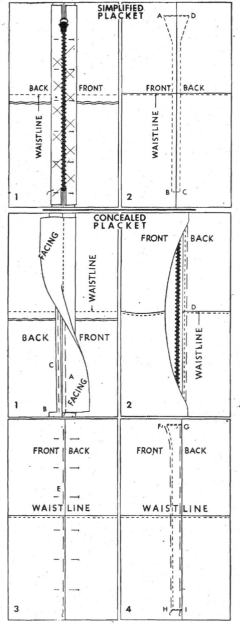

SLIDE FASTENERS

MANY TIMES, ALTERING a garment will require moving a slide fastener or putting one in where there had been none before. Of course, you will save all fasteners removed from discarded garments and keep them closed until they are needed for another use. The directions given here show how to apply the most common types of slide fasteners used in dresses and skirts. To change a placket from hook-and-eye or snap fastenings to slide fastener, remove fastenings and facings, baste and press the seam and apply the fastener according to one of the following methods.

DRESS PLACKETS

SIMPLIFIED PLACKET. This is used when the colour of the fastener matches and it need not be concealed. **Step 1.** Baste seam on left side of dress. Mark off the length of the slide fastener along the seam, approximately half above the waistline and half below. Stitch seam, except the length measured off for the fastener. Do not remove basting. Press seam open along its full length. Lay the closed fastener along the seam on the wrong side of the garment so that the centre of the fastener lies exactly over the seam line, with the slider side down. Pin fastener in place, easing fabric slightly and using pins crosswise to keep it smooth and straight. Catch-stitch the fastener in place, as shown. Remove pins. Turn dress right side out.
Step 2. Make a pocket at top of placket to conceal slider as shown. Begin basting $1\frac{1}{2}$ ins. below top of fastener and $\frac{1}{4}$ in. from the seam line, and make shaped end $\frac{7}{8}$ in. wide across the top. With cording foot of machine, begin at **A** and stitch down to **B**, across to **C**, up to **D**, across to **A**, and back to **D**. Stitch $\frac{1}{4}$ in. from seam line or centre of placket, except where you follow basting at shaped end. Pivot needle at each corner, and make square turn. Remove basting.

CONCEALED PLACKET. Used when fastener must be hidden, as when it does not match in colour.
Step 1. Baste seam on left side of dress. Mark off on this seam the length of the slide fastener, half above the waistline and half below. Stitch seam, except the marked-off length. Remove bastings. Then run a new line of basting stitches down both back and front edges of placket opening, to mark the natural seam line. Cut facing strip $1\frac{1}{2}$ ins. wide and same length as fastener tape. (If fabric is heavy, use matching fabric of lighter weight to avoid bulk. On sheer materials, use gros-grain ribbon.) Baste facing to front edge of placket opening; then stitch so that stitching line comes $\frac{1}{8}$ in. in from natural seam line. Turn facing to the inside. Press and baste in place, as shown in **A**.
Clip seam allowance of back edge of placket where facing ends, as in **B**. On this clipped seam, measure off $\frac{1}{8}$ in. from natural seam line. Crease seam along this line and baste, as in **C**.
Step 2. Lay fastener on table, right side up. Place dress right side up over fastener, with the turned-in back edge of placket $\frac{1}{16}$ in. from fastener teeth, as in **D**. Baste and then stitch back edge of placket to fastener tape, as shown.
Step 3. Close placket perfectly, lapping faced front edge over back. Pin in place; and baste along edge, as in **E**.
Step 4. From the right side, baste fastener tape to front

edge of placket, $\frac{1}{16}$ in. from metal, except at top which is shaped to fit around slider. Baste exactly where you intend to stitch. Stitch from **F** to **G**, back to **F**, to **H**, to **I**, and back to **H**. Remove basting.

SLIDE-FASTENER SKIRT PLACKET

Use a 7 ins. or 8 ins. fastener for the skirt placket. If the hip measurement is large, use a longer fastener.

The simplified manner given for the dress placket may be used in applying matching fasteners. Remember in doing this, to place centre of fastener directly over basted seam and place top of slider a seam's width down from top of skirt. Instructions given below are for a concealed fastener.

Prepare two selvedge-edged strips of skirt fabric, one $1\frac{1}{2}$ ins. wide and the other 2 ins. wide, and both 1 in. longer than the fastener. Fold the 2 ins. strip lengthwise through the centre to make a guard, stitch along the fold, and press. Turn skirt wrong side out. Baste left side seam. To measure off length required for placket opening, lay fastener on basted seam, with top of fastener $\frac{1}{4}$ in. down from top of skirt. With a pin, mark position of metal bar at lower end of fastener. Lay fastener aside, stitch side seam from pin to bottom of skirt.

Step 1. Press seam open its full length. Remove basting. Lay the $1\frac{1}{2}$ ins. wide facing strip along front side of opening, with selvedge edge along the seam edge of skirt. Baste together, making the seam $\frac{1}{4}$ in. wide on the facing strip and $\frac{1}{8}$ in. wide on skirt, as **A**; then stitch.

Step 2. Press selvedge edge of strip back toward the skirt, as in **B**; and stitch the strip along the selvedge to stay the front edge of the placket, as shown. This stitching comes on the seam allowance of the skirt (as shown by crease), and so the stitching does not show on the outside of the skirt when the placket is finished. Fold the facing back against the skirt, and press it in place along creased edge. On back edge of placket opening, turn raw edge back $\frac{1}{4}$ in. and baste, as in **C**.

Step 3. Turn skirt right side out. Lay closed fastener under the basted edge and pin in place, as in **D**. Place folded guard strip under fastener, with the selvedge edge of guard on top toward the back of skirt, and the folded edge of the guard even with the left side of the skirt, stitching through skirt, fastener tape, and guard.

Step 4. Close placket perfectly. Baste the front edge of the placket in position, basting from the bottom of the placket up to the waistline, as in **E**.

Step 5. Turn skirt wrong side out. Pin guard back, as in **F**. Turn raw edge of facing strip under—even with tape edge of fastener. Stitch on folded edge from **G** to **H**, stitching through tape and facing, but not through skirt.

Step 6. Turn skirt right side out. Baste in preparation for stitching. Stitch across the bottom, from **I** to **J** and back to **I**.

Pivot the needle at **I**. Stitch along the basted line from **I** to **K**. Move the slider down out of the way when you near **K**, so that you can stitch close to the fastener. Unpin guard, and slide it into position. Remove bastings. Pull thread ends through, and tie.

Step 7. Apply band or top belt to skirt, and conceal tape ends inside it. Place hooks and eyes on the band.

If the finished seams in the skirt are to be pressed open, clip the seam allowance at the bottom of the facing strip so that the seam will lie flat. Overcast raw edges. Press from the right side, using a damp cloth.

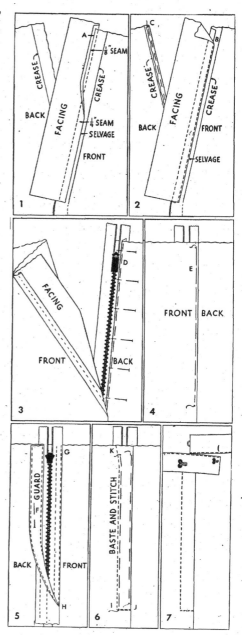

SLIDE FASTENERS—NECK, FRONT, BACK

Step 1. Cut a facing piece as wide as necessary. Crease this lengthwise through the centre. Cut down the centre on a thread, making the cut the same length as the fastener you plan to use. At the end, cut a ¼ in. diagonal line at each side, as in **A.** Turn the edges back ⅜ in. on the wrong side, as in **B;** crease on a thread, and baste.

Step 2. Place the slide fastener over this opening on the wrong side of the facing, with the right side of the fastener on top. Pin and baste in place, as in **C.**

Step 3. Turn down the tape ends at the top, as shown in **D,** so that they will be caught in with the stitching. Stitch as shown.

Step 4. Make a slash in the garment, exactly the same as in **A.** Turn the edges a scant ¼ in. to the wrong side, as in **B.** Baste. Place this opening, right side of fabric up, precisely over the fastener and facing piece. Baste and stitch, as in **E,** pivoting the needle at the corners. Remove bastings. Complete the opening by adding a collar or facing to the top or neck edge.

SLIDE FASTENERS—POCKETS, SLEEVES

Step 1. The slide fastener in a pocket takes the place of the welt. To make: Simply cut a line on a thread, making it ¾ in. shorter than the fastener. Cut diagonally on all corners for a scant ¼ in., as in **A.**

Step 2. Turn edges back, as in **B,** turning the seam 1/16 in. deeper at the front end of pocket to allow for the slider.

Step 3. Baste the fastener in place and stitch close to the edges, as in **C,** pivoting at the corners.

Step 4. Cut two pouch pieces, one the width of the slide-fastener tape shorter than the other. Stitch both pieces to the "slide"—shorter piece to the lower fastener tape, of course, and longer piece to the upper tape. Stitch the pouch pieces together, as in **D,** holding them away from the garment so that only the pouch edges are caught. The raw edges are notched or overcast.

Sleeve Fasteners. Concealed slide fasteners may be applied to fitted sleeves by the same method used for dress plackets. Use a fastener between 4 ins. and 6 ins. long. Place the closed fastener with the top of the slider a seam's width from the end of the sleeve. Use bias facing to finish the sleeve edge.

Fasteners for full sleeves with cuffs are applied

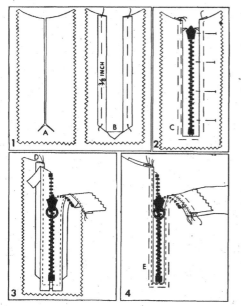

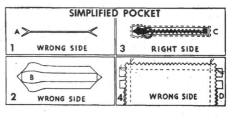

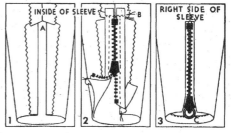

in the same way as for a neck opening. Face the opening with a narrow strip of fabric.

Decorative sleeve fasteners are applied as follows:

1. Measure the fastener and clip the sleeve to this length, as at **A**. Make a ¼ in. turn back on each side.

2. Baste and stitch the fastener in the opening, holding the edges away from the sleeve as you stitch. Turn back the bottom ends of the tape as shown. Stitch across and back at the top of the tape, as at **B**.

3. Use bias facing to finish the bottom of the sleeve; stitch the edge of the facing; and slip-stitch it in place, as shown.

LONG AND OPEN-END FASTENERS

For house-coats, lounging robes, hostess gowns, and daytime frocks, full-length and open-end slide fasteners are often used.

Long Fasteners. Long or full-length fasteners that are not open at the lower end may be basted in position over a pressed-open seam and applied exactly in the manner given for a simplified placket. Especially for a full-length fastener, take the precaution to ease the fabric slightly so that it cannot be tighter than the fastener.

Open-End Fasteners. For a closure that comes apart at both ends, use the open-end (or separating) fastener.

Baste both sides of the garment opening together on the seam line. Press open. Pin the closed fastener over the basted seam on wrong side of garment, with the slider side down and the centre of fastener exactly over the basted line. Baste through the fastener tape, easing fabric slightly. Fasten each lower end of fastener securely to garment. To do this: Draw a piece of strong tape through the metal hole, and baste ends of tape in position so that they will be caught in with the stitching when you stitch the fastener in place; or sew through hole with a strong thread, being careful not to let stitches come through to right side of garment. Turn garment right side out. Stitch the fastener in place, using cording foot and keeping the stitching ¼ in. away from the centre. To strengthen this, add a second row of stitching outside the first; or stitch a facing piece on to the inside, so that the stitching catches the fastener tape and serves to hold it securely. This is important in sports coats and children's play clothes, where there is hard wear and tear on opening.

Corded-Edge Application. If you want to conceal a fastener completely, cord both edges of the garment opening. Stitch these corded edges to fastener. The cording will conceal the fastener and will prevent the fabric from catching in it. Firm fabric is best for this type of application.

To Press Slide-Fastener Openings. Always close fasteners before pressing the opening. Lay a damp bath towel over the opening and press at each side and below the fastener but never on the fastener itself. Turn the garment to the wrong side, place the towel over the opening and press, still being careful not to touch the iron to the fastener.

★   ★   ★

39 .

SEWING-MACHINE ATTACHMENTS

THE SEWING-MACHINE ATTACHMENTS— "Fashion Aids," as they are rightfully called— provide you with the means of doing by machine what would demand real finger skill in hand-sewing. They save time and make it possible to do very professional-looking work in making ruffles, applying cording, motifs for decoration, and many other attractive fashion details. But you must first learn how to use each one, and then practise until you can use each one quickly and perfectly. Use your machine instruction book for reference or get instruction from the people at your local sewing-machine shop. A few of the favourite attachments are described here. These have helped us to save time, to do professional-looking work, and provided a measure of thrill for us, because that is exactly what you experience when you know how to speed these ingenious time-saving aids along your fabric to get a result quickly and perfectly. It does not matter what make of machine you use. (The attachments on all makes of machines are similar and work in much the

same way. Do you know your machine and its attachments; then these instructions will be easy to follow.)

A. The Cloth Guide. The cloth guide is a metal piece which is screwed to the base of the machine to help you place your stitching at the desired depth from the edge of the fabric. To adjust the guide strip for wide or narrower spacing, loosen the screw in the slot and slide the guide strip to the desired position. The cloth guide is invaluable for top and decorative stitching.

B. The Hemmers. Machine hemmers come in various widths so that it is easy to get the hem width you want. They are most useful if you have yards and yards of fabric to hem, as in making ruffles or flounces. The foot hemmer has a slot which will hold lace or braid in position so that it can be affixed to place as the hem is stitched. Clip the end of the fabric diagonally and turn about 2 in. of the hem to the width you want. Then slip the turned part into the hemmer, pull top and bottom threads back, and stitch.

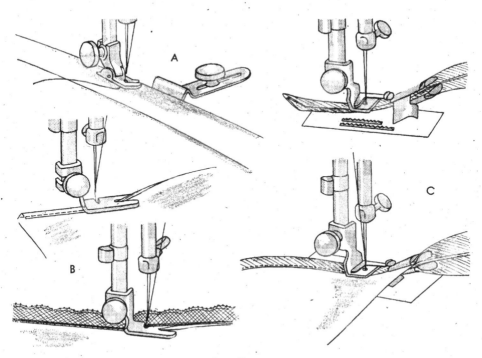

C. The Binder. The quickest and most efficient way to bind an edge is to use width No. 5 in a ready-made binding and apply it with the machine binder. Fold the binding in half lengthwise and cut one end to a point as shown. Put the point through the slot on the extreme right of the binder, attach the binder to the machine and slide the fabric inside the open side of the attachment so that it lies inside the binding and comes right up to the fold. Stitch. If the fabric is flimsy, turn one edge a scant ⅛ in. and stitch it first before binding. This not only gives more body to the edge but will insure the edges staying in the binding in wear and washing.

D. Gathering Foot. The machine gathering foot, like the cording foot, is an attachment that does not usually come with the machine, though it should be with every one, because it is indispensible in sewing-machine work. The gathering foot is as easy to use as the presser foot. You can make fine or coarse gathers simply by shortening or lengthening the machine stitch—a little practice on a scrap of ruffling is all that is necessary to insure efficiency with, and enthusiasm for it.

E. Cording Foot. There are two cording feet available, right-hand and left-hand. You may find it easier to use one than the other. Ordinarily, whichever you prefer is perfectly satisfactory. There are one or two cases in sewing which will require the use of both to finish the job. The cording foot enables you to stitch cording into a strip of bias so that the stitching is placed snugly against the cord. Use a short stitch and thread to match the colour of the bias strip. See the illustration for placing of cording in bias and the use of the cording foot.

F. Quilting Foot. This foot is purposely short and turned up at the front so that the padded fabric can slip easily under the needle. The guide bar of the quilter is arranged so that you can set it to space evenly between rows of stitching, as

*(Continued on page 42. Instructions for **G**, Singercraft Guide on next page.)*

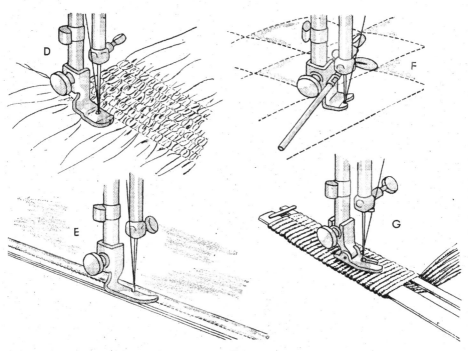

shown. This attachment can be used for decorating fabric when fashion favours quilted details and for making padded articles for the home.

G. Singercraft Guide. This is a metal strip with a slot through the centre. Thread, yarn, braid, binding or strips of fabric may be wound on it in various arrangements and stitched down through the centre slot. Extensions may be added to the craft guide to permit wider windings. The illustration shows how the presser foot stitches through the slot. Use your craft guide to make fringe and other edgings for garments and household linens, rugs and trimmings. The instruction sheet that comes with each machine when you buy it will tell you how. This again is an attachment well worth mastering. It has a multiplicity of uses and is a great time-saver.

H. Edge-Stitcher. This time-saver is used for joining edges of ribbon, braid, insertion, or lace to fabric or to each other. It holds the edges nicely one over the other while you stitch, so that you don't get too much overlap, but still catch the edges together. It can be used also for making pin tucks and for applying ribbon or braid smoothly and evenly to fabric. Illustrations show how to use it for two different types of stitching.

I. Braiding Foot. To apply narrow braid to fabric by machine, use the braiding foot. The stitching will be straighter and much more secure than hand-sewing. Apply the braid transfer-design to the right side of the fabric (wrong side, if the fabric is transparent enough to see the design through it) or mark the design on the fabric by running the unthreaded needle over the tissue design on the right side, as in **I-1**. Then slip the braid in the opening at the end of the braiding foot, draw it back and under the needle, and stitch on the line of the design as shown.

J. The Underbraider is a semicircular disc attachment screwed on the sewing-machine plate and used with the quilting foot to apply braid to

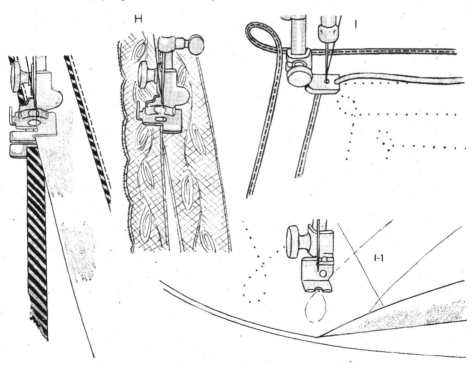

H

I

I-1

the right side of fabric as you stitch from the wrong side, following the design which has been transferred to it. If you do not wish to transfer the design to the fabric, make it on paper by stitching with the unthreaded needle, as described above. If you have a large surface to cover with the design, mark several thicknesses of paper and baste one piece on the wrong side of each section of the fabric. Then stitch on the paper. The underbraider will apply the braid along the design on the right side, as shown.

At the end of a line of braid pull the braid ends through a tiny hole in the fabric which you have made with a darning needle, and with needle and thread fasten the ends on the wrong side.

K. The Ruffler. This attachment enables you to make ruffles, tiny regular pleats, gathered ruffles, and group pleats with several stitches between. Practise on a scrap before using the ruffler to be sure you are getting the desired effect and are gathering up the right amount of fabric. To

attach the ruffler, remove the presser foot, then set the fork astride the needle clamp screw and the foot in position on the needle bar. Screw this in place just as you do the presser foot. Retighten the screw from time to time as you work, as the vibration sometimes loosens it in operation.

L. The Zigzagger. It is worth while to get complete instruction on the use of this attachment at the sewing-machine shop and then practise at home. The zigzagger is useful for many things and imitates hand appliqué in a very satisfactory way. If you like to make lingerie, children's clothes or dainty table linens, then by all means become expert in the use of this attachment. This is a most satisfactory way to join lace.

M. The Faggoter. This enables you to imitate hand faggoting. Wind the thread or yarn or braid for the faggoting back and forth over the prongs of the machine faggoter. Stitch it in position on paper. Place the fabric edges over this stitching and stitch down as shown. Remove the paper.

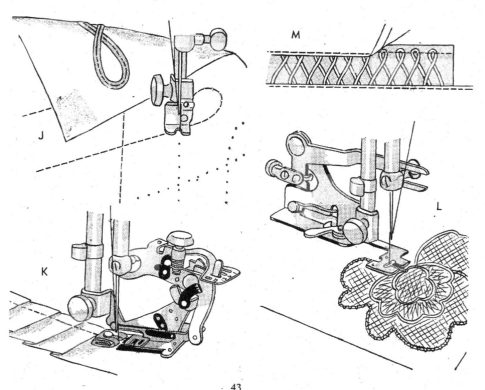

43

LET'S MEND IT

A STITCH IN TIME is a wise precaution. Mend if practicable as soon as there is a broken thread and thus prevent the loss of fastenings and save patching or major repair work.

We will concentrate at first on mending with stitches. Even if you have a make-over problem —a dress you want to turn into something quite different from what it is now—leave the pages that contain suggestions for such work for a little while and stay here. Learn first to darn, reinforce and patch. All of this experience will serve to give you practice and patience and insure a skill that will help you with a major job of reconditioning fabric.

We are not beginning our mending instructions in this book with stockings or socks, because you should be quite skilful with darning stitches before you undertake these. Feet resent any roughness or unevenness; and, to darn a sock or stocking so that it is completely smooth and comfortable, women must be skilful in handling the needle and thread, finishing off, drawing up the stitches—in fact, every step of the process. So we are going to begin with simple reinforcing at first, gain practice in that and, later, as skill comes, turn our attention to that all-important stocking bag or drawer, and do the mending needed there. Then, when we are quite expert at many types of sewing, we'll go on to remaking and refashioning garments.

Consider Your Fabric. No matter what method of mending you intend to use, always consider your garment or article and the fabric of which it is made. For mending fabrics of any fibre—cotton, linen, woollen, silk, rayon—the essential thing is to have a thread as nearly as possible the same in weight and colour as the warp, that is, the lengthwise thread, of the fabric. Whenever possible, it is desirable to unravel a thread of the fabric and use that for mending, especially if you are darning. The mend will be less conspicuous, wear more satisfactorily, and be in every way more practical. Often it is possible, in cottons, linens, and woollens, to pull out a warp thread along a wide seam edge to get a length of thread for reinforcing or darning. When only short ravellings are available for mending use a long needle, make your stitches on the needle, thread it and pull it through. Make the next row of stitches on the needle, rethread it and pull it through. By continuing to do this throughout the mend, the same scrap of thread can be used almost entirely.

Hand Darning. The principal stitch used in darning by hand is the running-stitch, which is placed in close parallel rows lengthwise on the fabric round and over the worn place and then crossed and interwoven by rows of stitches running crosswise. Many uses of this procedure are shown in the following pages.

If you are a novice at sewing, study the *Essentials of Sewing*, the *Stitches*, and the problems outlined in this section so that you may learn to work with skill and confidence. Learn to use all the tools of sewing—the darning egg, embroidery hoop, etc.—and to work with all types of threads and needles which are required by the actual work in hand.

Machine Darning. Living in the machine age as we are, it is logical that we should, when practical, mend by machine. This saves time and provides a very durable mend. The qualifications, when practicable, must always be considered. A machine mend shows—when thread matches perfectly, it shows little, but it does show. Many hand mends can be made invisible (or practically so).

You must decide how valuable your garment or article is, whether its mend can be worn proudly without concealment, as on a workman's overalls, or whether you want to keep your rips and tears to yourself and make them invisible. Study these points carefully before you begin to work.

To Darn by Machine. Regulate stitch as for regular sewing before starting to darn. See that tensions are correctly set and your machine is stitching evenly. Remove the presser foot. Attach the machine darning foot and the feed cover plate. Be sure this feed plate is precisely in place so that your needle goes directly into the centre of the hole. Put the fabric over an embroidery hoop, right side down, so that when the frame edge is turned up you can make your darn on the right side of the fabric. Be sure your fabric is tight in the embroidery hoop. Wrap one hoop, if necessary, to insure tightness.

Use a short machine-stitch and for white fabrics use a fine, white thread; size 100 is ideal. For colours, use mercerized sewing thread.

Bring the bobbin thread up and back from the darning foot. Pull the top and bobbin threads back out of the way so that these threads cannot catch in your darning. Drop the presser bar lifter down and proceed to stitch. After a row of darn-

44

ing, cut the threads off to prevent their interfering with your darning.

Move the work back and forth under the needle until the hole is filled in just as for a hand darn. Then turn and darn across these rows. In this way you make a sturdy darn, secure the threads and fill the hole. Stitching should extend five or six stitches beyond the hole all the way round so that the darn will hold through wear and washing. When darning by machine, your upper thread may break occasionally. This is because you are stitching backward or your tension is too tight. To correct, loosen the tension and turn your hoop so that you will stitch forward for each row, rather than forward and back. If the hoop is turned, always do this while the needle is down in the material so as to retain firmly your stitching position.

Darning can be done without the darning foot— or the feed plate. For this, unscrew the presser foot screw on the top of your machine head— unscrew until the presser bar lifter will not hold up.

EMERGENCY MENDING

IT WILL HAPPEN SOMETIMES! A garment will be torn in one of those long gaping rents that brooks no delay in closing it. With sewing equipment at hand, the problem is simplified, but it is well to know some quick, effective stitches that will keep the material in good condition until proper mending can be done. •

With Needle and Thread. A clean, straight, or right-angle tear may be quickly closed with diagonal-basting-stitches. If practical, turn the garment inside out, bring the edges smoothly together and baste, keeping the stitches reasonably short on the right side. Where the material is soft and a closer stitch is required to hold it, the catch-stitch is better.

If the material has become pulled or shredded, a regular darning-stitch will prove best, but make the stitches large so they may be easily removed when permanent stitches are put in.

When a piece of the garment has been torn out, try to cut a patch from some other part of the garment. The hem turn may supply it. Cut this, if possible, neatly enough so that it may be placed in permanent position later. Any scrap of material, whether it matches or not, will serve in an emergency.

Without Needle and Thread. A garment may become torn at one's work, play or when travelling. Quick mending jobs are possible with various kinds of adhesives usually available. Most of them can be removed satisfactorily with cleaning fluid.

Adhesive tape proves convenient for emergency mending. Bring the torn edges together so they just meet and apply small patches of the tape. This keeps the garment pliable.

Gummed paper tape, rubber cement or any similar adhesives will serve similarly.

Paste hardens, is likely to fleck off, and may not hold well on a straight-edged tear. However, a coating of paste on the back of a ragged or shredded spot will mat the material and hold it fairly well for a short time. Paste or soap on a stocking run proves a good stopper and washes out easily. Nail polish does not wash out and is likely to discolour the spot.

In some emergencies even chewing gum has been used to hold a rent that might prove annoying.

Tricks to Camouflage. In addition to tears in clothing there are times when accidents cause spots that must be camouflaged for a few hours. These people solved the problem:

The girl who dropped medicine on a light dress, made a bow from a lacy handkerchief.

The woman who caught a splash of chocolate on a white vest removed it and pinned in her husband's handkerchief.

The girl at the picnic who dropped a tomato in her lap pinned her soft sports hat at her belt to cover the stain and made it seem a new fashion whim.

The boy in the white trousers who sat on a berry pie tied his sweater round his waist knotting the sleeves in front.

The girl who nonchalantly looped her scarf through her belt to hide an annoyingly long paint stain.

The teacher whose light blouse was the target for a flying blot of ink from a youngster's pen cut a modish monogram from blue paper to paste over the stain.

Ingenuity is a necessity in mending, even in camouflaging until complete repair can be made.

REINFORCING

ARTICLES AND GARMENTS that grow thin or weak with friction or suffer accidental tears can be reinforced and the damage repaired easily. **Let's Begin.** Have you a thin place in the elbow of a long-sleeved dress? All right, turn it wrong side out. Slip a piece of cardboard, or an envelope, or any kind of firm, white paper into the sleeve. The white allows you to see just how worn the thin spot is, how large your reinforcement should be, where to place it, and where to begin with your stitches.

The Reinforcing Piece. Suppose the dress is wool. If you have an old piece of veiling, net, or chiffon of the same colour, you can fold it one or more times to make it strong enough to serve as a reinforcing piece. If you have an old piece of sheer stocking, use that. Try to use something that has some "give." For a thin elbow, a piece of georgette or chiffon cut on the bias is an ideal reinforcing piece, it will give with the garment.

Place your reinforcement over the thin spot, on the wrong side, as at **A.** Pin, then baste this in position. Knots, you know, are taboo in mending. For your permanent stitching, always start with the tiniest back-stitch you can make. Sometimes it is well to take three or four back-stitches to hold your thread and start you on your way.

Take tiny stitches through the reinforcement and the worn material so that they are not visible on the right side, but are from $\frac{1}{8}$ in. to $\frac{1}{4}$ in. long on the wrong side. Place your rows of stitches $\frac{1}{8}$ in. to $\frac{1}{4}$ in. apart, and sew back and forth, lengthwise of the fabric, until the reinforcement is securely in place. Trim off any frayed edges and press the reinforced part from the right side with a piece of fabric between the mended place and the iron. If preferred, the reinforcing stitches may be taken from the right as at **B.** The advantage of working from the right side is being able to see the worn spot. Your stitches can be made practically invisible.

Never draw stitches tight in mending. Make them easy, because there is a certain give in all materials that must be duplicated in your stitches if they are to become a part of that fabric and serve you for the remaining life of the garment. **Reinforcing Heavy Fabrics.** Cut the reinforcing piece large enough to cover the entire thin area. Pin, baste round edge of patch to hold it in place.

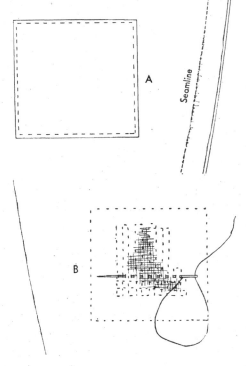

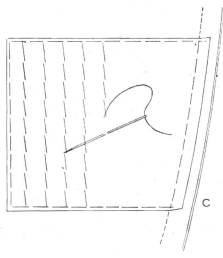

46

Use a diagonal basting-stitch on the wrong side, as in **C,** take a ¼ in. to ½ in. long stitch on the surface, barely catching a thread of the fabric being reinforced so that the stitches on the right side will be invisible. Make rows and rows of such stitches ¼ in. to ½ in. apart, this depending on amount of space to be covered. Also, if the worn spot is very weak, the smaller closer stitches are necessary. Make the stitches easy so that the stitches will not draw on the right side.

If the elbow of a man's overcoat is worn too thin for the above repair, place under it a piece of fabric slightly darker than the coat and four to six·times the size of the thin spot. Use thread of a little darker tone than the overcoat. Weave it back and forth, back and forth, so that it will not show from the right side.

Yarn Reinforcing. Use a strand of yarn from the fabric or a matching mercerized or woollen thread and darn the weak point. Doing this will give enough added strength to the threads in the garment and the yarn will not break apart into a hole.

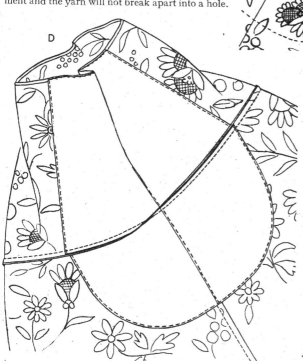

Shield Reinforcement. When underarm parts of blouses, dresses, shirts, etc., wear thin, they can be reinforced as shown here. This particular case was a sheer embroidered fabric which was worn and strained between the embroidered motif. A plain sheer fabric was used for the reinforcing section. The shield pieces were cut with the straight of the fabric and fitted to the underarm. The two halves were put together separately, then stitched into the underarm seam. Then the edges were attached to the garment with a running-stitch, as shown. **D** shows the wrong side with the sections all in place and the outer shield piece whipped in place at the sleeve binding. **E** shows the right side with the worn and strained places reinforced and caught with tiny stitches to the shield.

This type of repair can be done on many types of fabric—not necessarily only sheer fabrics.

EVERY TEAR HAS A MEND OF ITS OWN

Invisible Darn. To darn moth holes so that they are almost impossible to locate once the darn is complete, use a thread from the garment to be repaired. It is best to take a warp thread of the fabric, one from the side seam, if possible, for this usually will be a warp thread and stronger than a woof thread taken along the hem. Use a crewel needle, as small as will hold your thread. Then darn, from the wrong side, back and forth, beginning perhaps $\frac{1}{4}$ in. beyond the hole. Place the rows of stitches first lengthwise on the fabric, laying them carefully over the hole and going about $\frac{1}{4}$ in. beyond its edges all round. Darn in the crosswise rows of stitches, alternating the stitches over and under the lengthwise stitches. It is better to take your stitches gently, and a little too loose rather than draw them tight, because woollen fabrics all have a certain amount of give and you want your darn to have just as much elasticity as the rest of the fabric. If too tight, the edges may pull away and the fabric will be drawn round the darn. Bring all thread ends to the wrong side and snip them close to the fabric. Press the darn by placing it right side down on a well-padded board. Under a damp cloth press the darn gently.

your threads carefully to the fabric to make the work invisible. The darning may be done either by hand or by machine, according to the type of fabric you are mending.

Reinforced Darn. For a hole in a man's shirt, for example, baste a piece of firm bandage gauze or cheesecloth on the wrong side as shown in **A**, using thread to match the colour of the shirt. Use a fine needle and fine darning stitches with a medium-fine thread. Work from the wrong side; then your shortest stitches will be on the right side and less conspicuous. Darn back and forth, lengthwise of the fabric as shown in **B**. Place the rows of stitches through the hole just a little closer together than those on the sides.

Slashes. When you have to mend an accidental slash in a garment or want to draw together the edges of a long tear before sewing on the machine, it is sometimes practical to use a fishbone-stitch as shown here. It can be used on firm fabrics of cotton or wool without any other stitching if there is no strain on the slash. If the slash is rather long or on the bias, it may be advisable to pin or baste a piece of paper under it before starting to sew the edges together. To keep the stitches uniform, the edges must be held smoothly together. Take the stitches firmly but not so tight as to draw the fabric. If the place is subject to strain and needs further strengthening, darn back and forth over the slash in the usual manner after drawing the edges together with the fishbone-stitch. Match

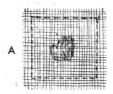

A

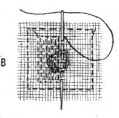

B

One-Way Darn. Some types of fabrics, particularly those in which the threads running one way are heavier than those running the other way, are likely to wear as shown here. One set of threads wears away, leaving the other set loose. To repair, simply stitch back and forth across the remaining threads, beginning a little back from the edge of the worn spot and stitching far enough past each side to prevent pulling out.

Corner Tear. This is the kind of tear most likely to result from catching a garment on something sharp, such as a nail, and snagging it. To mend it : Smooth the edges of the tear together and baste a piece of writing paper over the right side to hold it in place. Then, on the wrong side, darn back and forth across the tear, starting a little back from one end and working towards the corner. Make the rows of stitches a little deeper towards the corner for greater strength at the weakest spot. Cross the rows of darning at the corner, and continue to the other end, tapering the rows slightly as you get away from the corner and finishing $\frac{1}{4}$ in. or more beyond the end of the tear.

As you turn back from one row to another, leave a tiny thread loop at each turning so that your

stitching will have some give just as fabric does. Clip the basting stitches and remove the paper.

Runs in Knit Wear. Two ways to repair these are shown here. The run in **C** is simply whipped together as in **D**. This type of repair would be done on knitted underwear which did not require fine work or need not be mended invisibly.

The mend in **E** is more painstaking, and would be done on garments of more value and where it was important not to have the mend show. Use a very fine crochet hook, pick up the free loop in the knitting, and pull the threads of the run through the loop, one after the other until you reach the end of the run. Catch the last loop in place from the wrong side with needle and thread and secure with a few whipping-stitches.

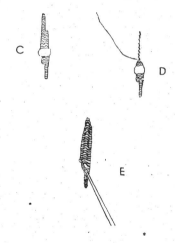

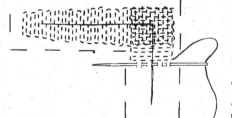

Crosswise Splits in Knit Wear. A long crosswise tear in fine-ribbed knit wear, glove silk, rayon underwear, etc., may be mended by machine, as in **F**. Pin the edges of the split together as shown, and stitch twice across the edge.

Coarser knit fabrics, woollens, etc., can be inconspicuously mended as in **G** or **H**.

G shows the fabric folded along the split and whipped together by putting the needle through the loops along the edge. Use matching thread. Be sure to catch all loops of the fabric to prevent runs. *(Illustrations **F**, **G** and **H**, on page 50.)*

(Instructions for F and G on page 49.)

Stocking Grafting. The stitch shown in **H** should be done with matching thread to make it invisible. Catch the needle through two loops on one side of the split, then two loops on the other, alternating all across the split. Secure the thread on the wrong side at the end of the mend.

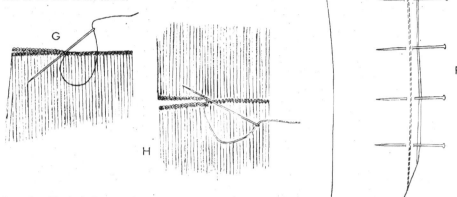

Irregular Machine Darn. This type of ragged tear occurs frequently in underwear, particularly at the end of a placket or in the crotch of men's shorts. The method of darning shown here may be used for many tears of this kind. Pin or baste a piece of similar fabric under the hole on the wrong side. Set your machine stitch at about twelve to the inch. Stitch on the right side, beginning a bit back from one end of the tear and going back and forth over the edges as shown. Continue this, changing the direction of the stitching as the shape of the tear requires, until all torn edges are stitched. Trim off excess from the reinforcing piece, and whip the edges down.

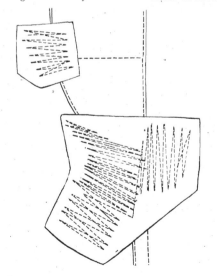

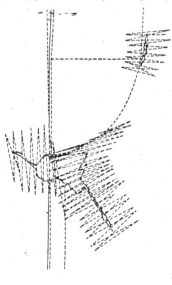

DARNING IS A FINE ART .

DARNING, like embroidery, needs, for perfection, pride in the accomplishment of truly beautiful work. The right materials, care in doing, and an appreciation for appropriateness are essential in good darning.

If you have a new garment that has met with an accident, then consider that to have a hole or tear repaired professionally would cost several shillings. If your skill is sufficient to do it so that the mend is nearly invisible, then consider that such work is well worth your time and trouble, and proceed to do it so that you can take pride in it.

to avoid a thick mend, and to prevent the hole from becoming larger and so save extra work.

Stocking Patch. This patch is good for large holes in the heels of men's and children's socks because it gives so much elasticity. Cut away round the worn part to get a round or oval hole. Cut the patch piece to fit into the hole, with the rib of the knit running the same way in the patch as in the sock. Baste paper under the hole and join the edges with the laced seam. For instructions on this seam, see page 20. Remove the bastings and paper when the patch is complete. This seam is good to use in applying a new foot to stockings. However, it is better to darn and mend stockings before they need such extreme repair as a whole new foot.

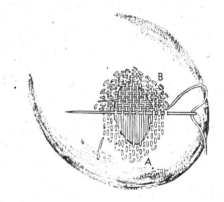

Woven Darns. When a stocking needs darning, do it so smoothly that there can be no rough places and so that the stitches do not show at the top of the shoe. The surest way to do this is to use thread that matches and separate the strands so that you use not more than three at a time. Two strands usually make a softer, less conspicuous darn. Work over a darning ball or egg to prevent drawing the threads. Lay the stitches lengthwise over the hole as in **A,** then weave the crosswise threads in by picking up every other thread. As your thread turns to go back with each row you will have some stitches that are at variance with your weaving as at **B.** The stitches in the illustration are enlarged in order to see the process.

Mesh Darning. Use a single strand of darning cotton. Do not draw mesh together. Darn with the weave of the stocking rather than draw the break together with whipping-stitches. The purpose of such a darn is to hold the threads together,

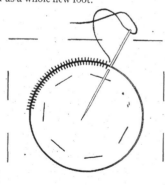

Stitch Stocking Runs by Machine. Thread your machine with mercerized sewing thread in a colour to match your stocking. Adjust machine for a very short stitch. Turn the stocking wrong side out. Lay the run together as for a seam. Pin it as

shown in **A**. **B** is the regular stocking seam at the back of the stocking. **C** shows the run being pinned in preparation for stitching. **D** shows the run, stitched. You begin 2 ins. above the run as at **E**. Take a seam as deep as necessary to take in all of the run. Taper the seam down to the stocking seam, or to 2 ins. below the run as in **F**. Stretch the run lengthwise as you stitch so that the stitching line will have elasticity to match the weave or "give" of the stocking. Some women prefer to stitch such runs on news or tissue paper. Once you develop skill with such runs, you will be able to do it without the paper and will consequently have less ripple in the seam.

If you must sew a run by hand whip it as in **G**. Do this from the right side of the stocking and stretch the run lengthwise as you proceed with the seam.

Runs in Stocking Hems. Runs occur in all silk or all rayon tops, more readily than in cotton. When they do occur, as in **H**, stitch, as in **I**, doing this as you would a run in the leg.

When there are many runs in a hem, as in **J**, stitch across these runs, as at **K** and **L**, to prevent their spreading and to keep them within the hem. Do not try to mend them all separately, as this will make this part of the stocking too narrow for the leg. Often such precaution will save the stocking from leg runs.

M shows a hole caused by strain on welt of stocking where the suspender hooks on. **N** shows how edges should be whipped together very securely to prevent serious run. If the stocking welt does not bind, the edges of the opening can be whipped together as at **O**. This will give extra protection when suspenders are worn.

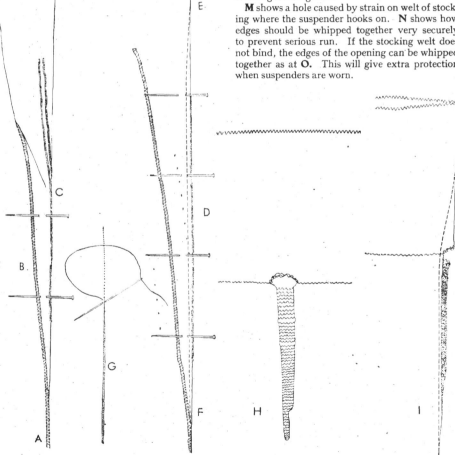

Stocking Welt Patch. When a hole is torn in the stocking welt, as it may be by a suspender, mend it as shown here. Cut a patch from an old stocking, place it over the hole on the wrong side, and pin, then hem it in place, as in **P**. The right side of such a patch is shown in **Q**. Hem round the hole on the right side, and if a run has started from the hole, darn it neatly as at **R**.

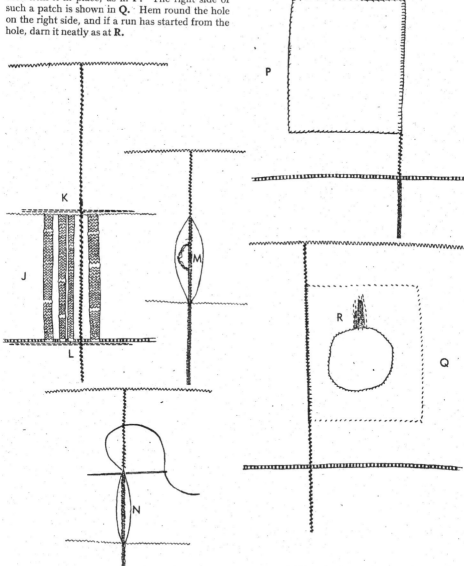

WOVEN DARNS IN KNITTED WEAR

Chain-Stitch Darn. The darn when done with matching yarn and a little care can be almost invisible on knitted articles such as gloves, sweaters, etc. Begin by securing the yarn with a few stitches through the loops, as at **B.** Then weave the needle in and out of the loops across one edge of the hole, as shown, being sure to catch each loop. When one row is caught, turn the garment round and go across again. Catch each single loop in each row. Go back and forth until you have laid threads across the entire hole, as in **A.**

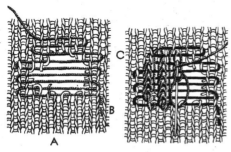

Do not cut off the yarn, but bring the needle out at the corner of the hole, as at **C,** and begin making a series of chain-stitches, as shown, utilizing the threads you have laid across the hole as foundation for the stitches. When the end of a row is reached, bring the needle out in the next row of loops. Working the needle over and under the threads, go up to the top of the darn and begin the next row of chain-stitches. Continue until the hole is covered.

This method gives an excellent imitation of the original ribbed knitting, and if the correct weight of yarn is used and the stitches are neither too tight nor too loose, no one will ever see the darn.

Stocking-Web Darn. For darning sweaters, gloves and other hand-knitted garments, this method is very satisfactory. It takes considerable time and skill, so don't do it unless the garment is worth the effort. Use wool that exactly matches that of the garment to make the darn invisible.

Cut away worn and broken threads round the hole, pull out loose thread ends and leave the loop formation of the knitting clear on each side. With regular cotton sewing thread of the same colour as the wool, put in supporting strands, as shown in **D,** to connect the free loops at each end of the hole and to give a basis on which to place the new loops that will fill the hole.

Hold the fabrics so that the ribs run up and down. Then, with your wool darning thread, begin at the top right of the hole and one whole loop to the right of the edge, as shown in **E,** and cover the row of loops to which the supporting strands are fastened. Work across from right to left, putting your needle through as shown in **F** and leaving the loops loose enough to match the original knitting. When you have gone one whole loop beyond the left edge, turn the work round and go back, placing the next row of loops on the supporting threads and connecting the preceding row of loops as shown in **G.** The work must be turned at the end of each row.

Continue until you have covered the row of free loops at the opposite end of the hole.

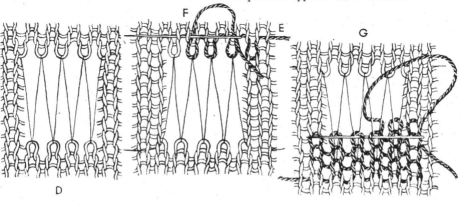

54

PURPOSEFUL PATCHES

Material for Patching. Cut a patch piece from a facing or from under a hem, or from the underside of the back of a collar, or from the tail of a blouse or shirt. Cut this to match the warp and woof, or the print pattern, of the part to be patched. This makes it necessary also to patch the garment where you procured the patch piece. You can do this with any fabric of similar colour and texture.

If you are patching a child's play suit, or linen slacks, you can "go gay" and use other colours for the patches, putting them on in the shape of leaves or diamonds or in crazy-quilt style. See *Amusing and Decorative Patches*, page 63. Take a note from this and patch decoratively.

Rip off a pocket, if this is practical, to provide the patch. Or take a piece from the scrap bag. New cotton or wool pieces should be washed to prevent shrinking after they are applied. If the garment is faded, place the patch in the sun to fade it. Match stripes and figures accurately.

Hemmed Patch. This type of patch is best used on very firm or heavy washable fabrics, such as linen, seersucker, etc., and on articles on which you don't mind having the stitches show. Begin by cutting away the frayed portion of the fabric round the hole, as in **A**. Cut a square or rectangular hole, using the threads of the fabric as a guide to get the edges straight. Clip each corner of the hole diagonally about ¼ in., as at **B** and turn the raw edges under all round. Cut your patch about 1½ ins. longer and wider than the hole with its edges turned under. Be sure to cut the patch so that the fabric threads and any design or print are matched to the part of the garment to be patched. Baste the patch in position under the hole and then, from the right side, hem the turned-under edge of the hole to the patch, as at **C**. Remove the bastings. On the wrong side, turn under the raw edges of the patch and hem them down as in **D**. We show this patch put in by hand, but it may be done by machine in the same way.

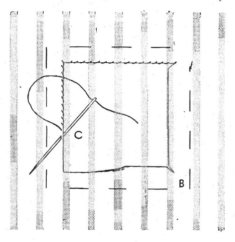

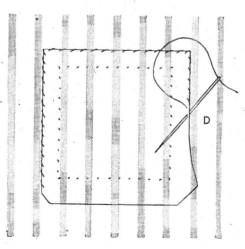

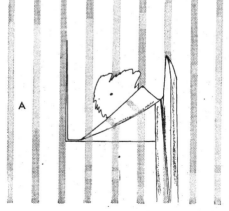

Oversewn Patch. This patch is less conspicuous than the hemmed patch, but is not so strong. It should be used on garments that are not washed often. Prepare the hole as for the hemmed patch. Clip the corners of the hole diagonally, as shown, and turn the edges under. Press this turn to get a nice straight line on each side of the patch. Lay the fabric for the patch piece under the hole and match it carefully against the edges of the hole for design and fabric grain as in **A.** Pin the patch in place and then slip-baste it to the edge of the

hole. Turn over to the wrong side. Trim the edges of the patch to $\frac{1}{4}$ in. and crease them back away from the edge of the hole as in **B.** Press this turn back if necessary. Fold back the fabric along one side of the hole as shown and oversew the two folded edges together from the wrong side. See oversewing, page 13. As you turn the corner, take several extra stitches to give strength at this point. Continue oversewing all round, folding the fabric back along each side as you come to it, and putting in the extra strengthening stitches at each corner. Clip the corners of the patch as at **C.** The raw edges of patch and hole may be pinked if the fabric is firm. If the fabric is loosely woven and tends to ravel, overcast the edges.

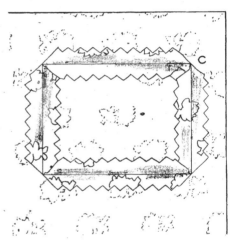

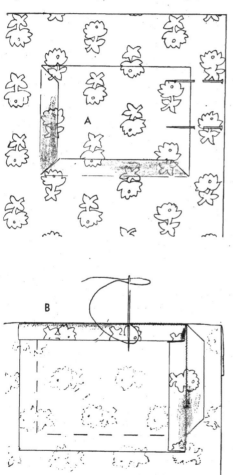

Flannel Patch. This makes a substantial patch for flannel or other fabrics that do not fray. Prepare the hole just as for the hemmed patch, by cutting the edges along a fabric thread. Lay the fabric for the patch over the hole, matching it to the garment both for pattern and for fabric grain. Then cut it from $\frac{3}{8}$ in. to $\frac{1}{2}$ in. larger than the hole. Baste the patch in position on the wrong side without turning in the edges of either the patch or the hole. Work from the right side first and herringbone-stitch the raw edges of the hole to the patch, using matching thread. Turn to the wrong side and herringbone-stitch the raw edges of the patch to the garment, as shown. Always try to make your stitches neat and inconspicuous.

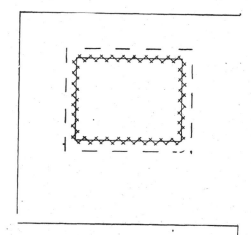

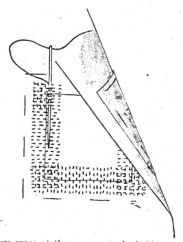

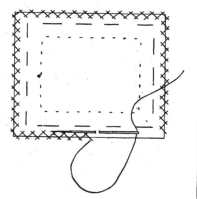

they cross at the corners to look like the fabric. For knitted underwear and for elastic foundation garments a **round underlaid patch,** herringbone-stitched in place, gives the maximum stretch. Cut away the worn part to make a hole round or oval. Cut the patch piece about **an** inch bigger in diameter than the hole. Baste the patch under the hole with the ribs parallel. Herringbone-stitch the edge of the hole to the patch as in **A,** using small stitches and a strong thread—button-hole twist, or mercerized cotton. Then, on the wrong side, herringbone-stitch the edge of the patch to the fabric of the garment, as in **B.** For herringbone-stitch see diagram page 13.

Underlaid Patch. When you need something stronger than a fitted patch, and still do not want any extra bulk, the underlaid patch is practical. You can use this on knitted fabrics, table linens, loosely woven woollens, etc. Cut away the frayed part round the hole, following the fabric threads to make the edges true. Make your patch about an inch larger than the hole, matching the fabric carefully for grain and pattern. Baste the patch in position under the hole. Then, from the right side, darn back and forth across the joining as shown, using matching thread to make your darning as inconspicuous as possible. Run your rows of stitches $\frac{1}{4}$ in. or more beyond the joining on each side to hold the patch securely and prevent ravelling, and weave the stitches in and out where

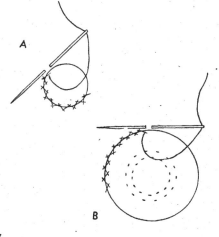

57

Tailored Patch. This type of patch has the advantage of being less conspicuous than the hemmed patch, and yet is strong enough to bear considerable strain. It can be used on any fabric. You begin, as you did with the hemmed patch, by cutting out the worn part round the hole, following the grain of the fabric to make a square or rectangular opening, as in **A**. Clip the corners as shown at **B**, turn under the raw edges, and press the crease with your iron. This pressing will insure your getting a neat turn under and will serve as a guide for stitching. It is especially advisable if you are working with woollen or some other fabric which is not readily creased by hand. Cut

your patch 1 in. to 1½ ins. longer and wider than the hole, being careful to match the grain or the printed or designed pattern of the fabric to the garment. Place the patch in position and, from the wrong side of the garment, baste it along the crease you have pressed in, as in **C**. As you baste, take a small back-stitch at each corner, as at **D**, to prevent the patch from slipping while you stitch. Then stitch it on the machine.

There are three ways of finishing the wrong side of this type of patch. If your fabric ravels and you don't mind having one row of stitching on the right side, you can do it as in **E**. Clip off the corners of the patch as shown, turn the raw edge

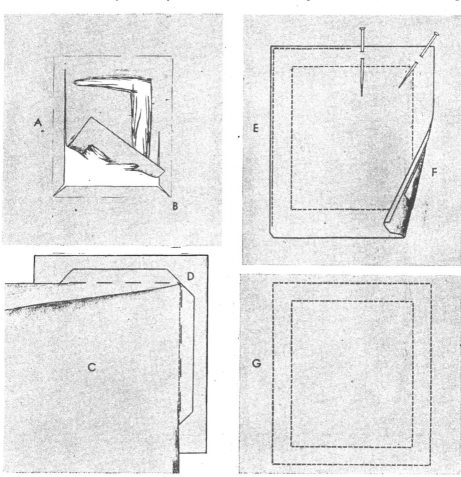

58

under as at **F,** and pin it in position; then stitch all round, close to the edge. The right side will then appear as in **G.** If your fabric does not ravel easily or if you prefer to have no stitching show on the right side, you can finish the wrong side as in **H.** Strengthen the corners by whipping just over the stitching as at **I** (do this in all cases to prevent pulling away). Trim the edges of the patch to the width of the hole turn-back, and overcast the two raw edges together. The method shown in **J** is similar, but a little stronger. You trim off the edges of the patch and herringbone-stitch the two raw edges to the garment. No stitches will show on the right side if you do this carefully, picking

up just a thread of the fabric with your needle. The right side should appear as in **K.**

Corduroy Patch. Cut the hole for the patch in a square or rectangle with two of the edges coming between the wales of the corduroy. Clip the corners of the hole diagonally and turn the raw edges back. Lay the patch piece under the hole and match the wale, as in **L,** before cutting. Baste the patch piece in place. Then, on the wrong side, stitch the patch to the turned-back edges. Press the seams open and clip off excess fabric at the corners, as in **M,** but leave enough overlap and overcast edges to prevent the corners ravelling.

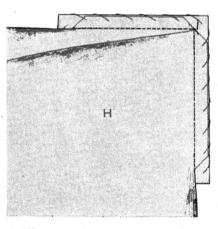

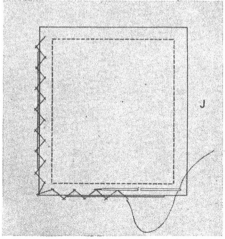

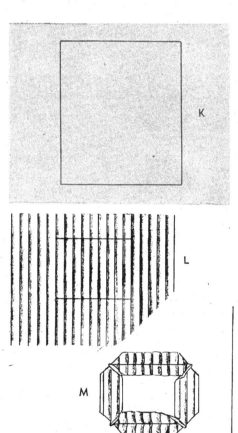

Fitted Patch. This is a patch cut to fit exactly into a hole. It eliminates all extra bulk and makes a perfectly flat patch. If you take care in matching the colour and weight of your thread to the fabric, and practise the stitching on scraps until you can do the work perfectly, this type of patch can be almost invisible. Prepare the hole just as you would for any patch. Then place the fabric for the patch under the hole and, with chalk, pencil, or tracing wheel, draw the shape of the patch. Match the patch to the garment fabric in grain or pattern. Now cut it out and fit it into the hole.

If your fabric is damask, round-thread linen, brocade, firm tweed, or bulky woollen cloth, you might use the fitted patch **darned in,** as in **A.** For this you cut a piece of paper an inch or two larger than the patch and, working from the wrong side of the garment, baste it under the hole to the right side. Fit the patch in place, right side down, and tack or baste it to hold it securely. Now run your darning-stitches back and forth across the slit, starting at the centre of one side, as shown. Where the stitches cross the slit, alternate them over and under the edges so that both sides of the patch will be supported. The stitches should extend $\frac{1}{4}$ in. or more beyond the joining on each side to be sure the edges are well caught.

Weave the rows of stitches in and out across each other at the corners, to make them show as little as possible and to give support where the strain is greatest. Be sure to hold your work flat as you do this so that the edges will come together straight and the fit of the patch will be perfect. Remove the paper when the patch is complete.

For heavy-napped fabrics, felted fabrics, broadcloth, etc.; the fitted patch with herringbone-stitch makes it possible to have no stitches showing on the right side. It is very satisfactory when used in a place where there is no strain.

Prepare the hole and the patch as described for the hemmed patch. Baste a piece of paper over the hole on the right side, just as for the fitted patch darned in, and fit your patch into the hole. Then, working from the wrong side, herringbone-stitch across the slit, concealing your crosswise stitches within the thickness of the fabric. Take care that your needle comes out at the cut edge of the hole or patch, and never goes all the way through the fabric; then, when you have finished, there will be visible only two rows of tiny stitches on the wrong side, as in **B.** Remove the bastings and paper.

The strongest of the fitted patches is the **machine-stitched** fitted patch. It can be used on most fabrics. If the garment or article you have to patch is to be used a great deal, laundered or cleaned often, then by all means machine-stitch the patch. Test a scrap of the material and thread you are going to use in the machine to see how much the stitching will show. Some fabrics show the stitching very little and others more, and if that is a point to consider, the best way to make sure is by testing. Don't attempt to do machine darning without mastering the instructions on page 44, because successful work depends entirely upon your skill with the machine. For the machine-stitched fitted patch, prepare the hole and fit the patch just as for the other fitted patches.

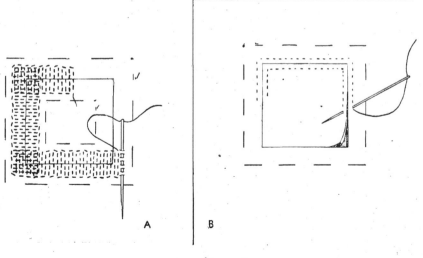

A   B

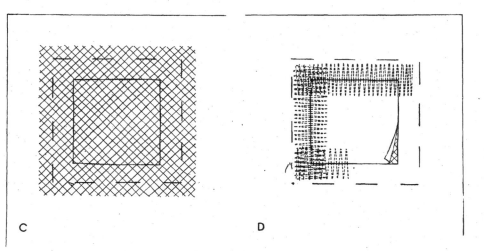

C   D

Cut a piece of cheesecloth or old curtain mesh about an inch larger than the patch, and baste it over the patch on the wrong side, as shown in C. Then put the work in an embroidery hoop to hold it perfectly flat and taut under the machine needle. Stitch back and forth across the slit on the right side of the fabric, extending the stitching about five stitches beyond the edges on each side, and crossing the rows of stitching at the corners for strength, as in D. Trim off the edges of the cheesecloth or mesh close to the stitching, and if you wish to remove all of it, do so by pulling out the threads from under the stitching.

Flat Fell Patch. This is similar to the hemmed patch, but it is put in with flat fell seams. The illustrations show how such a patch is fitted into a garment and how it can be made in other shapes than square or rectangular. Begin by opening

the seams of the garment E and F to a distance of 1½ ins. beyond the section to be replaced. Cut across as indicated by dotted lines in the first drawing and remove the torn section. Lay this piece on the fabric for the patch and cut the patch piece, fitting it exactly on the curved sides but leaving a ¾ in. seam allowance on each side of the length. Put the patch into the garment with flat fell seams, see page 20, stitching seams G and H across before doing the curved ends. Then turn your curved seams and stitch them neatly into the seams of the garment itself, as originally.

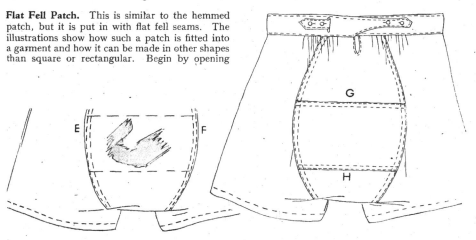

Half-and-Half Patch. The type of patch shown here may be useful in mending print fabrics if you haven't enough of the print to match the design. The particular case illustrated was a light-weight print blouse with a large hole on the edge of the yoke running into a part of the printed design. The patch piece was cut from under the collar but did not provide enough of the print design to match it all. The print part, therefore, was left when the fabric was cut away round the hole. The seam at the yoke was opened and the patch was pinned in place. The patch was stitched along the edges as at **A** and **B** and into the yoke seam. The upper half of the patch which reinforced the worn print section was held in place by running stitches following the line of the print, as shown. On the right side, the curved line round the design was turned under and hemmed down to the patch by hand as at **C**. The raw edges were overcast as shown on the wrong side. To replace the piece cut from under the collar, a piece of fabric matching in colour was used, making a fitted patch in the way shown on page 60.

This patch—half patch and half reinforcing, half machine-stitched and half hand-sewn—would vary a lot with the particular problem at hand.

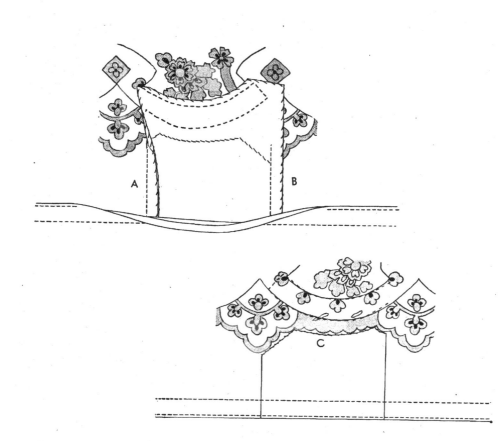

AMUSING AND DECORATIVE PATCHES

SOMETIMES PATCHES can be used to turn a disaster into almost an advantage. Instead of trying to conceal the mend, you come right out and show it boldly, but do it as decoration so that the patch looks as if intended from the beginning as a part of the garment. This is especially worth doing if the garment is practically new and even careful mending would rob it of its newness, or if the damage occurs in a spot that cannot be mended inconspicuously.

Appliqué Patches. These are appropriate for casual clothes and children's garments. Mend the spot by hand or machine and trace off on paper the size of the patch needed to cover it. Cut a silhouette of a conventional design—flower, fruit, animal, etc.—large enough to cover the mend. Turn in the edges of the patch and secure it to the garment. It may be applied by machine or by hand with a slip-stitch, whipping-stitch, running-stitch, blanket-stitch, long-and-short-stitch or any type of feather-stitch. Use more than one appliqué piece if necessary to balance the first and make the design seem planned.

A girl once had a hole burned in the front part of her sweater. She cut out a felt heart and appliquéd it over the hole with blanket-stitches, and no one was the wiser. When using felt or felted fabric it is unnecessary to turn in the edge of the patch.

The appliqué flower shown here illustrates how to turn under the edges, clipping or pinching in as necessary round curves. The right side shows how various stitches may be used to apply the

motif. A long-and-short-stitch is used round the blossom, while the stem and leaves are put on with a running-stitch.

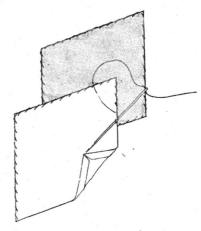

Hobo Patches. These are square, rectangular or diamond-shaped patches, usually entirely different in colour or fabric from the garment, whipped in place on the right side without any attempt at concealment. They serve a practical purpose when used to mend holes in knees, seats and elbows, and they have even been used, without the necessity of mending, just as a fashion feature on summer sports dresses, etc. Sometimes they are applied with thread of contrasting colour to carry out the carefree spirit of their use.

Reinforcement Patches. Generally these patches are applied to sports, play or work clothes when they are made to reinforce points of greatest wear. They are usually cut in ovals or rectangles, either from the same material as the garment or sometimes from leather, and stitched on the right side. Boys' and men's sports jackets can often be reinforced at the elbow with neat patches made of small pieces of leather or suede.

You can imitate these in mending for decorative effect. If there is a thin spot in the elbow of a little boy's sweater and you can't reinforce it to your satisfaction, take a piece of felt or leather from an old glove and apply a patch on each elbow. It is a good idea to cut suede patches of appropriate size and colour to be applied to elbow or knee.

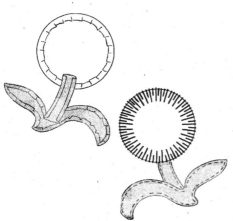

Trimming Patches. For mending garments or household articles that require more precise handling of a damaged spot, this type of patch is suitable. Patches may take the form of straps, bands, panels, medallions, pockets or yokes, so that they appear to be a part of the actual construction of the article. Make them of the same fabric as the article to be mended or of contrasting fabric or lace or anything that will blend properly.

The drawings **A** and **B** show a dress that was torn on the skirt and was patched in this way. The belt was opened up and pressed out so that two panel pieces could be cut from it. The top of each panel was shaped to a point that matched the lines

of the pocket on the blouse part. Then the two pieces were stitched in place so that they appeared as a part of the fashion detail of the garment.

C shows how a decorative patch can be applied over a worn edge of a jacket or dress with tabs that cover worn or shabby buttonholes. New buttonholes are worked on the new fabric.

D shows a type of patch that can be set into the front of a skirt to cover a worn spot or hole. The edges are stitched into the seams of the gores and the pointed lower end is top-stitched as shown. The top is worked into the waistband.

E is a panel patch that can be used to mend a blouse or dress that is worn out under the arms. Fit the panel into the line of the armhole and use top-stitching on the long edges of the panel to make it appear a planned part of the garment.

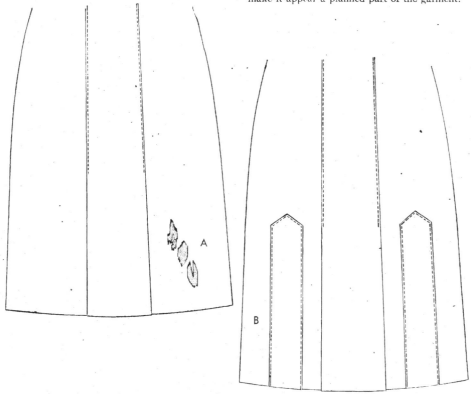

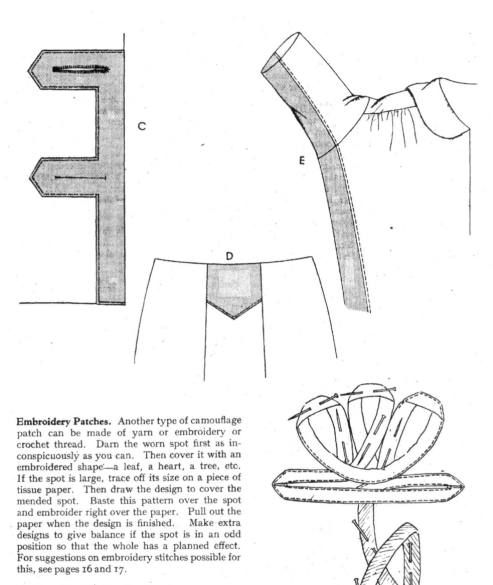

Embroidery Patches. Another type of camouflage patch can be made of yarn or embroidery or crochet thread. Darn the worn spot first as inconspicuously as you can. Then cover it with an embroidered shape—a leaf, a heart, a tree, etc. If the spot is large, trace off its size on a piece of tissue paper. Then draw the design to cover the mended spot. Baste this pattern over the spot and embroider right over the paper. Pull out the paper when the design is finished. Make extra designs to give balance if the spot is in an odd position so that the whole has a planned effect. For suggestions on embroidery stitches possible for this, see pages 16 and 17.

Braid or Bias Binding Patches. Large trimming motifs or patches may be made from bias binding or braid. Plan the shape to cover the worn or mended spot. Pin the motif in the desired shape and stitch both edges of the binding as shown.

ESSENTIALS OF WEAVING

IN ORDER TO DO GOOD invisible mending and reweaving, you must examine the weave of your fabric carefully and understand its construction. Use a magnifying glass if the weave is very fine, so that you will surely know how to duplicate it in your mending. It may help you to distinguish between the threads to separate them and pick them up with a needle.

You have read, in the paragraph on *Fabric Grain*, page 8, how the loom is threaded for weaving with the lengthwise (warp) threads and how widthwise (woof) threads, carried in the shuttle, are run back and forth, over and under the warp. The number of warp threads over and under which the shuttle passes at one time determines the surface pattern of the fabric. Since that is what you need to know to reweave the fabric, we illustrate here six fundamental weaves, with the threads drawn very large to show how they are placed.

Plain Weave. The simplest weave is this one, in which each crosswise thread alternates over and under the warp threads, making an even fabric.

Satin Weave. In this weave, each thread of the woof passes under several threads of the warp before going over one, or vice versa. The effect of these long threads on the surface is to make a very smooth and glossy fabric.

Twill Weave. In this weave the woof threads are woven over and under the warp threads so as to form diagonal ribs in the fabric. The number of threads passed over or under by the woof determines the width and slant of the twill.

Herringbone Weave. This variation of the twill weave has a zigzag rib made by changing the direction of the twill at regular intervals.

Basket Weave. This is a variation of the plain weave. Two or more woof threads are woven over and under an equal number of warp threads to give a latticed effect.

Figured Weave. This weave has a design worked out by the arrangement of the interweaving threads. There is an almost endless variety in the possible figures to be made—small geometric designs, dots, plaids. checks, borders, bands, etc. The design may be a self-figure—that is, one made all of the same yarn—or a design introducing another colour or yarn of a different character.

Of course there are many variations on these types of weaves. Study the fabric you have in the light of what you know about these basic weaves, and you will be able to count the threads and replace correctly the ones that are worn.

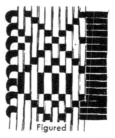

REWEAVING

REWEAVING MEANS REPLACING worn places in a fabric by weaving in new threads of a similar weight and colour so that they duplicate the original fabric threads.

When there are holes in a valuable garment, such as a coat or suit, reweave it yourself, provided you can do the work skilfully and with pleasure, or have it done professionally. In every city there are firms that do reweaving at prices varying with the size of the hole. Find someone reliable, ask the price before leaving your garment, and, as it may cost several shillings for one hole, be sure the garment is worth the expense.

Many women say that they would like to know how to do reweaving, but few will take the time and have the patience that the work demands. First one should study the weave of the fabric so that no one stitch that is put in will stand out and be different from the woven pattern of threads. When one learns reweaving professionally, the first lessons are devoted entirely to imitating fabric weaves.

Several examples of reweaving are illustrated here. The illustrations are made bold so that the threads are easy to follow and the same weave, a diagonal twill, is shown throughout for comparison of the various types of repair. Study the illustrations as you work. The invisible patches, though not strictly reweaving, are included in this section because of their close relationship.

If possible, pull threads from an edge of the fabric for the reweaving. Otherwise use yarn as of nearly the same weight and colour as you can get. When only short ravellings are available for reweaving, put the needle in as you want to place the stitches, then thread the short end of thread into it and pull through. Work carefully and do not pull the threads tight or leave them too slack. . Work in an embroidery frame or pin to a cushion. Do not hurry. Practice makes perfect, you know!

Repairing a Pulled Thread. This is not illustrated. It is simply threading into the fabric one matching thread to replace one that has been pulled out. Do it exactly as you would any one thread in *Reweaving a Hole*, following the weave to make it conform to the other threads in the fabric.

Reweaving Over a Thin Spot. This is different from reinforcing a thin spot, see page 46, which is simply darning back and forth over the worn area for strength. In reweaving, the new threads are actually woven in to match the fabric construction. Thin spots, such as that in **A,** are most likely to appear in woollen fabrics and are most easily rewoven in such fabrics. Hold the fabric right side up, bring the needle up from the wrong side and lay the new threads over the worn ones, as at **B,** which shows five new warp threads in place. **C** shows how the new thread ends are

A

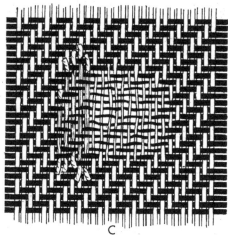

C

concealed on the wrong side and how the old threads lie under the new ones. Weave the new threads in so that the edges of the repair are uneven. This will help to blend the repaired spot into the garment without leaving a definite edge. Trim off any long threads extending out from the edge of the mend on the wrong side.

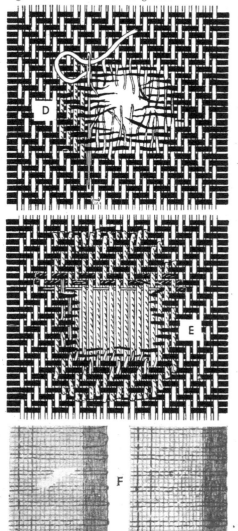

Reweaving a Hole. To hide the worn threads round the hole and make a completely invisible repair, work from the right side over all surface threads, then work the yarn into the fabric on the wrong side. Use a needle that is long enough to go from one side of the hole to the other, as in **D**. After laying the new thread across the hole, pull the needle through to the wrong side and weave it in and out of at least five or six threads to secure the new thread. Put in all the necessary warp threads first, as in **E**, and then weave in the crosswise threads.

Invisible Mend on Sheer Fabric. The type of fabric shown in **F** is very sheer, with an irregular plaid design. Replace the black threads that are torn by taking stitches across on one black line until you reach a black line running up and down. Then go down that line until you come to another black cross thread that is broken. Go back on that to another up-and-down black thread, and so on. Follow the same principle in replacing broken grey threads. Thus the darn is concealed by the design of the fabric and can be detected only when you hold the fabric up to the light.

Invisible Patches. These patches are useful chiefly for holes in woollen garments, such as that in **G**, that you want to repair invisibly, though other fabrics, such as rough-textured rayons, can be patched in this way also. Cut a square patch piece from under a pocket or collar, from the hem, or a facing or above a pleat. The piece must be large enough to cover the hole amply and allow about ½ in. additional on each side. Ravel the threads on each side of the patch, as in **H**, to the depth of about ½ in. Lay the patch piece over the hole on the right side, matching it to the fabric grain, and baste it in place. Then, with a fine steel crochet hook, reach through from the wrong side as in **I**, catch one thread of the ravelled edge at a time, and pull it through to the wrong side. Follow the weave in pulling the threads through. This will mean that the edge of the patch will be uneven, as at **J**, where one thread is pulled straight through, the next crosses two threads before being drawn under, and so on. In this way the weave is matched accurately and the patch is made inconspicuous. When all threads have been pulled through, turn to the wrong side, which is shown in **K**, and darn the thread ends to the fabric with short stitches.

The **woven-in patch** is another invisible patch, more difficult than the preceding one, but better if

68

your garment is valuable enough to warrant the extra pains it takes, because it is even less conspicuous. .It is to be preferred for more closely woven fabrics. This takes a larger patch piece, allowing 2 ins. if possible on each side beyond the hole. Ravel the sides of the patch to a depth of 2 ins. Match it to the fabric grain and baste it in on the right side as described above. Then thread the ravelled thread at one corner into a needle and weave it into the fabric. Insert your needle in the proper place on the right side, as in **L,** then turn to wrong side and weave it over and under the thread of the fabric, placing your stitches to correspond exactly to the weave for three or four stitches, and pulling the thread through so that the end is on the wrong side. Then take the next ravelled thread and do the same thing. Continue all the way round the patch. This is painstaking work, but the results are worth the effort, for the patch is truly invisible on the right side, with no line or extra thickness to show where the edges were. The patch is blended into the fabric and consequently is stronger than the patch shown in **K.**

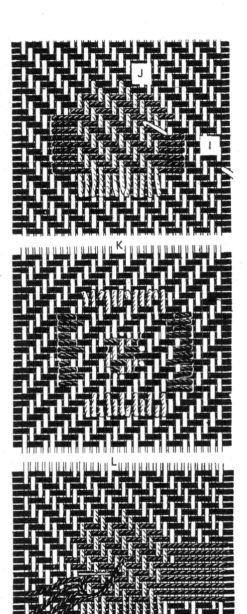

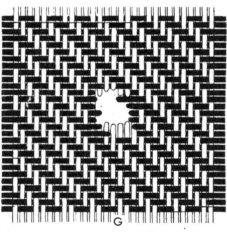

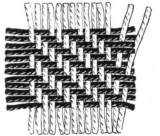

BUTTON, BUTTON, DON'T LOSE IT

IN REPLACING BUTTONS on a garment, always sew them on exactly as the other buttons are sewn on. Place the thread through the same holes. Sew with the same stitch length so that the button will not appear too tight or loose alongside its companions. If one button comes off or is loose, the chances are that all should be inspected and resewn in place. If you cannot match the original thread used for buttons, it is best to sew all the buttons on with the new thread. The buttons of a garment must look alike in every detail.

Place Buttons Exactly. Mark the position for the button. To do this, bring the buttonhole edge over the button edge of the garment and pin the opening together top and bottom. Put a pin into the fabric through the buttonhole. Small buttons should be placed in the centre of the buttonhole, but to insure a correct closing for larger buttons, put the marking pin close to the front end of the buttonhole.

Make Your Button Stay. A button must have a little stem left in sewing it on so that it will allow room for the fabric round the buttonhole to fit under it. Do this either by holding the button a little away from the fabric as you sew, or by using pins as illustrated here. Use a sufficiently strong, medium-short thread, doubled, and begin with a back-stitch, bringing the needle up through one hole of the button. Put pins across the button, as in **A**, to keep the stitches easy as you put the needle through the other hole. Take enough stitches through and through the holes of the button to

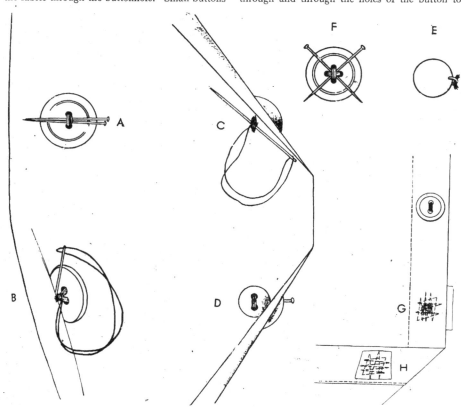

make it secure and then bring the needle out between the button and the fabric. Remove the pins, draw the button away from the fabric and complete the stem by winding the thread round the stitches that hold the button, as in **B**. Bring the needle to the wrong side and finish with overcasting-stitches, as in **C**. If you have a row of buttons close together, don't break off the thread between buttons, but carry the thread along from one to the next for strength and speed in sewing. If, as in unlined jackets, housecoats, or coats, the inside must look as nice as the outside, sew a small button on the inside, just under the outside button, as in **D**, or keep your stitches under the facing so that they cannot show.

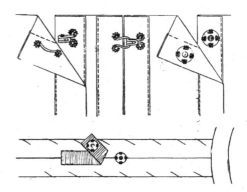

Shank Buttons. Mark the position for the button and pin it in place from the wrong side. Take short stitches through the shank, as in **E**, and finish with tiny back-stitches on the wrong side.

Four-Hole Buttons. Stitches should be placed in an orderly manner on buttons of this type. The usual placing of stitches on tailored garments is shown in **F**, where the pins are placed criss-cross and the stitches are criss-crossed over them. On tailored washable garments the stitches are usually placed either parallel, linking the holes two and two, or boxed, going continuously round the square formed by the four holes. On embroidered or smocked garments, buttons are sometimes sewn on with thread of the embroidery colour and the stitches are placed so that they radiate from one hole to the other three.

Button Pulled Out. When a button has pulled off, leaving a hole in the fabric, first repair the hole by placing a piece of fabric or tape under it, and stitching back and forth over it, as at **G**. The wrong side will appear as at **H**. This will fill the hole and make the spot strong enough for the button to be sewn on again.

Hooks and Eyes. You can buy these in sizes o, double oo and triple ooo, the last being smallest. A card usually has both round and straight eyes, so that you can choose the type suited to the opening. The illustrations show both types as used in the openings appropriate to them. Utilitarian hooks and eyes are generally put on the inside of the closing so that they do not show. They should be placed quite close together to prevent gaps in the closing, and the hooks and eyes must be exactly opposite each other to keep the line

straight. Mark the positions with chalk and then overcast all round the loops of each, using a strong thread. The hook should have several strong stitches taken through the hump to hold it in place. Be careful that the stitches don't go all the way through your fabric and show on the right side.

Snap Fasteners. Measure the spacing and mark the position for snap fasteners very carefully. Hold the fastener exactly in place and take several stitches through each hole to secure it. Do not let the stitches go all the way through the fabric.

Tapes to Hold Shoulder Straps. These may be bought ready-made at haberdashery counters. To make your own, use ¼ in. firm grosgrain or satin ribbon or tape. Cut a 2 in. length of ribbon, turn one end under and whip it to the shoulder seam at the place where lingerie straps cross the shoulder. Turn the free end of the ribbon under and sew a small snap fastener there. Sew the other half of the snap to the seam, as shown.

Covered Buttons. These may be made for you on a button machine, from scraps of your own fabric. Or, you may cover wooden, or composition moulds yourself.

If a shank pulls out of a machine-made button, use a scrap of the same fabric and re-cover it yourself. If you have none of the material, cut a circle of fabric as near like it as possible, and slightly larger than the tin or composition backing, turn in the edge, and blind stitch or whip it underneath, catching it at the extreme edge of the top covering. This is not a strong button, but another may be moved and replaced by the repaired button.

FRAYED BUTTONHOLES

THE ILLUSTRATION at **A** shows perhaps the most common ailment of buttonholes—the split at the end. The best way to remedy this is to darn it by machine, as shown in **B**, stitching back and forth across the tear from ¼ in. beyond it up to the proper end of the opening.

If the buttonhole is frayed all round, either whip round it by hand, as shown, or strengthen it by machine, as in **C**. This machine-stitching is especially good for such garments as play clothes, overalls, dungarees, etc., in which the fabric is tough and strong, gets a lot of wear, and is difficult to sew by hand. Place two rows of machine-stitching round the buttonhole, as shown; then stitch across these two rows, back and forth, as in **D**, so that you get a really secure edge. The easiest way to do this is to grasp the fabric at the sides of the opening to hold it apart and move the work from side to side under the machine needle as you stitch, being careful not to let the needle stitch across the opening.

When a buttonhole is badly frayed, as in **E**, it can be very successfully mended with tape. Choose your tape to match or contrast with the colour of the fabric. Cut two pieces of tape as long as you want the opening to be, plus ¼ in. on each end for turning under. Turn under the ends of the tape and fold each piece in half lengthwise. Put one edge of each tape through the opening, covering the frayed edges of the hole as with a binding. The two folded edges of tape must be brought evenly together to form the new buttonhole opening. When you have them properly placed, baste them in position, as in **F**; then stitch all the way round with the machine, as in **G**. Whip the corners on the wrong side, as in **H**, to give strength and make the hole exactly the right size for the button. If you are repairing several buttonholes on the same garment in this way, be sure to measure the width you want and make all alike.

Another way to repair a frayed buttonhole is shown in **I**. This is good for sleeping garments, as it is similar in appearance to the frogged buttonhole often used on these. First darn the torn end of the buttonhole by machine, making it the right length for the button. Then cut a piece of narrow ready-made bias binding about four times the length of the buttonhole. Fold it in half lengthwise. Mark the middle of the piece and pin this in place on the right side at the front end of the buttonhole. Fold the ends back to lie along the edges of the buttonhole and cross the ends in a curve as shown. Turn the raw edges under at each end. Pin this in place; then baste. Stitch carefully all along the edges of the binding. Then, on wrong side, whip the buttonhole edge to binding

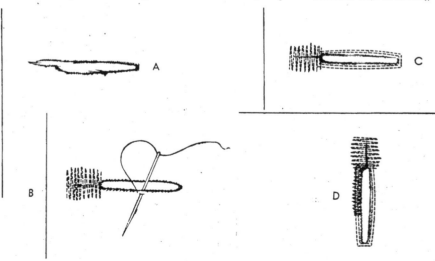

72

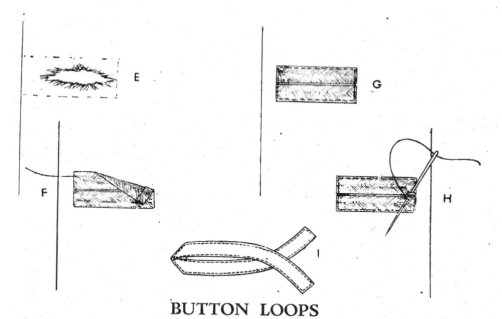

BUTTON LOOPS

Button Loops. At a closing point where there is not too much strain, form loops of thread to fit buttons. Use four strands of buttonhole twist, firm cotton, or linen thread, and over these strands work a close blanket stitch as in **A**.

Fabric Loops. Take a ¾ in. strip of bias. Fold it together over a cord—wrong side out. With the cording foot on your machine, stitch along the cord; and stitch twice or three times across the end, through fabric and cord, as in **B**. Then turn this tubing right side out, as in **C**. When the cord has been pulled out, clip it off, as it is not used further. (Its purpose is to keep the tubing an even

width and to make it easy to turn it right side out.) Mark the opening for the position of buttons on the right side. Lay the tubing so that it will form a small loop, as in **D**, with ¼ in. allowed at each end for stitching it in place. Cut the amount off the tubing, and use it in measuring and cutting the number of loops required. Pin and then baste the loops in place, so that they will be even in size as well as an equal distance apart. Stitch along them, as shown, stitching slowly and lifting the presser foot frequently, if necessary, to keep each loop in position. The facing is then stitched on over the button loops to neaten off the ends, as in **E**.

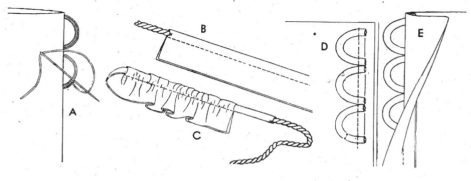

WORKED BUTTONHOLES

MARK THE POSITION and length of buttonholes carefully with chalk or pencil. In most cases, buttonholes should be placed on a lengthwise or crosswise thread of the fabric. Cut with sharp-pointed embroidery scissors or razor blade, cutting along a thread and to a thread at each end of the buttonhole. Stay it as illustrated in **A** and **B**. First take a tiny back-stitch on the wrong side, bring the needle through, and lay a long thread on each side of the opening about ⅛ in. from the edge, as in **A**. Overcast the edges, as in **B**, finishing with a back-stitch. When buttonholes have to be placed on the bias, mark the position of each buttonhole and machine-stitch round it, as in **A1**, before cutting. The machine-stitching will take the place of the laid thread, so that you can just proceed with the overcasting.

To work the buttonhole, use a thread heavier than for sewing the fabric. Begin at the inside end of the buttonhole by taking a back-stitch on the wrong side. Bring the needle out on the right side about ⅛ in. to ⅛ in. from the edge of the slit, depending on how deep you want the stitches to be. Put the needle through the buttonhole, bringing it out just beside where you brought it out before. Take the thread near the needle and draw it round towards you and under the point of the needle, as in **C**. Then pull the needle through. Repeat this all round the buttonhole. Flare your stitches slightly round the outside end of the buttonhole and then continue back along the other edge. The finish for the inside end, shown in **D**, is the easiest and most satisfactory. To make this, lay two bar threads across the end, and then blanket-stitch over them with close stitches. Finish with a back-stitch on the wrong side.

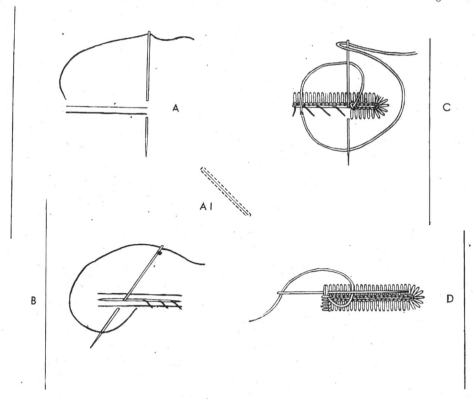

BOUND BUTTONHOLES

BRAID, RIBBON, OR SELF-FABRIC may be used to bind the slashed edges of buttonholes. The width of the binding showing on the right side is generally about ¼ in., but it may be narrower or wider, according to the weight and weave of the fabric and the size of buttonhole desired.

The first step is to mark carefully the position of the buttonhole. Cut a piece of fabric eight times as wide as the finished binding is to be. If you want a ¼ in. binding, for example, cut the piece 2 ins. wide. Cut each piece 1 in. longer than the length the opening will be. You can cut the piece lengthwise, widthwise, or on the bias of the fabric, depending upon the desired grain and type of buttonhole.

Place the binding piece right side down on the right side of the garment, centred over the marked buttonhole. Baste it in position. With chalk or pencil, draw a line meticulously through the centre where the buttonhole opening is to go, and across each end to mark the length of the opening. Stitch with the machine along each side and across the ends of the chalk line, placing your stitching line as far from the buttonhole line as the width of the finished binding. You will see these steps, the basting and the stitching, illustrated in **A**.

Remove the bastings. With sharp scissors, cut the openings, clipping diagonally towards each corner of your stitching, as in **B**. Take care not to cut the stitching line. Pull the edges of the applied piece through the opening to the wrong side, as shown.

Use a warm iron to press open the seams, but do not press the little triangular end pieces. Smooth out the edges. You will find that, when the folds of the binding meet along the opening on the right side, as in **C**, little pleats are formed on the wrong side, as in **D**. Fasten the tiny triangular ends with a few stitches; then overcast the edges of the pleats together, as at **E**. Tack the pleats together at the ends of the opening.

The wrong side of the buttonhole may be covered by a hem turn or a facing of the garment. In either case, baste round the buttonhole as in **F**; then, from the right side, cut through the buttonhole to make the opening in the facing or hem turn. Clip diagonally to the ends, as before. Turn the raw edges under and whip them down on wrong side, as shown at **G**. Take out bastings and press.

If the wrong side is not covered by a hem turn or facing, stitch round the outside of the binding with the machine to give a finish, as in **H**.

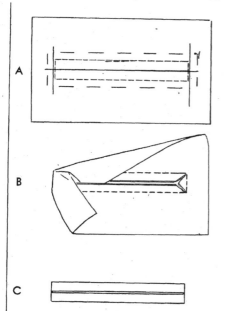

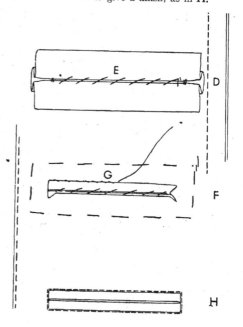

NEXT TO YOUR SKIN

When Your Slips Show. Some people always have "slipitis"—their slips always show. There are several possible reasons for this—the slips may be too long or too loose in the body or waist; the hips of the wearer may be small in proportion to her other measurements; the waistband of the skirt or dress may be too tight and hike up; the slip itself may have an uneven hem.

"Slipitis" is a habit—one to be avoided. Never be guilty of it. Adjust the shoulder straps; take a tuck above the hem, or darts in the back; buy a smaller size—any one of the several things that may be required to correct the difficulty for you. No matter how well groomed you are—if your slip hangs, you do not look smart.

Never allow beautiful underclothes to waste from disuse. Do whatever is necessary to make them right for the clothes you are wearing, and have lingerie that you can wear proudly rather than apologetically.

A. If you have a trousseau or gift slip that you have treasured for years or one you have saved because the bottom was beautifully trimmed or hand-finished, but have not worn because it was too long and you did not know what to do about it—cease your pining. Get the slip out and shorten it today. Here are three ways to do it:

1. Put the slip on and have someone fit it. If it is small round the hips, lift the slip and take the length out in the upper part by pinning a tuck just below the bustline. Be careful, in pinning all round, that the lower hemline is even. Remove the slip and baste the tuck on the wrong side, making a nice even line all round. Stitch this tuck from the right side directly on the folded edge. Cut away the fold underneath to within a scant ⅜ in. of the stitching line, and overcast neatly; or run a row of stitching round the seam itself to prevent fraying. A slip can be lengthened at the same place—mark and cut a line under the bustline all the way round and add a band of insertion lace, ribbon, or similar fabric.

2. If your slip fits round the hips, pin a tuck six or eight ins. above the lower edge. If only a small tuck is necessary, run it in by hand on the right side. Do not cut the fold away in case you should want to lengthen the slip again at some future time. If you have 2½ ins. or more to take out, pin the tuck in, cut away the underside of the tuck, and make a French seam, see page 19. If it would be suitable to the finish on the bottom, finish this seam on the right side of the slip and go over it with a shell-edge, see page 24.

3. If your slip has a shadow panel in front or back, make a seam at the waistline in order to cut away the surplus length. Fit the slip to your figure with darts; then make an opening at left side.

B. Almost every person at some time has a weak moment when she succumbs to the appeal of a frivolous piece of lingerie and buys it, only to find, after a relatively short period, that the frail trimming sections have begun to melt away. If you have such a frivolously trimmed slip that has given

way, replace the worn parts with new lace, or with eyelet embroidery or fabric. Use the original worn parts as a pattern for cutting a new top. If necessary, remove the original trimming at the bottom and apply a new piece.

If your slip is too short—and many slips either shrink or prove too short after a few wearings, especially those cut on the bias—it can easily be lengthened with an extension of lace or embroidery at the bottom. It may also be lengthened at the top by a longer bras line. Sometimes the original straps may be used, but more often it pays to buy new ribbon and make the entire top new. There is always the good psychological effect of working for dainty newness in remodelling delicate garments.

C. Very often the nicer the slip, the more frail it is. And lace-topped slips that are worn under blouses frequently wear out quickly. If you have a slip with bras top of lace, use the original as a pattern to cut a new lace top, laying little darts in the lace to shape it accurately to the bras outline. It may also be desirable to cut the bras part a little deeper than in the original garment.

D. When extra width is needed in a slip because of increase in weight or pregnancy, it can easily be gained. Open out the side seams and run strips of lace insertion up the sides. It is possible thus to add as much as four ins. or six ins. to the all-round size of the slip. In applying insertion or ribbon in this way, pin the garment seam edges to pieces of paper and baste the insertion strips in position. Then stitch through both fabric and paper. This will make the seams perfectly straight and the stitching line even and smooth. The paper pulls away easily after the stitching is complete.

If your slips are of fine material and you are determined to reduce your weight, or if you are pregnant, put the nicer slips away until you can wear them as they are, and alter those that are less important. The method suggested in **D** may be used for princess slips of which the seams have pulled out in wearing. Stitch ribbon or lace insertion over the seams and cut the frayed seams away.

E. Some slips wear out first under the arms and across the back. Frequently, also, they wear out at the waistline under the pressure of the belt line of skirts. If you have a slip that is worn beyond repair, or that has already been repaired many times, cut away the upper part and make a petticoat. See instructions on page 84. This is a practical way to salvage a slip and have service for a long time.

F. If you have a slip that has given way under the arms or at the front where you have pinned big clips or brooches, appliqué lace over the frayed parts, see page 106. Do this very neatly, and then cut away the ragged parts underneath. It is possible to appliqué lace so well that it looks as though it is a part of the design. Lace is lingerie's perfect complement. You can buy it in a colour to match the fabric you have, and it is very easy to apply either by hand or machine. When you can mend an undergarment with lace, use it by all means in preference to patches, because it can make your garment look new rather than mended.

G. Sometimes a slip is trimmed at the top and bottom with lace or net footing which becomes worn when the fabric part is still quite good. In such a case, buy new lace or eyelet embroidery to make a new top and hem finish. If you need to add length to the slip, buy your trimming band wider than that which trimmed the garment originally. Stitch the lace on from the right side, using the machine edge-stitcher, which allows you to stitch directly on the edge, see page 42. Always stitch lace on top of paper so that the lace will not tighten under the machine needle.

H. This shows you how to build up the top of a slip to be worn under a sheer dress by adding a top of eyelet embroidery or of all-over lace.

The slip in **I** has had a row of narrow lace stitched over a worn edge. This is a simple way to renew a garment if the fabric is good but the trimming worn before its time.

J. This slip was made from an old evening dress, recut entirely, with the lines of the slip conforming to the lines of the dress—a simple procedure.

K. Many women find that the back of the skirt is the part of a slip that wears out first. When the fabric there wears thin or shows signs of strain, repair it by inserting a panel of new fabric or material from an old slip, as shown. Cut the new fabric so that the grain matches that in the part to be repaired. Use the same type of seam as is used in the rest of the garment.

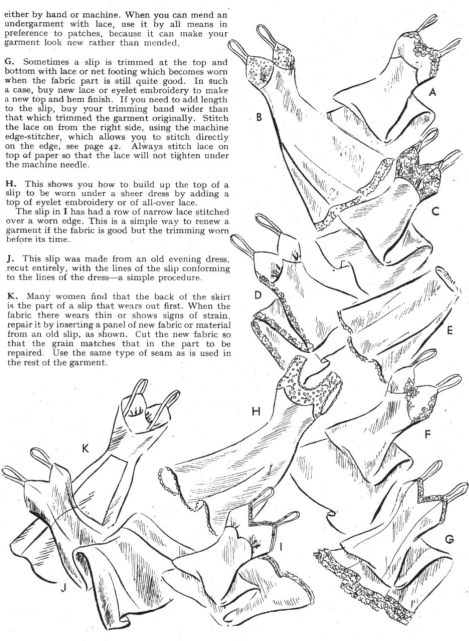

Reinforcing Straps with Machine Mending.
Straps often wear out first. Many slips require strap repair and some slips will require two or more sets of straps. Straps usually wear out where they join the garment. A shows how the slip may wear at the joining point. Machine-stitch back and forth over worn spot and frayed strap, as **B**.

Concealing Hole When Straps Pull Out. When the strap has torn completely out, leaving a hole in the fabric, mend as follows: Rip stitching back 1 in. each way from the strap, as in **C**. Turn the frayed edges in. Cut off the worn part of the strap or use new straps and pin in place as shown. Baste the turned-in edges together, as in **D**; then, using a short stitch, 12 to the inch, restitch across the point. A second row of stitching just below the top one is used to secure the strap.

Renewing Adjustable Straps. The type of strap shown here is most often found on camisole-top slips, though the same principle applies to any adjustable strap with two slides. New straps may be made of ribbon or fabric. To replace such straps: Remove one strap from the slip, leaving the other in place so that you can use it as a guide in arranging the slides and strap section. Open the seam where the strap joins the slip. After drawing the strap end **E** through the slide **F**, insert the new strap ends into the seam and pin, baste and stitch, as in **G**. Stitch back and forth across the strap, as at **H**, to hold the slide in the desired position. Then put the second slide on the end of the long strap piece, as in **I**. If you are using fabric straps, it is a good idea to make several rows of stitching along the strap, as at **J**, to prevent the strap from rolling into a string. Do this before attaching straps. **K** shows the right side with slides and stitchings in place. Replace the other strap in the same way.

Reinforcing Pulled Adjustable Straps. Straps with the type of adjustable clamp shown in **L** are apt to wear at the back joining, **M**. When this happens, fold the worn part down to the wrong side and whip it in place, as in **N**. Then whip the edge to the strap on the right side, as in **O**. If preferred, this mending can be done on the machine.

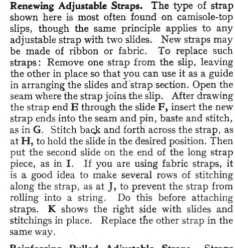

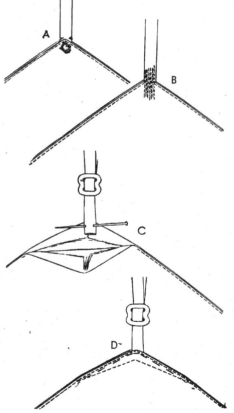

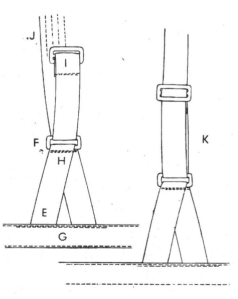

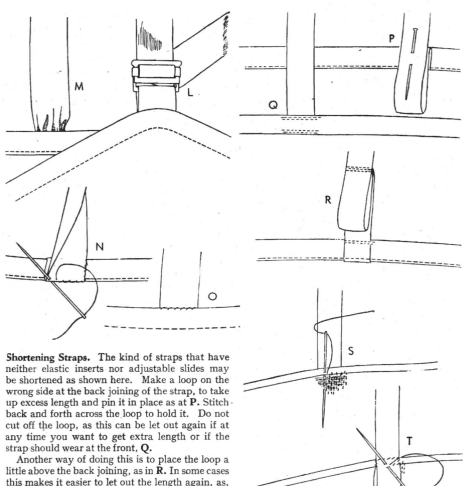

Shortening Straps. The kind of straps that have neither elastic inserts nor adjustable slides may be shortened as shown here. Make a loop on the wrong side at the back joining of the strap, to take up excess length and pin it in place as at **P**. Stitch back and forth across the loop to hold it. Do not cut off the loop, as this can be let out again if at any time you want to get extra length or if the strap should wear at the front, **Q**.

Another way of doing this is to place the loop a little above the back joining, as in **R**. In some cases this makes it easier to let out the length again, as, for instance, if the strap should wear through at the joining.

Reinforcing Straps with Hand Mending. Worn spots in the garment caused by strain on straps can sometimes be mended by hand and concealed as shown here. First fold the strap to the wrong side and darn the worn spot to it, as in **S**. Then turn down a loop of the strap over the darn on the right side. Whip it in position, as in **T**. On the wrong side, make a few stitches, as at **U**, through all layers except the top loop on the right side.

79

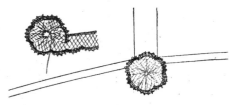

Rosette to Cover Darn. If the strap cannot be looped to conceal a darn, as shown on preceding page, a small rosette of ribbon or lace can be made to cover it. Draw up the edge of the lace or ribbon, as shown, joining the ends of the piece to form a rosette shape. Place this over the darn, fasten it at the centre with a few secure stitches, and then whip it down to the garment round the edges.

Renewing and Strengthening Straps. On this type of bras it is often necessary to give extra strength when replacing straps. The straps usually break off as in **A.** When making new straps, use heavy satin ribbon or fabric like that of the bras. For strength at the joining point of the strap, stitch a piece of ribbon over the point on the wrong side, as in **B,** turning the edges under and turning off the corners as shown. Insert the end of the strap under the piece and pin it, as in **C.** Then turn the strap up and stitch, as in **D,** to strengthen the whole point and joining.

For ease in movement, an insert of elastic at the back joining of the strap may be advisable. Stitch ribbon and elastic with wrong sides together, as at **E.** Fold the ribbon edge over the elastic, turn it down, and stitch, as at **F.** Then stitch the end of strap to back of bras, as at **G.**

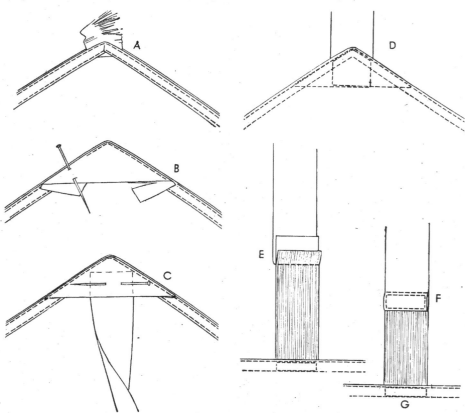

Frayed Lingerie Edges. Worn binding on the edges of lingerie may be re-bound with ribbon, as in **A.** Remove the old straps before binding, but leave the old binding and simply cover it with the new. This will help to retain the shape. Baste the new binding on, as shown, mitreing it neatly at corners, then stitch. Replace the straps or pin on new ones. This type of repair can also be done on different kinds of edges, such as that in **B.**

Worn edges can be made like new by applying a narrow lace edging on the right side, as in **C.** Baste it on, mitreing carefully at corners. Stitch twice along the basted line to hold it securely over worn edge and prevent lace from rolling up, as **D.**

Scalloped embroidered lingerie edges have a tendency to split. To prevent this and to add strength without bulk, apply a narrow net edging along just under the embroidery. Baste first, then stitch. **E** shows how this should appear from the right side. The wrong side is shown in **F,** with two rows of stitching and the neatly mitred corners.

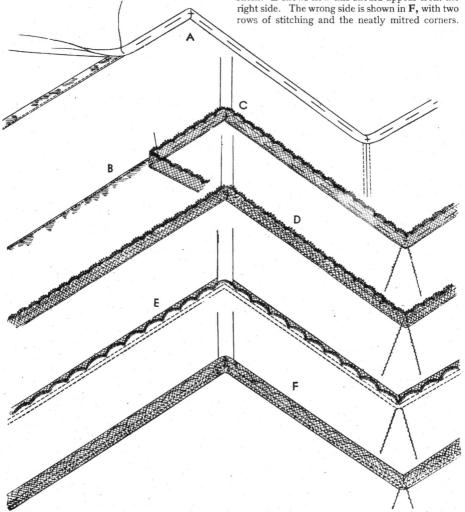

81

Worn edges can also be covered with strips of either matching or contrasting fabric. The strips may be straight, as ribbon, or bias. A plain nightgown is attractively edged with a band of printed satin or crepe. Mitre the bands of fabric, as in **A.** Turn the raw edges under and baste if the strips are bias, simply press if they are straight. Pin in place on the garment and top-stitch, as in **B.**

If the garment is frayed only under the arms, a piece of ribbon the required length may be stitched in place to form a protective shield.

Mending Brassière Cup. Brassière parts of foundation garments, being frequently made of lace or of fabric sheerer than the rest of the garment, often wear along the seam line, as at **C.** Do not try to rip this seam to mend it, as an inside stitching is used on this line in most cases. Simply turn the torn edge under and whip it down, as at **D,** beginning and ending the stitches about $\frac{1}{2}$ in. beyond each end of the tear.

Reinforcing and Repairing Slips. Slips often wear out first under the arms. The way one works or the type of work one does may be responsible for the type of wear, especially when only one side of the slip is worn, or it may be too tight.

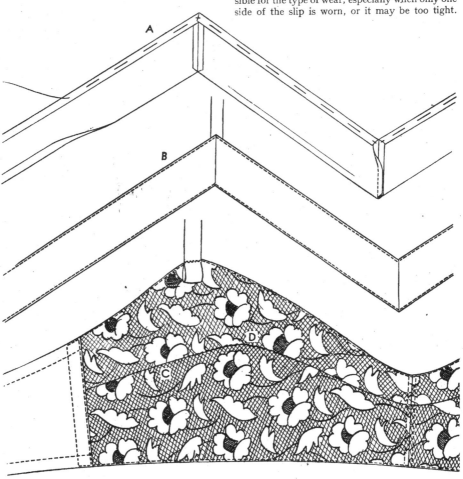

Underarm Reinforcements. When the slip has worn thin or the fabric has broken at the underarms, apply a patch, as at **B.** This shows the wrong side; **A,** the right side. For the patch, use a piece of fabric of similar quality and colour or use a piece of net, lace or ribbon.

Make the patch large enough to cover the worn area; pin, baste and stitch it on as shown. Machine darn over the thin part to hold it intact and secure it to the patch.

Waistline Reinforcements. Often slips wear along the side near the waistline where skirt fastenings rub. **D** shows net applied on the wrong side over such a worn part. **C** shows how the machine darning appears on the right side. If there is a hole too badly worn for darning, apply a patch of net or fabric to the wrong side of slip, trim away the edges of the hole, on the right side and clip the edges at intervals, then turn them under towards the patch, and stitch down firmly, as at **E.**

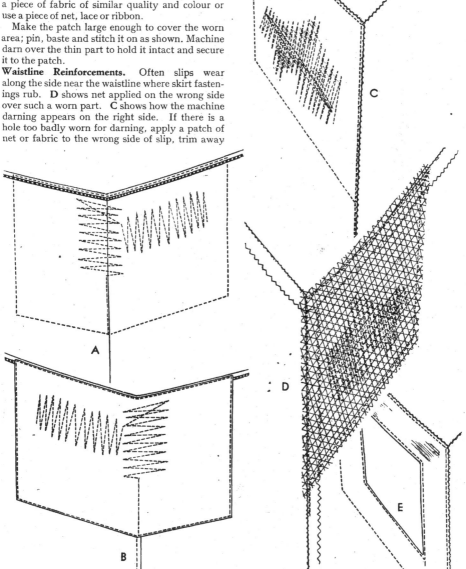

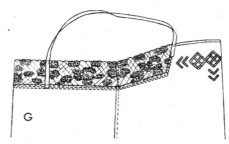

Above. F and G show the right and wrong sides of a slip repaired across the top with lace. When the straps have pulled away and the underarms are thin, this provides a very simple, practical way to repair the top. In the slip illustrated the drawn-work front was kept, the lace terminating at a point just in front of each front strap. Lace 3 ins. to 4 ins. wide is usually ample for such repair. All that is necessary is to baste it on, stitch it twice all the way round the sewing edge of the lace, turn in the ends, stitch these; then trim the fabric away underneath lace and overcast raw edge. Notice that the ribbon straps are fastened to the machine stitching line and then at the top edge of lace. This eliminates strain on the lace.

Below. A suit slip often wears out both at the underarms and waistline, as in I. A very satis-factory short petticoat, as in H, may be made by laying the slip out, as in I. With side seams together, pin bottom edges together as shown. Measure up from the bottom an even distance all the way round and mark with pins or chalk. Cut off the worn section. Baste and stitch bias binding or ribbon to the edge of the petticoat at the waistline, as in J. Turn it back on the slip and stitch it flat. top and bottom. Insert a narrow piece of elastic about ¼ the length of the waist measurement across the back, as in K. Pin, then stitch it at each end, drawing the waistline in as necessary. If elastic is not available, use a strip of narrow tape and insert it through two eyelets which you make at the back, a distance of 12 ins. or 14 ins. apart. Draw the tape ends together through the eyelets and tie them in a bow knot, for easy untying. Use a long tape that will not pull out.

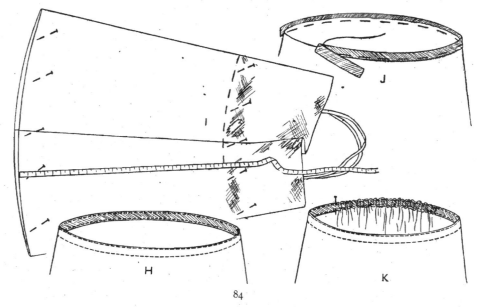

84

Bar Faggoting on Bras and Slips. When this type of seam breaks, replace the threads as neatly as possible so that the line is intact again. To do this, thread your needle with a thread of a suitable weight and colour. Insert the needle from the wrong side, as at **A,** cross to the opposite side. Put the needle in and bring it out at the line for the next bar, as in **B.** Cross over and put the needle in again, as in **C,** and continue down the seam until all broken stitches are replaced. Finish off with back-stitch, as in **D.**

Broken Seams in Foundation Garments. Some foundation garment seams are joined by faggoting. To repair a break in such a seam, work from the right side and beginning, as at **E,** several stitches above the break, go over the original stitches along the seam. The overlapping of the original stitches will secure them and prevent fraying. Follow the original needle holes along the edges as a guide for the new stitches. To reinforce the end of the seam, use ¾ in. ribbon or a square of strong fabric and whip this in place on the wrong side, as in **F.**

Ordinary seams that split may be repaired as in **G.** Use strong thread and sew on the right side as shown. If the strain is great, reinforce the seam on the wrong side with twill tape, turning the end under and stitching in place, as in **H.**

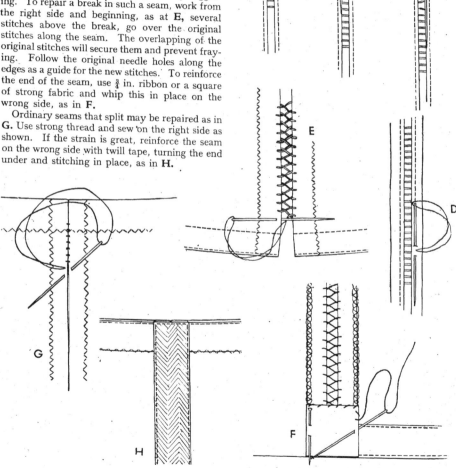

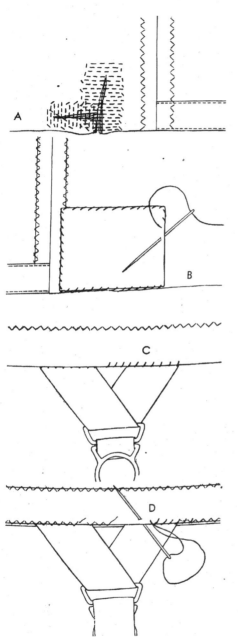

Strained or Torn Elastic in Foundation Garments

The elastic sections which are often strained or torn by pulling the garment on may be mended by hand, as in **A**. This is a regular hand darn for a corner tear or an irregular tear. Machine mending should not be attempted here, as it tends to cut the rubber strands of the fabric. Reinforce the section on the wrong side with ribbon or fabric hemmed in place, as in **B**.

Holes in elastic sections of garments can be mended by using the round underlaid patch for which instructions are given on page 57.

When elastic panels are badly torn, it may be better to take the garment to a corset department where the damage could be repaired with a zigzagger machine. However, if you are skilful using your zigzagger attachment, do this at home.

Reinforcing Suspender Joining. When a suspender begins to pull away where it joins the foundation garment, reinforce it as shown here. Sew it firmly on the right side, as in **C**. Then turn to the wrong side and whip the binding in place, taking stitches through the fabric of the garment, the suspender elastic and also the binding, as in **D**.

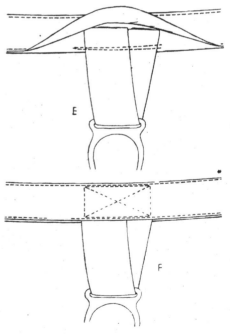

Replacing Suspenders by Machine. Turn back the binding and stitch twice across the suspender joining, as in **E.** Stitch the binding back in place and reinforce stitch over the section, as **F.**

Replacing Suspenders by Hand. When a suspender has pulled off and torn the binding, as in **G,** it can be mended by hand. Replace the suspender and whip it in place as shown. Then resew the binding over this with back-stitches. To reinforce the mend, put a piece of matching fabric over the spot, hem it on, and then take strengthening stitches across the piece, as in **H.**

Replacing Adjustable Suspenders. This type of suspender can be replaced with a new one or only the elastic renewed. Rip the stitching that holds the suspender to the garment. Pull the worn elastic out of the slide, as in **J.** Pry up the prongs holding the elastic, as at **I.**

Put the new elastic in and hammer the prongs down. Insert the free end of the elastic through the slide, as at **K.** Then stitch the suspender to the garment, and then resew the binding, as at **L.**

Suspender Belts. The suspenders on these can be mended generally by the same methods described here for those on foundation garments. The chief difference is that the suspender straps are much longer on the suspender belt. In many cases this length is partly elastic and partly tape. In replacing such suspenders, follow directions on page 88, **M** and **N,** for joining tape and elastic. Sometimes it may be convenient, in repairing suspenders that were originally all elastic, to use part elastic and part tape. Another small repair on the type of suspender belt that has a fitted fabric section at the waist is to adjust the waist size. This is done by making small darts in the fabric section.

Children's suspender belts and attachable suspenders may have the elastic renewed as shown.

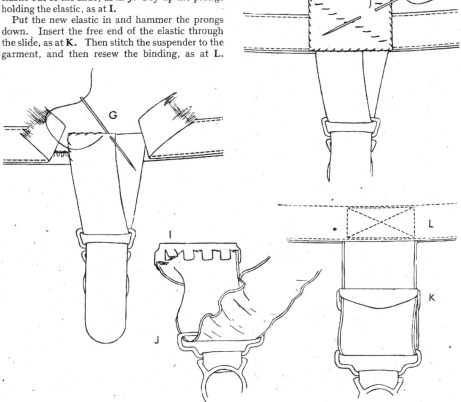

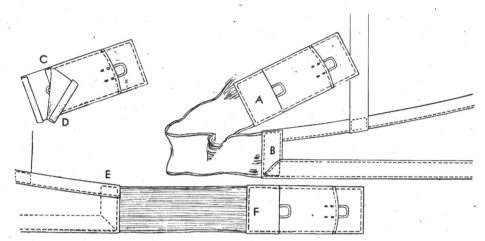

Brassière Fastenings. Because of its close fit, there is a certain amount of tugging required to open and to fasten a brassière, and this usually causes the fastenings to show wear first.

Replacing Elastic at Back. The method shown applies to all fastenings with a straight inserted piece of elastic. Twill tape may be used if elastic is not obtainable. If the elastic is only frayed at ends, it is ripped out, clipped off and replaced.

Rip the stitching at both ends of the elastic insert, **A** and **B.** Rip no more than needed to remove the piece. Do not rip stitching from **C** to **D** on the fastening end, as this seam holds the eye in place. Cut new elastic of required length and insert the ends into the seams. Restore the original stitching, as at **E** and **F.**

Elastic Torn at Fastening. G shows elastic torn out on one type of fastening. To repair this, begin

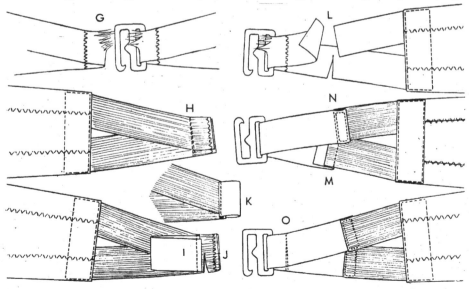

by stitching across the elastic on the loop side (the left side) about ¼ in. from the original stitching, as at **H**, to form a new loop for the hook. If the loop is too much worn for this, or if greater strength is needed, proceed as in **I**. Take a piece of tape 1½ ins. long, fold it in half, and stitch it to the end as shown. Then cut off the ends of elastic, as at **J**. Turn the tape under and stitch twice across to hold it in place, as in **K**.

On the hook side of the fastening, cut across the elastic on the straight, as at **L**. Cut a piece of tape about 2¾ ins. long and stitch it to the elastic, as at **M**. Then fold the tape end over the elastic end of the seam and make a flat fell, as at **N**. Put the tape through the loop of the hook and join the second end in the same way. Stitch up and back on the tape, as at **O**, to hold the hook in place.

Torn Hook-and-Eye Fastening. P shows a worn fastening of the two-hooks-and-eyes type. The method of repair shown above may be used on all similar types. Trim away the worn part of the guard, as at **Q**, and overcast the raw edge, as at **R**. Take a piece of ribbon about as wide as the end of the fastening and long enough to be folded in half to serve as a new guard. Stitch round the

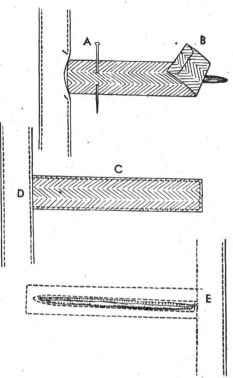

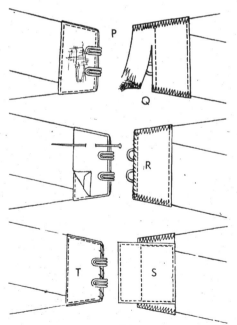

edges. Apply as at **S**, stitching slowly and carefully across the eyes to avoid blunting the needle.

Use ribbon to cover the worn part on the hook side of the closing, as at **T**. Stitch round three sides and whip the fourth side by hand over the hooks.

Tear in Fabric of Foundation Garment. The type of split shown here usually occurs along a fold and is caused by friction and perspiration rather than hard wear.

Rip the stitching of the binding a short distance on either side of the tear, as at **A**. Pin a piece of matching twill tape over the tear, sliding one end under the binding, and turning under the other end, as at **B**. Stitch all round the edges of the tape, as at **C**, and replace the stitching of the binding, as at **D**.

Turn to the right side and stitch round the tear, as at **E**. Trim away ravelled threads. If there is much ravelling, the raw edges of the split may be turned under before the final stitching.

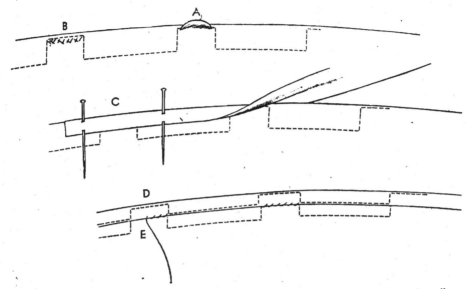

When Bones Push Through Foundation Garments. **A** shows the bone forced through the fabric on the right side of the garment. Sew the edges of the tear together, as at **B**. Pin twill tape over the edge, as in **C**. Stitch this in place, as in **D**, turning round the ends of bones, as shown. Hem down the tape edges across the bones, as shown in **E**.

F shows stitching at the end of a bone on the wrong side. This stitching sometimes rips, allowing the bone to slip down in the casing. When this occurs, force the bone up as far as possible and hold it with a pin, as at **G**. Stitch across several times, as shown.

If the bone has pushed through the casing, put a piece of tape over the tear, as in **H**. Stitch round the tape; then back and forth several times at the end of the bone to hold it in place, as shown.

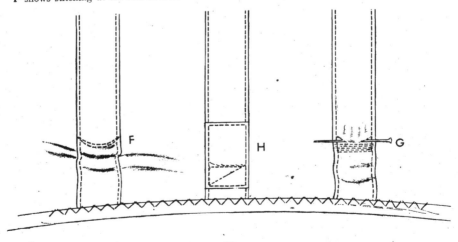

Elastic in Knicker Legs. Sometimes the very narrow elastic used in some knicker legs parts at the seam but doesn't tear the stitching that held it on the edge. To repair this, start by pulling one end of the elastic out of the threads for about an inch. Sew the end to a bodkin, as in **A**, and draw the elastic back through the threads. Lay the end over the other end and whip the two elastic ends together, as in **B**.

If the original threads have broken along the edge or if the elastic is pulled out too far to be easily drawn through, overcast the elastic along the edge, as in **C**. Overcast first one way, then the other, as shown. This gives a good, firm finish.

To repair this by machine, whip the ends of the elastic together, as at **D**; then stretch the elastic so that the fabric lies flat along it and stitch, as at **E**, making sure that the fabric overlaps the elastic enough to be caught to it in the stitching.

Elastic at Top of Knitted " Woollies." Elastic threads may break at centre-back seam and pull out, as at **F**. To repair this, start at the lower edge of the elastic band and thread each thread of elastic in turn on a large-eyed needle, as at **G**. The elastic need not be pulled far through the eye as a short end will hold. Using the head of the needle, weave through the threads where elastic originally was, as at **H**. When the thread is replaced all along, pull through on wrong side; remove needle, and with another needle and thread whip the end of the elastic thread to the centre-back seam. Don't break off this thread, as it can be used to fasten all the elastic thread ends. Don't snip off end of elastic thread if there is any extra length, as it is likely to pull out if too short. To prevent the same thing happening to the threads on the other side, reinforce them with whipping stitches made in a similar manner.

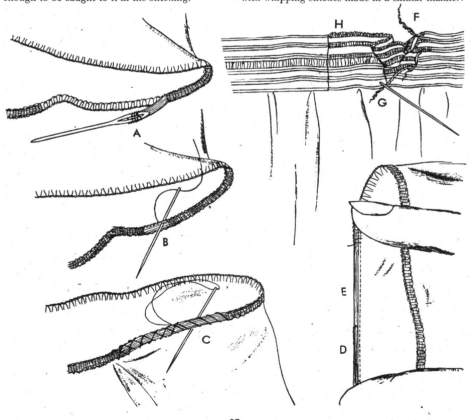

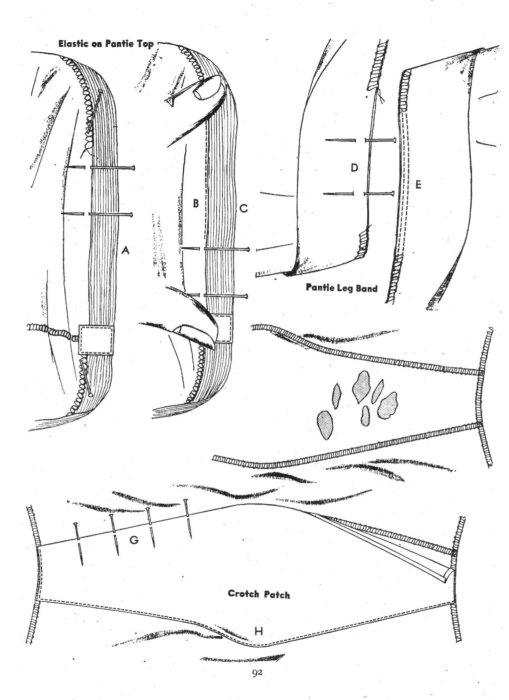

Elastic on Pantie Top

A

B

C

D

E

Pantie Leg Band

G

Crotch Patch

H

92

Elastic on Pantie Top. When the elastic has pulled away from the fabric along the waist of panties, re-stitch as shown here. Lay garment on surface into which pins can be stuck. **A** shows how to stretch the elastic while pinning fabric and elastic together. Stitch this on the machine, as in **B**, holding the elastic stretched out with the fingers, as in **C**.

Pantie Leg Band. Sometimes the stitching that holds the leg band on panties breaks and the band starts to come off. Turn the band back on the right side and lay the edges of pantie and band together. Pin them, as in **D**. Stitch twice along the edge, as in **E**.

Crotch Patch. **F** shows holes worn in the crotch panel of panties. To repair, cut a patch from an old knitted undergarment, shaping it according to the original and leaving seam allowance. Pin this in place as at **G** and stitch as at **H**, putting the new stitching along the old seam to give body.

Elastic in Men's Shorts. Elastic inserts in men's shorts may be replaced when they wear out. Rip out both ends of the elastic, as in **I**. Cut away the elastic along the seam edge **J**, rather than rip it. if several rows of stitching hold it.

Insert new elastic of the correct length, stitching the ends, as at **K** and **L**. Stretch the elastic, to pin the fabric along it, as in **M**, and when stitching the seam **N**, hold the elastic stretched as shown so that the line of stitching will not break with the stretching of the garment when it is being worn.

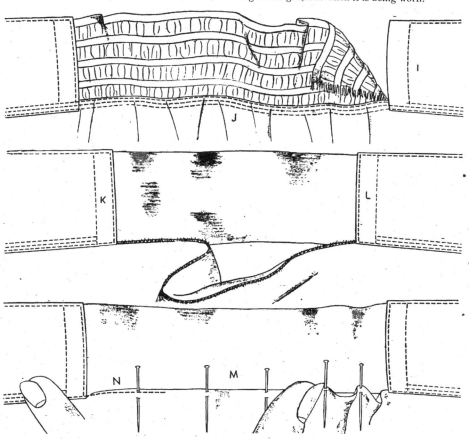

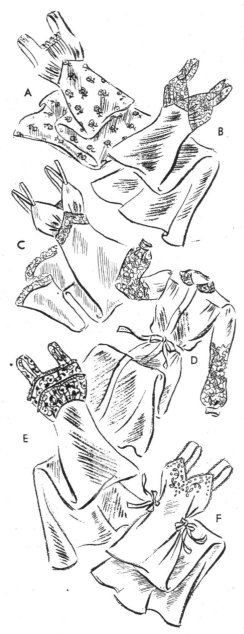

COUNT STITCHES

IF YOU WANT to sleep well, put on an attractive gown or pyjama suit and play that you are a beautiful angel floating away on the clouds of sleep. Never allow yourself to wear unmended or unattractive night clothes. You cannot readily put yourself to sleep with the repetition, " Every day in every way I'm getting better and better," when your night clothes need repair.

Nothing seems more bedraggled than once-dainty and lovely nightwear that has begun to wear and tear, and yet a few stitches and the addition of a few scraps of new material, ribbon, net or lace can make it fresh and like new in a jiffy. Very often beautiful new nightgowns can be made of old evening gowns or evening slips that have served their purpose in their original guise. The sketches show how really rewarding a little effort and ingenuity can be.

A shows an old print gown, the top of which was completely gone. With a new and dainty bodice section of georgette, it is prettier than ever.

B was a satin evening dress that had gone out of fashion. It was completely recut and given a new top of all-over lace with lace shoulder straps.

C was a nightgown that needed lengthening and new straps. The length was provided by a lace insert at the joining line of the bodice and also on the lower edge. New double straps were made of ribbon.

D shows a long-sleeved gown with new half-sleeves and collar of lace. The old sleeves, which had become badly worn, were cut off above the elbow and new sleeve bottoms were added. Detailed instructions are given on opposite page. The lace collar was substituted for the original badly worn collar to complete the rejuvenation.

E has a new camisole top of printed fabric replacing the upper part of an old gown.

F shows how new fabric straps edged with narrow heading were used to replace old worn straps. The same heading gave a new edge to the top of the gown.

No matter what type of garment you have there is a way to mend it attractively. Do not put too much handwork on fragile fabrics.

Never use trimmings on night apparel that do not conveniently wash and iron. Shabby " finery " is too expensive in more ways than one. Throughout this section are shown delicate and sturdy garments that have been repaired practically and with a minimum of time, effort and expense.

The pyjama mends shown are applicable to men's, women's and children's apparel. Learn how to do practical mending. Then, no matter what the rip, tear or damage, you can mend it appropriately and without it being obvious.

—NOT SHEEP

Two rewards can be yours in mending: (1) to prolong the wear of something you like and value, and (2) to get a real thrill out of your ability to mend effectively so that the garment never looks as though it had barely survived a mending routine.

To Mend Long-Sleeved Nightgowns. If the elbow of a long-sleeved silk nightdress wears out, as in **A**, don't reinforce it. Add decoration rather than a patch, because a silk nightdress is more or less a luxury item and needs to be kept so to the last. If the elbow is thin, the rest of the garment is also likely to be fragile. Appliqué a piece of lace over the thin spot, and then cut the spot away; or, appliqué a piece of chiffon or ribbon, or add a new half-sleeve as shown. Cut away the worn part and use the new fabric, as in **B**, keeping the cuff, if it is still good, to make the whole appear as if intended. See instructions for finishing sleeve on page 33.

Tight Sleeve Band. This shows how to insert a piece of ribbon at the seam of a sleeve band if the band is too tight for comfort. Rip the seam in the cuff and a few of the stitches joining the band to the sleeve, let out some of the fulness held in there. Insert a piece of ribbon or a strap of fabric of the right width into the band and hem it in place, as at **C**.

New Shoulder Straps for Nightgowns. When the shoulder of the type shown in the small sketch is worn or is too tight, it may be replaced in this fashion. Cut away the worn part or open the shoulder seam. Turn the edge under. Take two pieces of ribbon of the necessary length, place them at the edges of the strap, as in **D**, and stitch across. Then turn the whole seam down, with the ribbon folded in, as in **E**, and hold with pins. Stitch as in **F**, on the right side to secure the straps.

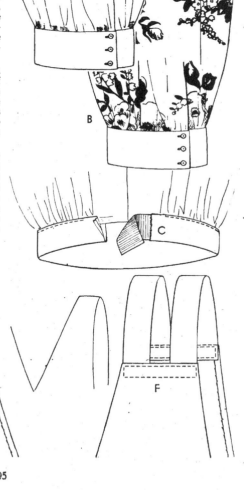

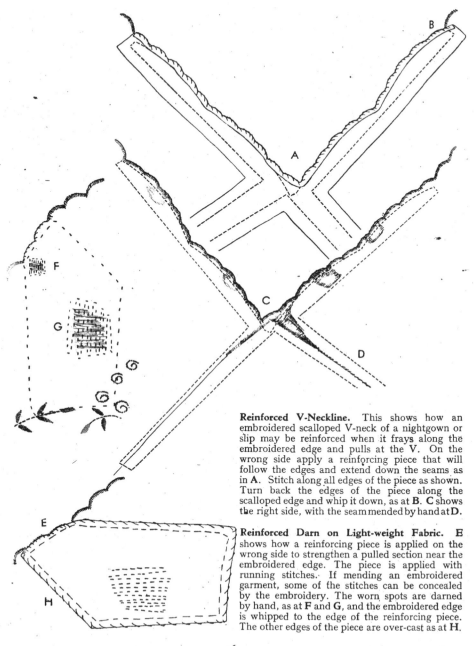

Reinforced V-Neckline. This shows how an embroidered scalloped V-neck of a nightgown or slip may be reinforced when it frays along the embroidered edge and pulls at the **V**. On the wrong side apply a reinforcing piece that will follow the edges and extend down the seams as in **A**. Stitch along all edges of the piece as shown. Turn back the edges of the piece along the scalloped edge and whip it down, as at **B**. **C** shows the right side, with the seam mended by hand at **D**.

Reinforced Darn on Light-weight Fabric. **E** shows how a reinforcing piece is applied on the wrong side to strengthen a pulled section near the embroidered edge. The piece is applied with running stitches. If mending an embroidered garment, some of the stitches can be concealed by the embroidery. The worn spots are darned by hand, as at **F** and **G**, and the embroidered edge is whipped to the edge of the reinforcing piece. The other edges of the piece are over-cast as at **H**.

96

Pulled-Out Tie Ends. Tie sashes on nightgowns often pull out at the seam, as in **I**. This may be mended either by hand or machine. **J** shows the hand-sewn repair. Insert the sash end into the seam and back-stitch it in place from the wrong side as shown. For extra strength the edges may be overcast together. **K** shows how the sash may be re-inserted into the seam and stitched in place from the right side. Place the new stitching exactly in the original line.

Torn Seam in Quilted Robe. Seams in quilted garments generally are bound on the inside with bias binding. Occasionally strain on the seam will break the thread holding the bindings, as at **L**. Unless this is mended quickly, the quilted fabric may tear at this point, as at **M**.

To mend such a tear, take a tiny seam from the inside in the right side edges of the tear, as in **N**; then lap the raw wrong-side edges over this and top-stitch, as at **O**. Replace the binding and stitching, as at **P**.

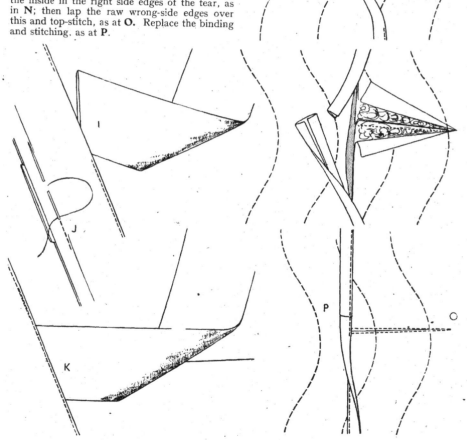

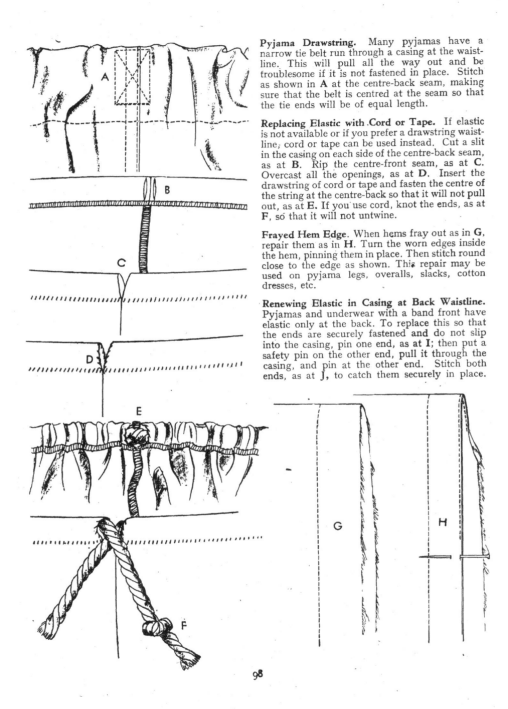

Pyjama Drawstring. Many pyjamas have a narrow tie belt run through a casing at the waistline. This will pull all the way out and be troublesome if it is not fastened in place. Stitch as shown in **A** at the centre-back seam, making sure that the belt is centred at the seam so that the tie ends will be of equal length.

Replacing Elastic with Cord or Tape. If elastic is not available or if you prefer a drawstring waistline, cord or tape can be used instead. Cut a slit in the casing on each side of the centre-back seam, as at **B**. Rip the centre-front seam, as at **C**. Overcast all the openings, as at **D**. Insert the drawstring of cord or tape and fasten the centre of the string at the centre-back so that it will not pull out, as at **E**. If you use cord, knot the ends, as at **F**, so that it will not untwine.

Frayed Hem Edge. When hems fray out as in **G**, repair them as in **H**. Turn the worn edges inside the hem, pinning them in place. Then stitch round close to the edge as shown. This repair may be used on pyjama legs, overalls, slacks, cotton dresses, etc.

Renewing Elastic in Casing at Back Waistline. Pyjamas and underwear with a band front have elastic only at the back. To replace this so that the ends are securely fastened and do not slip into the casing, pin one end, as at **I**; then put a safety pin on the other end, pull it through the casing, and pin at the other end. Stitch both ends, as at **J**, to catch them securely in place.

Strain at Centre-Front Seam. Garments that have elastic only across the back of the waistline sometimes show strain and wear at the centre-front seam. To prevent having this pull apart, the hem can be reinforced by inserting seam binding or twill tape, as at **K**. Rip only the bottom row of stitching along the hem, as at **L**, insert the tape or binding and restore the stitching. To reinforce the centre seam still further, stitch across the joining and back, as in **M**.

Underarm Patch. When pyjamas are torn out under the armhole, they may be patched, as in **N**. Follow instructions given for Flat Fell Patch on page 61. The patching material in this case may be cut from the bottom of the front facings.

Split Pyjama Shoulder. Some people wear out pyjamas particularly at a spot just in from the shoulder line. The pyjama top always splits lengthwise at this point. A suggestion for mending this or preventing such wear in the future is to insert a narrow panel of knitted fabric as in **O**. This will provide enough give to prevent wear.

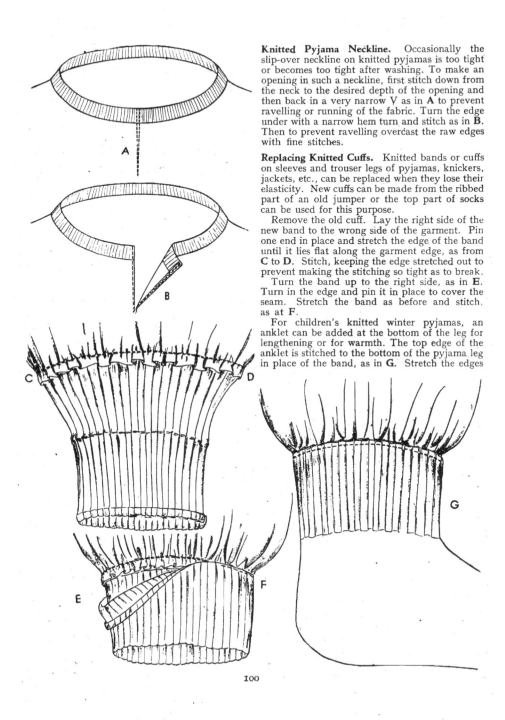

Knitted Pyjama Neckline. Occasionally the slip-over neckline on knitted pyjamas is too tight or becomes too tight after washing. To make an opening in such a neckline, first stitch down from the neck to the desired depth of the opening and then back in a very narrow V as in **A** to prevent ravelling or running of the fabric. Turn the edge under with a narrow hem turn and stitch as in **B**. Then to prevent ravelling overcast the raw edges with fine stitches.

Replacing Knitted Cuffs. Knitted bands or cuffs on sleeves and trouser legs of pyjamas, knickers, jackets, etc., can be replaced when they lose their elasticity. New cuffs can be made from the ribbed part of an old jumper or the top part of socks can be used for this purpose.

Remove the old cuff. Lay the right side of the new band to the wrong side of the garment. Pin one end in place and stretch the edge of the band until it lies flat along the garment edge, as from **C** to **D**. Stitch, keeping the edge stretched out to prevent making the stitching so tight as to break.

Turn the band up to the right side, as in **E**. Turn in the edge and pin it in place to cover the seam. Stretch the band as before and stitch, as at **F**.

For children's knitted winter pyjamas, an anklet can be added at the bottom of the leg for lengthening or for warmth. The top edge of the anklet is stitched to the bottom of the pyjama leg in place of the band, as in **G**. Stretch the edges while stitching. Then closely overcast the seam edges on the wrong side.

Torn Placket. The tear at the end of a placket, as shown here, is a common trouble with pyjamas and underwear. Because of the wear and tear on such spots, it is necessary when repairing to reinforce well. To do this, place a piece of twill tape or bias tape under the torn edge, as at **H**, and stitch it as shown. Then lap the edges of the placket and stitch, as in **I**, replacing the original stitching, as at **J**, and fastening the joining securely to the reinforcing tape as shown.

Lengthening Pyjama Placket. If placket opening is too short, it will tear along seam. Make it longer by ripping stitching as far as necessary. Secure end of stitching well. Mend any frayed or torn edges by hand or machine. Join placket piece, or bound edge, as shown at **K**. This piece may be taken from a ripped-off pocket, or it may be any scrap similar to pyjama material. Turn in raw edge and continue line of stitching, as at **L**. Add as many snaps, or buttons and buttonholes, as necessary for the length of the placket.

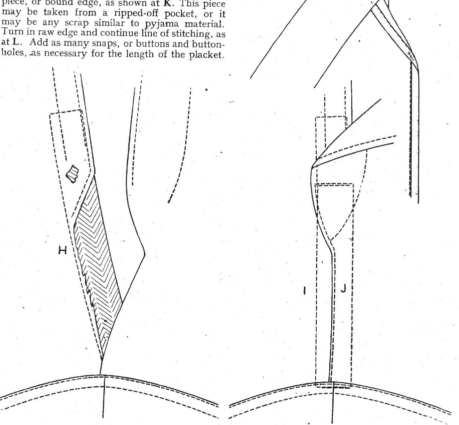

MENDING

Torn Patch Pocket. When the garment fabric tears at the corners of a patch pocket, mend it with cotton tape. First, rip the corner of the pocket from **A** to **B**. Cut a strip of tape long enough to cover the tear and place it on the wrong side. Fasten it in place with small running stitches, using matching thread, as at **C**. Then, working from the right side, darn across the tear, as at **D**. Finally, re-stitch the pocket corner as shown in **E**.

Torn Welt Pocket. These often pull out at the top, as in **F**. To mend this, pin and stitch a small piece of matching fabric under the hole inside the lining, as in **G**. This stitching will not show on the right side. Turn to the right side and catch the piece in place with small running-stitches and matching thread, as in **H**, and darn the hole to the piece, as at **I**. Make the stitches as small and inconspicuous as possible.

Crow's-Foot. If the garment is worth the extra work, a crow's-foot may be made over the mended part. To do this, draw a triangle of the desired size, as indicated in **J**. Work from corner to corner—from **K** to **L** to **M**, and back to **K**, turning the work as you go and bringing the needle out at each corner in the same way. Make

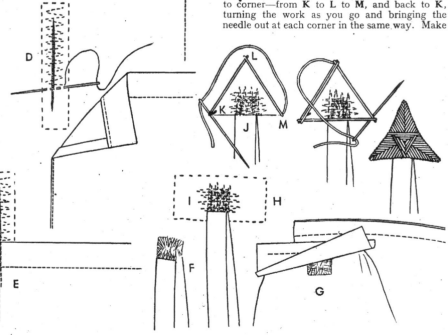

POCKETS

each stitch just below the one before it. All corners cross, as shown, and as the crow's-foot is filled in, the threads draw in towards the centre.

To Mend Stand Pocket. Such pockets, found in some suits, tailored dresses and nurses' uniforms, may tear at the corners, as shown in **A**. Remove all stitching, as in **B**, unless the stand has been entirely ripped out. Turn to wrong side and take up a narrow tapering seam, as in **C**, catching in the torn section. Be sure to hold the stand section away so it will not be caught in the seam. Finally stitch the stand section back in position, as in **D**. If all torn edges have not been caught in well, reinforce by hand at the corners, as at **E**. Any slight pucker or pleat that may form at the point of mending may usually be pressed down satisfactorily. If necessary, reinforce the pocket end further by placing a piece of tape underneath the corner of the pocket and catch it in the stitching **D**.

A pocket corner may wear above the pocket, as at **F**. Mend by hand, using a fine running-stitch, or by machine if the worn area is large and the type of garment permits. If badly frayed, reinforce underneath with tape or fabric.

Split Pocket. Once in a while a patch pocket, especially one on a jacket or coat, is torn through the body of the pocket, as in **G**. The simplest way to repair this is to use mending tissue or one of the tapes which can be pressed on. Slide a piece of cardboard into the pocket. Then lay the mending tissue under the tear. Bring edges together and lay a piece of tissue paper over the pocket. Then press carefully so that the edges will adhere to the adhesive. Replace the stitching along the top of the pocket with back-stitches and, if possible, darn back and forth from the underside, as at **H**, to reinforce this point.

If the pocket can be ripped off and replaced easily, repair it in this way: Make a narrow seam, as in **I**, tapering it to nothing, as shown. On the opposite side of the pocket, make a tapered inside tuck, as at **J**, to balance the first seam. Pin the pocket back in position and stitch as originally. If there is another pocket on the garment, remove it and make tucks so that the pockets match.

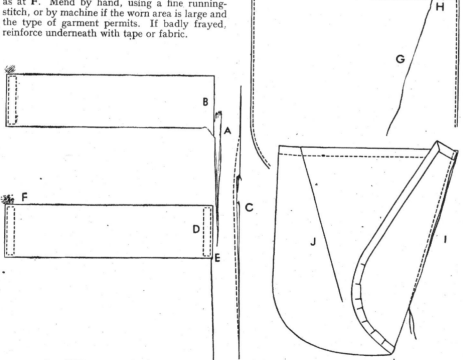

PULLED SEAMS

Broken Stitches in the Seam. Nothing is more annoying than broken places in a seam. You will hear many people say this is caused by bad thread. Possibly once in a thousand times this is so, but usually it is because the fabric has more elasticity than the stitching line. The tension on the machine may be too tight, or the fabric was not stretched enough in stitching to give a sufficiently long stitching line. A good seamstress will stitch her fabric over newspaper or tissue paper. This stretches the seam slightly and thus avoids breaking the thread when the seam is opened.

If you have a tight seam and need to restitch it, stretch the seam just a little as you stitch. Then, when you press it, shrink up all the stretch you have put in. Too many people, when they have a broken seam, will stitch the seam twice, generally just as tight as it was originally. Then, when the seam is pressed, there is the same danger of breaking the stitching line.

In stitching, avoid too long or too short stitches. Stitches that are too long do not hold the fabric securely enough, and too short stitches hold it too tightly. For chiffon, 16 stitches to an inch is right; for sheer woollens, 10 to 12 is ideal; and for cottons, it is best to have 9 to 11 stitches. On draperies or fabric furnishings 6 to 8 stitches to the inch is allowable.

Pulled Seams. When a garment is tight or when the fabric is loosely woven, fabric threads sometimes separate along the seams, as in **A**. Ordinarily this cannot be repaired by taking a deeper seam, because the garment is already too tight. Turn to the wrong side, which will appear as in **B**. Stitch on the seam side of the pulled-out part, as in **C**. Then take a needle and use the point to flick the fabric threads back towards the seam. Open the seam and catch it down over the frayed part with uneven basting-stitches in matching thread. Press the seam from the wrong side, as in **D**.

When considerably more ease is needed in the seams, let them out, as at **E**, and cover the pulled part with a band of fabric, braid, ribbon or bias binding, as at **F**. This repair can be made to look as if it is a decorative feature of the garment.

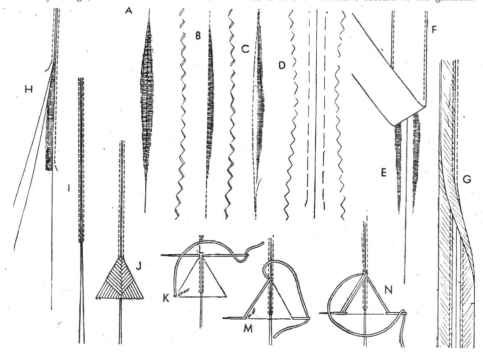

Pulled Pleats. Pleats occasionally pull out where they are stitched down, as in **H.** If the skirt is amply large, the pleats can simply be set over ¼ in. to cover the pulled part, and restitched. However, the reason they pull, usually, is that the skirt is a little tight and there is no room to spare for such repair. In this case, rip out the stitching for some distance from the bottom. Pin a piece of seam binding along the pulled part on the wrong side. Baste this; then restitch the seams from the right side, as in **I.** If the strain is caused by tightness of the skirt, let out the side seams.

Arrowhead. For extra strength at the end of the stitching on the pleats, an arrowhead can be worked, as in **J.** To make this, begin by drawing with chalk, a triangle of the size desired and taking stitches, as at **K,** with buttonhole twist. Take a straight stitch across the point of the triangle, as at **L,** then another through the fabric across the base of the triangle, as in **M.** Continue as in **N,** until the triangle is filled in.

Let-Out Seams. When a seam has been let out so far that the edge is very close to the seam, bind each edge, as in **G,** to prevent pulling away.

DROOPING HEM LINES

HEMS THAT DROOP are dangerous, untidy, unattractive, and careless. So look over the hem of every garment you have, and put in staying stitches to be sure your hem line does not sag.

Don't say that you can't do a slip-stitch. It is very easy. With your needle and thread, take a lengthwise stitch in the seaming ribbon or edge of the hem, and then a tiny stitch in the skirt. You will soon learn to pick up just half a thread, and to make your stitches so loose and easy that they will not be visible on the right side. This stitch is illustrated on page 14.

Because your skirt had a hem when you got it, don't think you have to keep the same hem until the garment is discarded. Nothing gives new life to an old skirt more readily than a new hem line. Look at yourself in the mirror. If your skirt sags, get someone to turn a new hem.

It is no trick to put up a new hem line. First, pin it at the new even length. This can be done by measuring from the floor with a stick and putting a row of pins around where the new hem is to be. Or you can use a piece of chalk to mark round the hips; then measure an even distance down from this line to the hem line. Or you can stand before a mirror and pin the points that sag until you have a perfectly true line. Review all your hems in your full-length mirror. Make sure both dresses and slips are the correct length and that the hem lines are even. In tailored

skirts or narrow skirts, even a slight sag will be conspicuous as there is no fulness to hide it.

To Let Down a Hem With a Worn Edge. Sometimes the lower turned edge of a hem, especially in a washable dress, is worn thin from constant laundering. If the dress is to be lengthened, it would not be practical to have this worn line showing above the hem. Then, too, the fabric that was on the under side may appear less faded.

You can camouflage this and also insure a sturdy finish by stitching a narrow tuck near the original hem turn, to hide the worn edge. Apply a facing and catch the upper edge of it just below the tuck, stitching as at **A.** This stitching is not taken through the tuck but under it, as at **B.**

To Mend a Worn Hem Edge. The worn edge may be drawn up underneath by taking out the hem and making it slightly deeper. If it is too badly frayed for this treatment, split the hem at the turned edge and fold in the two split edges ¼ in. to ⅜ in. or just enough to catch the worn edges. Under the garment edge, slip a piece of bias strip of any light-weight fabric, as at **C,** so that one edge of the strip is even with the fold, and baste. Catch-stitch the raw edge of the turned portion to the bias strip as shown. Do not catch through to the right side. Turn under the hem piece, as at **D,** so that it is slightly above the new hem edge as at **E,** and fasten with slip-stitching, avoid catching stitches to outside.

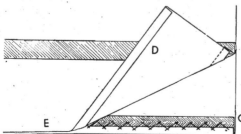

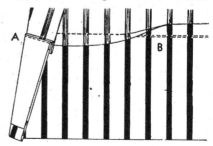

MENDING LACE

Repairing Lace Edging. Where lace edging is severely torn, it may be patched, as shown, by placing a new piece over the torn spot, matching the design carefully, and whipping it down around the motif. The torn section may then be cut away.

Repairing All-Over Lace. All-over lace may be repaired in much the same way. Lay the new piece over the torn spot, matching the motifs to those in the garment. Whip around the motifs and then trim off the worn section on the wrong side.

Lace Appliqué. All-over lace, such as that used to make new slip tops, lace blouses and dresses, should be appliquéd at the seams, rather than stitched. Allow enough overlap at the seams so that you can cut around the design on the edge. Baste the edges to paper and whip the seams around the designs as shown above so that the

joining is invisible. Even darts and tucks in lace should be cut away and appliquéd in this way to prevent a heavy overlapping that would detract from the beauty of the lace pattern.

If the motif has a heavy outline thread, you can imitate this by laying a heavy thread around edge of cut out design and overcasting over this.

Inserting a New Section of Lace Edging. When the edging has been completely torn off or is so worn that a piece must be replaced, the new piece should be inserted as shown. Whip the edges of the lace together, as at **A.** Gather it to the required length by pulling a thread in the lace edge and sliding the lace on the drawn thread. Then roll the fabric edge with the left thumb as you whip the gathered lace to the garment with a fine thread, as in **B.** Make the whipping stitches blend invisibly with the mesh of the lace.

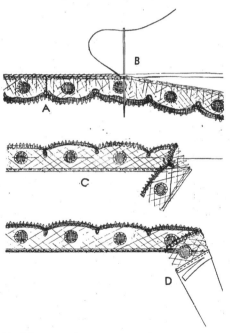

Applying Lace by Machine. Lay the lace right side up on the right side of the fabric and stitch with fine thread, as in **C.** Turn and stitch back. Trim away surplus fabric from seam edge, as **D.**

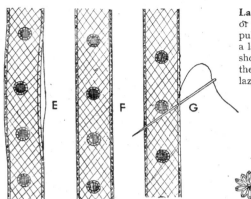

Lace Pulled Away at Corner. At the armhole òr neckline of a slip or nightgown the lace may pull away from the corners. To secure it there, a lazy-daisy stitch may be worked, as in **H**. This should be repeated at matching corners to give the effect of decoration, rather than mending. The lazy-daisy stitch is given on page 16.

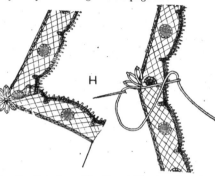

Repairing Insertion. When insertion is pulled away from its stitching, as in **E**, it may be repaired either by hand or by machine, according to the original stitching. When repairing by machine, as in **F**, stitch on the right side with fine matching thread, beginning a little back from the break and stitching a little beyond it. Pull thread through to the wrong side and tie. When repairing by hand, whip the edge back in place, as in **G**.

Appliquéing Lace Banding. Use banding from 4 ins. to 6 ins. wide. Cut it through the centre, as in **I**, cutting around motifs and being careful not to cut the threads that form the design. Thus you have two lengths of banding, each with an attractive irregular edge. Pin and baste the banding along the edge to be covered, letting the uncut lace edge extend $\frac{1}{4}$ in. to $\frac{1}{2}$ in. beyond the fabric edge. Oversew along the irregular edge, as in **J**, with a matching thread. Then cut away the surplus fabric under the lace, as in **K**. Press from the wrong side over a Turkish towel.

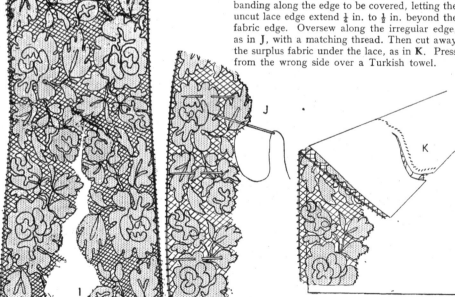

REPAIRING BELTS

Shortening Buckle Belt. Remove any extra length from the buckle end of the belt so as not to affect finished end. Remove buckle. Cut off excess, allowing enough extra length to hold the buckle. Make two holes about ½ in. apart, as in **A**. Then with a razor blade cut a slot between the holes, as in **B**. Replace buckle, putting tongue through slot, as in **C**. Fold end under and stitch, as at **D**. Move belt-hold up near buckle, as at **E**, and stitch, as at **F**.

Lengthening Buckle Belt. Belts in which buckles are used are generally of leather or stiff fabric-lined material. If they require lengthening, put an insert at each side under the arms. This may be of the same dress fabric, leather taken from an old purse, or grosgrain ribbon, as shown in **G**.

Belt Worn Near Buckle Holes. A belt may crack or wear where it is drawn through a slide or buckle, as at **H**. Remove stitching from **I** to **J**. Cut away worn part. Lay one end over the other and stitch from **K** to **L**. To restore the stitching exactly, place the belt under the machine needle, insert the needle into one of the original stitching holes, and adjust the length of the stitch to the one previously used. Then thread your machine with matching thread. If the stitching cannot be duplicated exactly, stitch twice in the same holes. This will give much the same effect of weight in the stitching as the original had.

This same plan may be used to lengthen a belt. Simply stitch an extra piece of dress fabric or double ribbon as from **M** to **N** on end of a belt. If of fabric make worked eyelets for buckle holes.

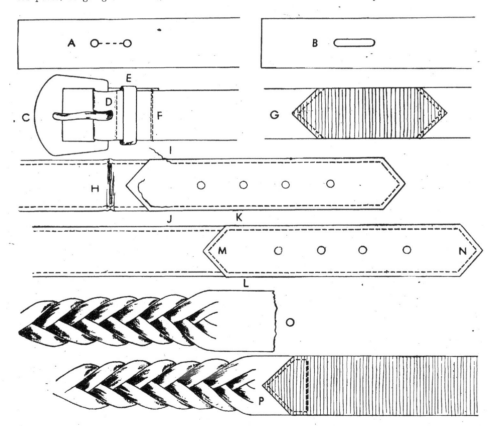

To Repair or Lengthen Belt Ends. If a belt of leather or fabric wears at the ends, or if it requires extra length, it may be made wearable with new ends of grosgrain ribbon. Remove slide or other fastener. Cut away worn sections, if necessary, as at **O**. Cut two lengths of ribbon, making them long enough to tie in a bow, to lap or to accommodate a buckle, as in **Q**. Finish ends of ribbon by rounding them or with points, as shown at **P**, and stitch to the belt securely.

To Lengthen Narrow Fabric Belt. A firm, narrow fabric belt may have length added, as shown here. Cut a slit in each end and finish it with a buttonhole-stitch, as in **R**. Through the slits run a tie strip of the dress fabric, ribbon or silk cord, as in **S**. This is tied in front.

Loose Belt Lining. Belts having hooked closings are often lined with leather or fabric which is glued in. If this lining separates, as in **T**, use rubber cement or any suitable adhesive, moisten both parts of the belt, allow it to dry, then press together, as in **U**. Lay it flat with a weight on it until it has set. If a belt lining must be replaced, rip out the old one and replace with grosgrain ribbon. It can be glued or stitched in place, depending on the materials you are working with.

Loop Belt Carrier. For some dresses, belt carriers made of thread are most satisfactory. They are particularly desirable in "make-overs" where extra material may not be available. Use buttonhole twine or cotton thread in the same colour as the belt. Make four to six easy stitches about 1½ ins. above, and 1½ ins. below waistline, as in **V**, and work a close blanket-stitch over these to form a firm strand a little wider than the belt.

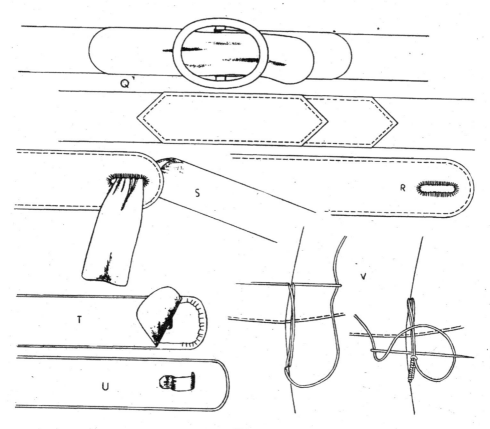

"ALL HANDS ON DECK"

THERE ARE ANY NUMBER of conditions that cause wear and tear on gloves so that they need mending. Seams split from the breaking of faulty threads, from lack of care in pulling gloves on and off, from some unpredictable strain on the seam or because gloves are too tight or some parts are too small for the hand or fingers. Holes result from hard wearing or from pulling the glove too tight or too hard at some point.

A glove, although utilitarian, must never be soiled or untidy and never unmended—and never, never should mending stitches be recognizable as such. To insure this it is well worth your time to learn at the outset to do such mending in a truly professional way.

Glove Seams. The instructions that follow cover different types of seams commonly used in both fabric and leather gloves. For repairing your gloves, as nearly as you can, use the type of stitch and seam that was used originally.

Overcast Glove Seam. To mend a seam, as in **A**, pull the threads of the original stitches back two or three stitches. On the wrong side of the glove, with an unthreaded needle, take several stitches in the seam, then thread the needle with the end of the thread and pull it through, as in **B**. Do this at each end of the broken space. Now thread your needle with a double thread of matching colour. Take a back-stitch on the wrong side of the glove

to fasten the thread. Bring the needle out to the right side, at the end of the stitching, through one of the holes made by the original thread. Take one overcast stitch at a time and imitate the original as nearly as possible, as in **C**. This is most easily done if you slip one of your fingers inside the finger that is to be mended. In leather gloves take each stitch in the original holes. This insures an even spacing of the stitches and keeps you from working too many or too few. Do not draw the thread tight. When the last stitch is complete, turn the wrong side out sufficiently to allow you to finish off the thread on the underside, using an inconspicuous yet secure back-stitch.

Blanket-Stitched Glove Seam. Many gloves have a machine-stitch on the seams that resembles a hand-made blanket-stitch, as in **D**. To repair such a seam by hand, proceed as for a hand-sewn glove. Secure the end of the original thread at top and bottom of the break. Mend with a double thread in matching colour. Bring your needle through from the wrong side, and begin to make a blanket-stitch as shown. Insert the needle straight through the two edges of the seam; do not put it in slanting. Take your stitches in the original holes. Complete all the rips; then take the needle inside, turn the glove wrong side out, and fasten off the thread with tiny inconspicuous back-stitches. If you crochet, and if the glove fabric is not too closely woven, you can crochet

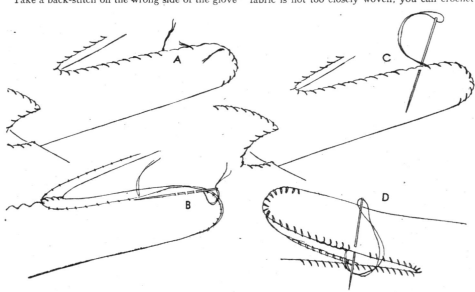

this blanket-stitch in and do it more quickly than with sewing needle. Use a fine steel crochet hook and take the stitches in the original holes. A good glove has a long life, so take pride in your repair stitches and only you will know that your gloves have been mended.

Restitching Glove Seams. Very often the stitching thread in gloves breaks, as in **E**. The best way to mend such gloves is with machine-stitching, as in **F**. To do this, thread your machine top and bottom with a thread as nearly like the original thread as possible. Test the length of your stitch on a scrap. Make it as near the length of the glove stitch as possible. Clip away the broken threads, begin two or three stitches back, and put the machine needle in a hole made by the original needle. Continue stitching in the original holes until the seam is again complete. Pull the machine thread end through to the inside and tie at both ends of the repaired seam, so that the new stitching of the seam will not pull out.

Restitching Gloves by Hand. Sometimes a machine-made seam is ripped in such a way that the mending is best done by hand, as in **G**. In such a case, thread your needle, tie a knot, bring the needle through from under the glove finger, begin to make stitches in the original stitching holes in the seam. Make a row of regular running stitches along the seam. When this row is in, go back again and just reverse the process, filling in all spaces between stitches so that the new seam corresponds as nearly to the original as you can make it. This stitch is called a double running stitch, it is very strong and neat. This method is used also to stitch hand-sewn fabric or leather gloves.

Hand-Sewn or Saddle-Stitched Seams. These should be repaired with a plain running-stitch. Usually the stitches are spaced a distance apart so that both sides of the seam will appear alike. Insert the needle straight through the two edges of the seam.

Lapped Seam. This seam, shown at **H**, because of inaccessibility must be back-stitched by hand.

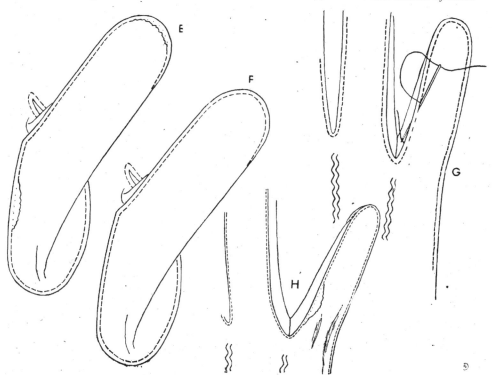

Repairing Leather Gloves. Use a fine short needle for such work. Bring your needle through from the inside of the glove finger and finish the seam in a manner as nearly as possible the way the original glove was sewn.

A shows how a seam is rewhipped. This method of repair also may be used on fabric gloves with a whipped seam edge.

B shows how both edges of a pulled-out seam have first been buttonholed, and how the buttonholed edges have then been whipped together as the enlargement **C** shows. This buttonholing is to avoid tightening the seam at a point where the rip itself gave evidence of strain or tightness.

D shows a variation of the whipped seam **A**. Remember always to imitate the original stitching as nearly as you can, and to begin and end your repair stitching so that only you know where it is.

Laced-Stitched Seam for Gloves. When a glove rips because it is too tight, use the lace-stitch seam

to repair it and thus gain the extra width of the seams. The stitches should be made quite close together, as in **E**. See page 20 for instructions.

Patches on Gloves. Frequently gloves tear at the finger sections, especially when fingers of the glove are too short, or over the fat part of the thumb, as at **F**. To repair, cut away the point of the cuff, as at **G**. About ½ in. on the side gloves, of course. Take a piece of this patch material and carefully place it under the tear that is to be mended. Whip the tear to this patch; make your stitches close together and avoid drawing your thread too tight. Leather gloves that are tight across the palm often tear out at the top of closing, as at **H**. Placing a patch underneath is the only way in which this can be repaired. Do this in the same way, as in **F**. Sometimes a little beeswax rubbed on to the thread makes it smooth and easier to pull through.

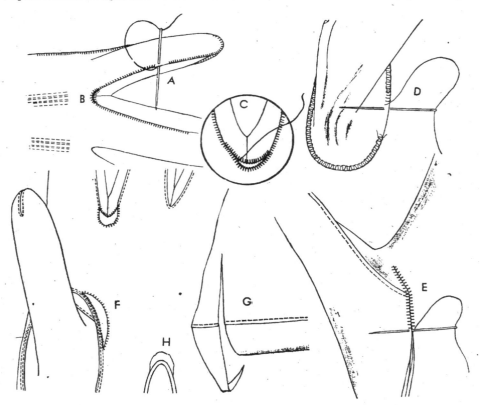

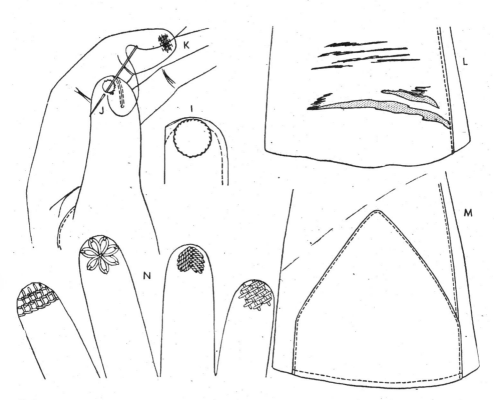

If the glove has a bound or hemmed bottom edge, then use leather from an old glove or pocketbook that is of a matching colour to the glove, for the patch piece.

When Finger Tips Give Way. Gloves often wear thin or a hole is worn through at one or more of the finger tips. The value of the gloves and the time you have to spend in the mending are points to consider before undertaking the repair. A simple way to repair such tears is to cut a patch from a fabric that harmonizes with the glove from a point of view of both colour and texture, making the patch twice as large in diameter as the hole. Turn the finger wrong side out. Slip one of your fingers in this, pin the patch in position over the hole and overcast it, as in **I**. Turn the glove-finger right side out—trim away any frayed edges around the hole. Then with tiny stitches whip the edges of the hole neatly to the patch, as in **J**.

If the fingers of the gloves are thin but not actually worn through, the ends may be reinforced with very fine darning-stitches, as shown in **K**.

Wrist Patches. When a glove gives way in the wrist, as in **L**, as a result of too strenuous pulling on or off or faulty leather, mend it with appropriate fabric—jersey, felt, grosgrain ribbon, velvet, firm crepe. If the fabric is light-weight, it may be necessary to apply a piece and then line it, to cover the seams and to give sufficient body. A pointed patch is shown in **M** and a slanting patch may be used as the dotted line shows. Shape your patch as your glove requires, just being sure of a neat secure job when finished.

Children's Wool Gloves. When children go through the fingers of their woollen play gloves, the holes are usually large. To conceal an extensive darn, decorative stitches may be used, as shown in **N**, either on front or back of the finger tips. First do the darn with matching colour and then place the decorative stitches, using gay contrasting colours. Then the effect will be one of intended decoration. The same thing can be done with adults' sports gloves and mittens, etc. For types of decorative stitches, see pages 16 and 17.

WHEN YOU MEND FOR MEN

EVERY NEW HUSBAND is happy about the first button that comes off. His bride will sew it on for him and he will revel in this special attention. If she continues to sew on every loose button, mend every tear, and darn every hole promptly, he is apt through the years to become so accustomed to such a model wife that he is not aware of the hours she spends in keeping his clothing in repair. On the other hand, more husbands have become aware of their wives disinterest in them through permanently missing buttons and ragged socks than in any other way.

A happy home must have no frayed edges—nerves are easily jangled by such things. Ugly words can be heard through stocking holes and sheet rents. Again, that little extra pin money that many women long for can be earned by keeping the linen and fabric of a home in a good state of repair.

Linens will last one-third longer if broken threads are reinforced as soon as broken; a shirt can have a life and a half if kept in repair and given a new collar or band and if cuffs are turned at the right time.

Suits can lead a double life if each little break is looked after—edges mended, frayed seats renewed, cuffs reconditioned, darns put in, reweaving done.

A good way to appreciate your own mending is to become an artist at it, and then put a price on your time and keep a notebook, say for three months, of the time spent in mending. You can then feel encouraged by knowing that you have not only salvaged your mended article, but saved the expense of paying for it.

One woman with husband and three children to sew for learned to mend, took the necessary time to learn to do it well. At the end of a year she showed her husband how she had really saved enough to warrant his buying a piano for her. Maybe you need and want something very badly for your home. Perhaps you can show your husband that you have earned its cost and more by your conservation programme of mending and making over.

Men's clothes are classic in line, traditional in finish and conservative in every detail. Custom has made them so.

This means that you must mend such clothing with precise care so that what is done is never conspicuous.

Threads must match exactly; stitching must be true and stitches of the same length as the original stitches in the garment. Don't experiment on a man's suit or favourite shirt no matter how badly it needs repair. Know what you are doing and why. Proceed with precision and care and don't hurry the work.

Remember, most suits are made by men tailors, and there is a certain deliberateness in their work which you must imitate, to restore a suit to a " good-as-new " condition and appearance

A TURN FOR THE BETTER

Reversing a Collar. To turn a collar, first slip the point of a razor blade under the stitches joining the collar and the band, and gently pull the point along under the stitches as you go. Because the stitches are fine and the collars usually starched, it is almost impossible to pick them out. The razor blade opens the seam efficiently. Be careful that you do not cut the fabric. Rip only from **A** to **B**, and not out to the ends of the collarband. When you have ripped the collar off, fold it in half, end to end, and put a pin at the fold to mark the centre. Fold the neckband end to end and mark its centre with a pin. Turn the collar to its good side and insert it back into the neckband, matching the pins in collar and band to centre it correctly. Pin the ends of the collar in place at **A** and **B** and place another pin, fastening it at the centre-back. Pin all the way along the neckband, as shown, and then baste, being sure that the underside of the band is caught by the stitches. Stitch carefully along the original line.

If the neckband is worn and must be turned with the collar, rip the stitches joining neckband to shirt, removing the collar and band. Pin the ends of the collarband to the front edges of the shirt, as shown at **C**, so that the collar fits the neck edge of the shirt. Place another pin at the centre-back, as at **D**. Pin the rest of the collar in place, slipping the neckline of the shirt inside the collar band. Pin exactly along the old stitching line on the neck of the shirt, as at **E**, so that the new band covers it but does not overlap more of the shirt than was included in the original seam. Then baste, making sure that the underside of the collarband is caught by the basting stitches. Stitch carefully along the basted lines. The button must be moved to the other end of the band, after this turning, and a new buttonhole made (see Buttonholes, page 74).

Ready-Made Collars and Bands. There are available at notion counters ready-made collars with neckband attached which you can apply to shirts. They come in white usually in two qualities—broad cloth and less expensive fabrics—and in regular neck sizes of men's shirts—13, 15, etc. Apply them as has been previously described.

Many men have shirts to be worn with separate collars that they no longer care to wear because they prefer the attached collar type. These shirts can be salvaged by removing the band and applying ready-made collars.

There are also available collarbands to be applied to the type of shirt worn with separate collars. Apply these in the same way as the collar with band.

Repairing Shirt Cuffs. There are three ways to turn a cuff. If the shirt has double cuffs, rip the cuffs off with a razor blade just as you do the collar. Turn the cuff over with the worn side inside. Pin, baste and stitch carefully along edge.

If the shirt has a single cuff that is badly frayed and the sleeve is none too long, bind the edge with bias binding as in **F**. Use a binding that matches in colour the shirt or the most prominent stripe. Bind the edge as shown. Ease the binding around the corners so it will lie perfectly flat. Unless you are quite expert with the machine-binder, baste the binding on before stitching.

When the cuff is frayed and the sleeve could afford to be slightly shorter, then turn in the edges, as in **G** and **H**. Rip both stitchings along the bottom edge of the cuff. Turn in the worn edges as shown. Pin, baste and stitch round corner and along the edge, as at **H**. The second stitching is same distance from edge as original, see **I**.

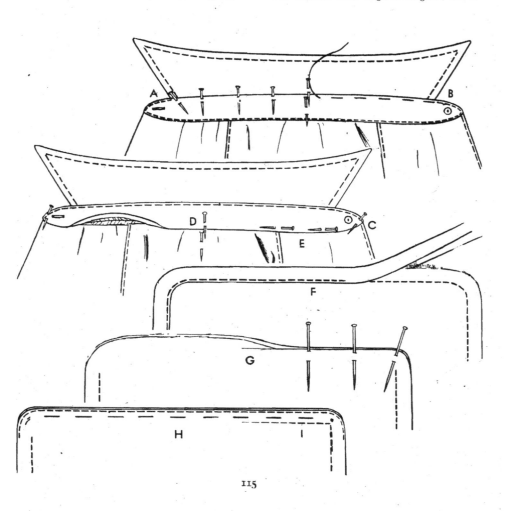

NEW LIFE FOR A SUIT

Frayed Coat Sleeves. No matter whether sleeves are long or short, whether they have starched or soft cuffs, or none at all, the edges of coat sleeves will fray after a time. The easiest, simplest repair is a new seam at the bottom of the sleeve. This will shorten the sleeve by the depth of the seam, but otherwise is scarcely noticeable.

A shows the frayed edges. B shows where to baste the lining and sleeve together with diagonal stitches before any ripping is done. To do this basting, slip one hand inside the sleeve and turn the sleeve as it is basted all the way round.

Rip the lining loose at the bottom of the sleeve. Press out the crease between hem and sleeve. Turn the hem over to the right side, folding the old crease in reverse, and put pins a little back from the crease, as at C. Baste just inside the frayed part, placing the basting from $\frac{1}{16}$ in. to $\frac{1}{4}$ in., as is required, from the frayed crease mark. Stitch on this basting line, as at D. Remove bastings. Turn the sleeve wrong side out, and press and baste the seam up against the sleeve, as at E. This prevents the seam from rolling inside the new hem. Trim from the interlining an amount equal to that taken up by the seam and catch the interlining to the new seam, as at F. Press the new hem in position. Catch it down with diagonal basting-stitches, as in G. Cut the sleeve lining off just enough to equal the amount taken up in the new seam. This serves to give a desirable new line to the lining. Bring the lining down. Pin it in place, as at H, and slip-stitch it to the hem, as at I. Then give a final pressing to the sleeve.

In some coats it may be necessary to remove the lower buttons on the sleeve to put in the repair seam. In such a case, sew the button back in place, carry your thread over to the second button, and finish off over its threads—this, because such buttons are usually sewn on with

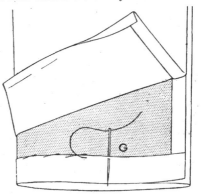

ead. Therefore, the other buttons might ose if not secured at this time.

Front Edges. Often a man's coat or waist- ears on the front edges, especially on the hole side, as in **A**. It requires skill and fine s to correct this condition. Some women k over the linen interlining to make it the ur of the suit and do not undertake to mend ll because the buttonholes are so close to the edge that it is difficult to get a seam.

If you wish to turn the frayed edge in, first cut with the point of a razor blade the seams that join the facing to the front. Do this ripping slowly, so that you will not cut the fabric. When you have the frayed part ripped, rip as much above and below as necessary to taper off the turned-in section and make the line appear straight. On hand-tailored suits you may find a linen tape directly along the edge, as in **B**. Clip the stitches that hold this and move the tape back ¼ in. In any case, clip stitches that hold the interlining and cut the interlining away a scant ¼ in., as at **C**. Whip the tape down again. Turn one edge of the coat over the interlining (usually ⅛ in.) and whip it down, using tiny diagonal stitches, as in **D**. Note how one edge is pinned back to make this sewing easier. Turn the remaining edge in the same amount. Line up the two edges perfectly and slip-stitch them together, as shown at **E**, using very short stitches so that the edges will really be stoated together. Use a damp cloth and press the edge carefully, from the wrong side.

Whatever stitchings you had to remove from the edge to make this repair should be put in again so that the edge finish matches all along. **F** shows two stitchings sometimes found in ready-made suits. Generally the second one nearer the buttonholes need not be removed, if it is, be sure to replace it as well. Join the new stitching to the old so that it does not show.

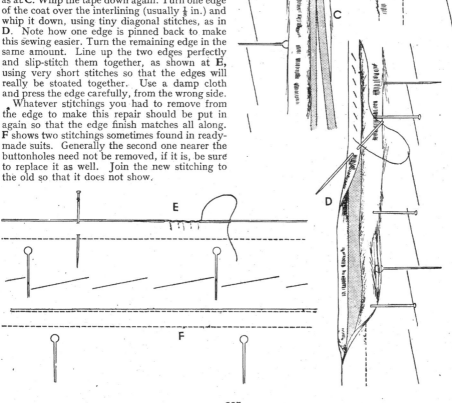

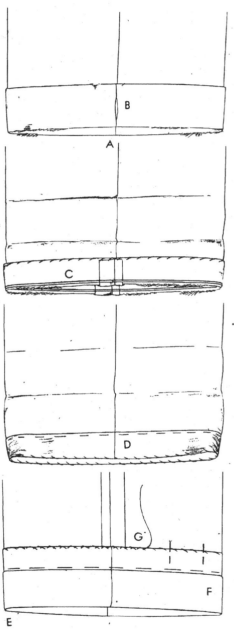

Plain Turn-ups. Most turn-ups on trouse[r]
and are cut from wear on the bottom e[dge]
shows a trouser leg with a break at the [...]
the turn-up and frayed edges at the bottor[...]

Rip out the tack at the sides of the tu[rn-up]
then remove the stitches that hold the hem. [...]
out the turn-up and brush out all lint and [...]
If there is a broken seam, as at **B**, reseam it be[...]
continuing with the turn-up.

Turn the hem over to the right side, folding
the old crease in reverse, as at **C**. Make a seam
just wide enough to take in all the frayed part—
$\frac{3}{16}$ in. to a scant $\frac{1}{4}$ in. is usually sufficient.
Double-stitch to insure firmness.

Turn the seam down towards bottom of trouser
leg, as at **D**. Baste, then press carefully. Leave
basting in until the leg is finished completely.

Turn the trousers wrong side out. Fold the
lower edge up on the crease that forms the top
of the turn-up, as at **E**. Pin this in place, easing
it in slightly, as at **F**. Baste. Hem down the edge
with small stitches, as at **G**. Do not draw the
stitches tight. Press well, then turn the turn-up
to the right side and press it in position. Retack
the turn-up at the side seams.

Flat Turn-up. Rip out the tacks at the side seams.
Rip the bottom hem and brush out lint. Press
well so that creases are removed.

Measure each trouser leg from the waistline
down to the correct length for finished trousers,
as at **H**. Mark with tailors' chalk around each leg,
making sure that the line is even. Make another
chalk line $\frac{3}{4}$ in. above the first line, as at **I**, and
a third line $1\frac{1}{2}$ in. below, as at **J**.

Turn the bottom under along line **H**. Baste
near the edge and press. Bring the creased edge
up to line **I** and pin. Baste this fold, as at **K**.

Turn the bottom edge under to the wrong side

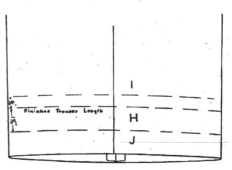

ιnd crease along bottom chalk line, as **J.** Pin and ρaste close to the crease, as at **L.** Press carefully, ιs this forms the lower edge of the trousers. Remove the basting. Turn the trousers wrong side ɔut. Fold the raw edge under and whip the two ſolded edges together, as at **M.** If the edge to ɔe turned under is too wide, cut off any excess so as to prevent overlapping of folds.

Turn to the right side and tack the turn-ups in position. Then give a final pressing. It is wise to protect the lower edge with a wear guard. Use twilled tape and sew it on by hand, as in **N.** A guard may be applied to trousers without any turn-ups, as in **O.** Stitch a short length of tape or braid to the lower edge and it will protect the back part of the trouser leg.

Taping the Edge of Hemless Trouser Legs. If you have removed the turn-ups to use the fabric for patching elsewhere, finish the trouser leg as follows: First brush the edge to remove any dust or thread ends. Press the edge. Use twilled tape of a colour similar to that of the fabric. Tape is made in comparatively few colours; therefore, look for a good match rather than an exact one In applying the tape, begin at the inside leg seam. Stitch the tape, as in **P**, $\frac{1}{8}$ in. above the original line (or more, if the edge is badly frayed). Do not allow the tape to become tight. To prevent this, ease the tape as you baste it on. Stitch precisely on the edge of the tape. Bring the free edge up, as in **Q.** Turn one end under. Whip it securely; then, with just a prick of the needle, catch a stitch in the trousers, take a real stitch in the tape, and so on, until the top of the tape is secured to the trousers. Press again. Turn them right side out, and press them very carefully, remembering the importance of the unbroken centre-line creases, front and back.

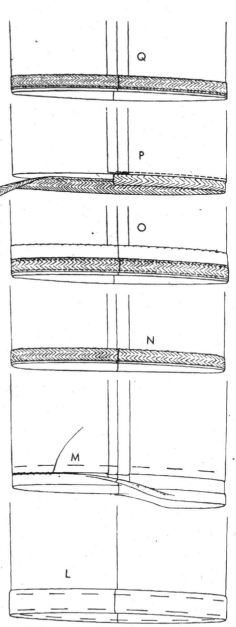

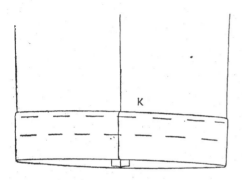

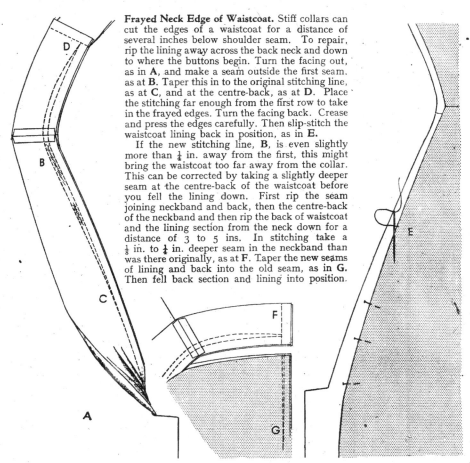

Frayed Neck Edge of Waistcoat. Stiff collars can cut the edges of a waistcoat for a distance of several inches below shoulder seam. To repair, rip the lining away across the back neck and down to where the buttons begin. Turn the facing out, as in **A**, and make a seam outside the first seam, as at **B**. Taper this in to the original stitching line, as at **C**, and at the centre-back, as at **D**. Place the stitching far enough from the first row to take in the frayed edges. Turn the facing back. Crease and press the edges carefully. Then slip-stitch the waistcoat lining back in position, as in **E**.

If the new stitching line, **B**, is even slightly more than $\frac{1}{4}$ in. away from the first, this might bring the waistcoat too far away from the collar. This can be corrected by taking a slightly deeper seam at the centre-back of the waistcoat before you fell the lining down. First rip the seam joining neckband and back, then the centre-back of the neckband and then rip the back of waistcoat and the lining section from the neck down for a distance of 3 to 5 ins. In stitching take a $\frac{1}{8}$ in. to $\frac{1}{4}$ in. deeper seam in the neckband than was there originally, as at **F**. Taper the new seams of lining and back into the old seam, as in **G**. Then fell back section and lining into position.

Renewing Velvet Overcoat Collar. Make a paper pattern of the collar to be covered, as in **A**. Fold the new fabric on a true bias; place the centre-back line of the paper collar at the true bias fold and pin in place. Baste; then cut, allowing for seams.

Fold the seam edge of the velvet over the underside of the collar, as in **B**. Catch-stitch the edge down. Cover the underside with a facing and whip it down, if it was that way originally. Finish the neckline of the collar as it was first tailored.

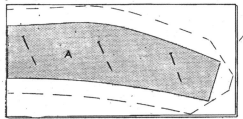

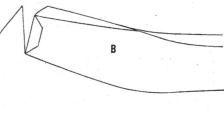

To Mend Trouser Knees and Sleeves. Machine mending is quick and sturdy for men's work clothes and boys' everyday suits that are worn at the knees and elbows. For trousers, use a patch large enough to reinforce the entire knee from seam to seam and long enough to cover the worn place. Stitch back and forth from the right side with matching thread, keeping the line of stitches close together. Reinforce worn coat sleeves in a similar manner.

Knee Stays. For trouser knees that tend to bag or show wear, use knee stays of firm light-weight lining. Cut these 15 ins. to 17 ins. long and as wide as the front trouser leg, plus seams. To finish the top and bottom of these pieces stitch in a single turned edge, as at **A**. For light-weight trousers on which this edge might press through and show, pink or overcast these edges.

Place the stay along the outside trouser seam. Pin and baste in position on the seam and across the top of the stay, as in **B** and **C**. Baste it down the front, along one side of the crease, as at **D**. Tack it with easy diagonal basting-stitches along the other side of the trouser crease, as at **E**, making them as inconspicuous as possible. These are left in. With the hand, smooth the stay over to inside seam and pin, baste, and trim, see **F**.

Slip-stitch the top edge of the stay to the trousers so that stitches do not show on the right side. The bottom is left free. Finally, stitch the stays in the side seams of the trousers, working from the back of the legs and stitching exactly in the original seam lines of the trousers, as at **G**.

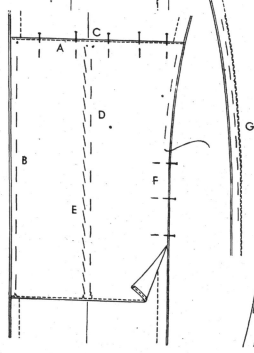

Frayed Trouser Pockets. When pockets are worn and the stay piece on the pocket shows through, as in **A**, repair it in one of several ways. **Bind with Braid.** We illustrate the simplest way of covering a worn edge. Take ½ in. wide twilled rayon or silk tape in a colour as near like the fabric as possible. Pin a piece of tape to the pocket, as shown in **B**. Turn the top end under and whip one edge of the tape to the edge of the pocket, as shown. Stitches are enlarged in the illustration to show how they are made. They should be made with a short needle and close together, and, of course, with thread of matching colour. Turn the raw end in at the bottom. Turn the pocket wrong side out and whip the tape down neatly, so that when finished it will appear as in **C**.

Bind with Trouser Material. For trousers of an unusual colour that you cannot match with tape, cut a strip of fabric ⅝ in. wide from the back seam. Turn the edges in ⅛ in. on each side and whip this over the worn edge of the pocket. This narrow width makes necessary a very short turn to the under edge of the pocket.

Rip the Pocket Edge and Reseam. This requires real skill and "a mite of patience." Rip the stitching along the edge. If there is a buttonhole bar at the bottom of the pocket, to prevent its

tearing out, rip this out—doing this so carefully that you do not damage the fabric. When you can get to the pocket edge inside, arrange the seam so that you can make a stitching line ¼ in. to ¹⁄₁₆ in. farther in from the first stitching. Curve the stitching line, as in **D**—so that you keep the pocket edge smooth at top and bottom. This deeper stitching will take in all the frayed part—when you turn the pocket to position again. Press it carefully—then stitch the edge as it was originally ⅛ in. to ¹⁄₁₆ in. from the edge.

Repairing Trousers with Half Pockets. Trouser pockets often wear out at the bottom, the fabric being cut by keys, coins, pocket knives—heavy articles. Often to mend them it is necessary to apply new bottoms to the pockets. Half pockets should be made of drill, fabric as heavy as was used originally.

Cut off the torn part and use it as a pattern. Allow 2½ ins. in length and ½ in. in width when cutting the new section for the pocket. This is ample allowance for the flat fell and French seams and will prevent your making the pocket too short. A pocket without sufficient depth is annoying to a man simply because he has become accustomed to pockets of a certain depth.

Cut the pieces and apply the patch with a flat fell, as in **E**, so that no raw edge or seam edge comes inside the pocket. French-seam the edge, as at **F**, so that it will match the original seam.

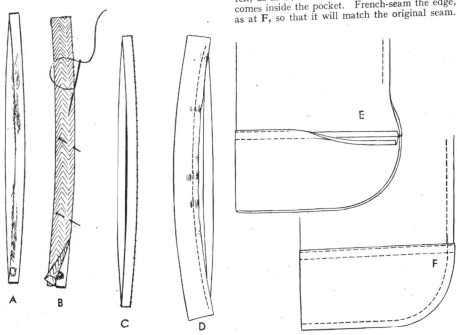

A   B   C   D   E   F

The " Thin Man's " Trousers. Sharp pelvis bones rub holes in their owners' trousers and often make unwearable a garment that seems reasonably good in all other parts.

If the man you mend for has the habit of wearing his trousers out in the seat, then take your " stitches in time," and reinforce the seat from the wrong side before it has a chance to wear thin. This can be done in several ways:

1. With bias pieces of georgette of a neutral colour, place pieces in the seat, catch the edge to the back seam and leg seams. Fit these in neatly so that they cannot draw or wrinkle.

2. Apply bias pieces of georgette directly to the area that will become thin in wear, secure in place, using thread that matches the trousers exactly. Use a diagonal basting-stitch on the wrong side of the trousers to hold the reinforcing piece in place, see *Reinforcing*, page 46.

Seat-of-Trousers Patch. A shows places where broken threads finally made holes necessitating tailored patches. Note here how chalk or basting outlines the area to be patched. The tailored patches must follow the same fabric grain as that at their location in the garment. B shows patch pieces cut from turn-up. Since they are necessarily narrow, each patch must be pieced, as in C. This piecing is made the narrow way of the turn-up, therefore, on the cross grain of the fabric. The seam is pressed open. The seat seam is ripped from D to E, to give room to work and to enable you to insert the patches accurately. See tailored patch, page 58. In F we see how the patch looks on the right side—how carefully the design of the weave was matched and the seams inconspicuous. Such a patch is really not noticeable, and the trousers can be made almost as good as new. If the turn-ups were removed to provide patch material, save scraps for further mending. See page 119 how to tape the edges of trousers.

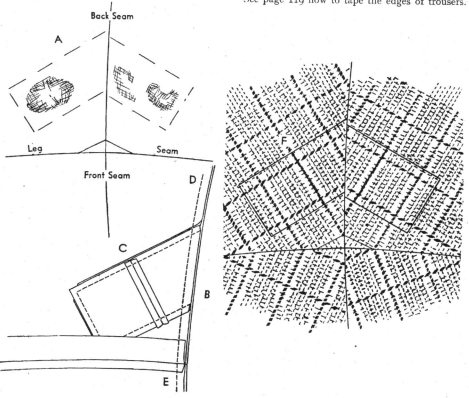

123

TIRED TIES

A MAN WHO OTHERWISE pays little attention to clothes, may cherish his neckties. Through his choice of tie he may express a mood or his artistic sense of the fitness of things. He may have bought a particular tie to go with a favourite suit, or one tie may be of sentimental value because he received it as a gift. He refuses to part with it even when it begins to show wear. What to do?

Good silk or woollen ties always deserve mending time. By ripping and cutting out the part worn thin at the knot, you may make ties as good as new. They may also be entirely ripped apart, washed or cleaned, and completely remade.

Grease from the chin sometimes soils the knot of the tie. Remove with cleaning fluid. If the edges are frayed, repair as below. When the knot is tied, the seam will be scarcely visible.

Repairing Ties. Rip the closing on the underside of the tie to about 4 ins. above the worn section. Pull out the thread carefully, as at **A**, so that it

can be re-used, for it is very strong. Turn the tie over and smooth out the bottom. Cut across the tie on the straight of the grain through the worn part. Fold along the straight of the fabric or on the edge of a stripe below the worn part. Bring this fold up until the pattern or stripe matches and the worn part is concealed, as in **B**. If more than 2 ins. to 2½ ins. of worn part has to be concealed, this method would make the tie too short. The tie in that case can be used by a young boy.

After the pattern has been matched, pin along the fold as shown, placing pins crosswise to the fold. Slip-baste along the folded edge. Then stitch along the basted line, as at **C**. Do this carefully, so that when you turn to the right side, the seam will be on the straight of the fabric and practically invisible. Trim away the excess of the under edge, as at **D**. Press the seam.

Fold the tie back to its original shape and measure length of interlining to be cut away. Cut the interlining on the same angle as the seam, as in **E,** lap it as shown, and stitch. Refold the tie.

BEST FOOT FORWARD

WE DO NOT RECOMMEND that you undertake to be your own cobbler, but a pair of shoes is so valuable that you should give some real thought and care to buying them and keeping them in good condition.

Buy Wisely. Buy first of all for good fit. A badly fitted shoe will not give you the wear you are entitled to. In fact, a good shoe salesman can tell by the way your old shoes are worn exactly where they did not fit correctly. Wrinkles, worn toes, loss of shape, and unsightly rubbed spots are often traceable to poor fit.

Then, buy shoes of as good quality as you can afford from a reputable store. The price of good leather and good workmanship will be repaid to you in looks, fit and durability

Keep 'Em Walking. Once you have bought shoes, give them the care that will keep them in good walking condition. Polish or clean them often with the type of dressing they require. Be sure that your shoe kit is well stocked with the polish or cleaner needed for each kind of shoe you are wearing, so that you don't put off caring for them too long. Check your supply of black and brown polish, neutral cream, white cleaner, suede dressing, cleaning fluid, saddle soap—whatever your shoes call for. And have brushes, polishing cloths, a bit of fine sandpaper for rubbing up the nap on suede, etc., all ready to work with. Don't use wire brushes. They tear the skins. Bristle or sponge will do the job safely. When suede shoes are worn beyond restoring by the sandpaper method, they can be made to resemble grain leather by rubbing with a cream dressing. This flattens the nap. When dry, polish thoroughly with ordinary shoe polish.

Keep shoes in shape with shoe trees or by stuffing them with wads of tissue paper and protect them from dust and lint by putting them in shoe bags or on shoe racks between wearings.

Snow, rain and mud don't do leather any good, so wear overshoes always in bad weather. Start out in brogues or low rubbers when showers are in order. If you do get shoes wet, dry them slowly, away from the heat, and stuff them with paper to preserve their shape. Some shoes are benefited by covering with saddle soap and rubbing; some can be restored to softness and pliability after a wetting, with oil or vaseline.

"**For Want of a Nail,** the shoe was lost," you remember, so have repair jobs attended to at once. Have heel lifts replaced when they begin to wear. Otherwise the body of the heel may be damaged and the whole shoe thrown out of shape. Watch for worn spots or broken seams in the lining. If they go far enough to roll up or crumple down, they can make a shoe extremely uncomfortable and ruin stockings. People who habitually wear out the sole at heel or toe should have metal plates put on at those spots. Your shoe-repair man will do this for very little.

What Glue Can Do. There are a number of little repairs you can make yourself with glue. One caution about this, though. Use a good household cement and put on just enough to do the job. Don't use so much that it squeezes out around the edges and smears the shoe.

Glue will take care of the little skinned pieces that sometimes are caused by catching your heel in a grating or rubbing against a concrete step. Put just a touch of glue under the piece, smooth it down and rub it into place. When the glue is dry, polish over the repair.

Often the lining and counter inside the heel will get loose. Repair this with glue and put a shoe-tree in to hold it in place until dry. You can also put down the inner sole in this way if it comes out or pulls loose in one spot.

Sometimes the leather covering the heel breast (the forward face of the heel) is loosened. Sandpaper the heel to remove old glue. Then glue the leather flap back in place; holding it firmly until dry with a rubber band or string around the heel. The same thing can be done if the covering of the heel itself has come loose.

There are available at haberdashery counters a number of shoe-repair sections that can be glued in—inner soles, lining sections for heels, slipper soles, etc. One of these would prolong the life of a shoe or slipper, do make the repair yourself.

What Dye Can Do. You can buy liquid shoe dyes that may sometimes put new life in an old shoe. Follow carefully the directions on the bottle, work to make the dye coating even, and perhaps the pair of shoes you can no longer call white or beige will be your new black, blue or brown shoes. These dyes are also useful for restoring colour to spots where it has worn or rubbed off.

REPAIR OF HOUSEHOLD LINEN

MOST LINENS have a sentimental value, as they are so often gifts for the bride's trousseau. Again, linen usually comes in a set and if one piece gives way or is damaged, it behoves us to put it in repair to carry on with its matching pieces. To this end, form the habit of always putting freshly laundered linens on the bottom of your stock, so that all of a dozen napkins, for example, will get equal wear.

Cigarettes often burn holes in good linen. For such damage the damask darn is in order. If a large hole is burned or an awkward tear made in washing or ironing, crochet a square or oblong of filet lace, matching the weight of the thread to the texture of the linen. No. 30 crochet cotton is usually right for damask. Use a fairly small square for the filet; whip the piece over the hole; then trim the fabric away under the crochet and roll and whip the raw edge, securing this neatly to the edge of the lace. Such a mend will last a long time and can be really decorative

A damaged place in a velvet or tapestry runner may be mended in a similar way, by making a patch of latticed ribbon and applying two or more to a runner, one being essential to cover the damaged place, the others to make the patch seem part of the design.

The will to mend so that the repair really adds to, rather than detracts from the article, must be the aim of all who would really restore nice things to a good-as-new status

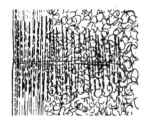

A

Terry Darn. Towels and wash cloths repay rough treatment by tearing at the edges. To repair, place a piece of tissue paper under the tear and bring the torn edges together; stitch back and forth across the tear and right through the paper, as in **A**, until it is secure. The stitching will cut away most of the paper and the rest may be pulled out after it has served its purpose of giving a foundation for stitching and frayed threads. If the selvedge is frayed, turn the edge once and stitch it back—use a No. 24 six-cord thread, and thus give strength to the edge for future use.

Damask Darn. For cigarette burns, place a piece of fabric underneath the hole, stitch or hand-sew back and forth. Then turn and sew across these stitches to fill in the hole securely, as in **B**

B

Scallop Darns. Embroidered scallops on the edges of table linens, underclothing and other articles sometimes fray out between the scallops, as in **C**. The methods we show here for mending such damage are best for articles that have already given good service and on which you don't want to spend too much time.

To strengthen the edge and prevent further fraying out, put two or three rows of machine stitching along the worn edge, as in **D**, and then stitch back and forth across these rows, as in **E**. Be sure the stitching runs far enough back from the edge to be firmly anchored; otherwise your whole darn will pull away on loose threads. If the damage has become more serious and a tear has developed up between scallops, as in **F**, proceed as in **G** and **H**. Hold the tear in place so that the scallops on either side lie flat, and stitch back and forth across the tear, beginning a little beyond the end of it and stitching a few stitches past each side. Then turn and stitch back and forth in the other direction across the first rows. In all of this work the better

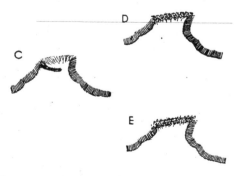

C

D

E

you match your thread to the fabric, the more inconspicuous the darn will be.

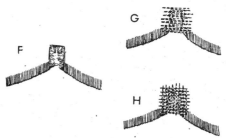

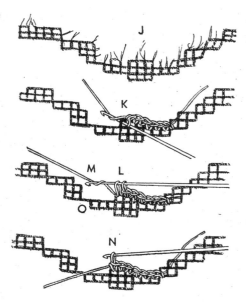

Triangular Tear. I shows how to mend this type of tear by machine. Page 44 gives general instructions on machine darning. Baste a piece of gauze under the tear and stitch zigzag across it to secure the torn edges to the reinforcing fabric. Remove basting and trim away edges of patch under tear.

Everyday articles can well be mended by machine. Valuable damask that would look embarrassed at having a patch, should be mended by hand as carefully as possible.

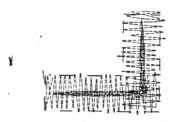

Worn Embroidered Edge. Many household linens are finished with open-work embroidery or heavy lace. When these become frayed, as in J, they can be given new life by crocheting along edges. Trim loose threads and worn eyelets away until you have a smooth and symmetrical edge on which to work. Insert crochet hook in eyelet and draw thread through from underside to form a loop. Then draw another loop through the first to fasten thread-end. Insert hook into eyelet of edge, as in K. Carry thread around needle and draw it through so that you have two loops on hook, as at L. Thread over hook, as at M, and draw thread through both loops to form one, as in N. Start again, as in K, and continue until entire edge is finished. If there are no eyelets to crochet through, as at O, needle can be inserted into the fabric itself.

Special Fabrics or Types of Work. There are a number of special problems of mending in household linens that can be solved only by trying to duplicate as nearly as possible the original fabric and stitching in each specific case. For example, hardanger work, the heavy square or diamond-patterned embroidery on hardanger cloth, can be repaired only by matching the thread as well as you can and following the original pattern. The cloth itself is a basket-weave type of fabric, see page 66, and should be rewoven as nearly as possible, see *Reweaving*, page 67.

This is the case also in repairing damasks, hand-woven heirloom spreads, etc. It may be possible to ravel an edge and obtain enough thread to mend, or, if the damage is extensive, even cut off an edge to obtain a patch piece. It all depends on the type of repair job you have and the use to which the article is being put.

Needlepoint and other embroidered work would have to have the damaged part reworked in the same stitch and matching yarn. Perhaps a piece of new canvas will have to be tacked under the hole to give a foundation for the new stitches. Whatever special problems you may have, look over the sections on weaves and reweaving and on stitches so that you can do a satisfactory and inconspicuous job of conservation.

WEARY BED LINEN

SOME SHEETS WEAR thin all over. When they start to tear, use them for bandages, for ironing-board covers or for pads. Turn the narrow hem to the top of the bed occasionally to distribute the wear. Never use a sheet for a laundry bag.

Hemstitched sheets usually break in the hem-stitching. For this reason many thrifty house-keepers use hemstitched sheets for the top sheet only. Hems may be re-attached in one of three ways: (1) Tear the hem off and sew the hem edge over the sheet edge, as in **A**, and baste and stitch it in place, as in **B**. (2) If you haven't a machine handy, take No. 30 crochet thread and overcast the hem to the sheet, as in **C**. Make stitches loose and even. When the hem is pressed out there will be only the slightest ridge where the edges overlap, and the stitches can be a decoration. Pillow cases can be done in the same way. (3) Use rickrack to join the edges, as in **D**. Baste paper under the open seam, placing the two edges the distance apart that suits the size of rickrack you are joining. Then stitch one side. Go back and stitch the other, starting from the same end of the seam.

When sheets are frayed along the hem edge, tear off the hem, as in **E**. Lay the right sides of the sheet and the torn-off hem strip together and stitch $\frac{1}{8}$ in. in from the frayed edges, as in **F**. Turn the hem over to the wrong side, folding so that the seam line falls $\frac{1}{16}$ in. from the edge, as in **G**. Then stitch the hem firmly in place.

To Repair Hemstitching. If only a small section of the hemstitching is broken, it may be worth while to mend it, as in **H**. Baste paper under the torn section and mend it by hand. Broken stitches can easily be replaced, as in **I**. Pick up several of the threads in the drawn thread line, as shown. Pull the needle through, drawing the thread close, and take another stitch into the hem edge. Pick up an equal number of threads and repeat, continuing several stitches beyond the break for strength. If the hemstitching is double, as in **J**, repeat the process on the inside edge of the drawn thread line, catching the stitches into the fabric. Between each group of threads, make one or two small whipping stitches to strengthen this side of the hemstitching.

Many mothers take the sides of the sheets that have torn down the centre, seam the selvedge edges together and make crib sheets of these. Such sheets can also be used for cots or three-quarter beds.

Remember our great-grandmothers made their sheets of 36-in. muslin, carefully felling a centre seam. Sheets 72 ins. by 90 ins. or 90 ins. by 108 ins. are our twentieth-century luxuries.

Other suggestions are: Take the sheet corners and make four pillow cases of them. Tear soft sheets into six pieces and use them for dish towels.

Attractive cottage curtains and aprons can be made of coloured sheets. Learn to use soft fabrics for your purposes and know the real satisfaction of such economies.

Pillow Cases. Pillow cases usually wear thin all over and, except those torn accidentally in laundering, are not generally mended for regular use. There are some uses, however, for which they are ideal; for example, bandages, ironing-board covers, or blued bags to keep summer clothes in. Old pillow cases and sheets are too linty for dusters. Your nearest hospital can always use old, clean, soft ones. Pass them along, if all yours wear out at once, as is sometimes the case.

Stitch split edges together on the sewing machine, dip in very blue blueing water, dry thoroughly, and use unironed as cases for white articles, wash apparel, heirloom linens and treasured lingerie, and baby clothes that are not in regular use.

Slip two worn cases together and use them as covers for home utensils that are seldom used, such as large roaster or picnic kit.

Repair of Blankets. Good wool blankets require your best care in storing, washing and even in using. Always try to have your top sheet long enough to cover the edge of the blanket generously. Even with the best of care the binding becomes worn and soiled in time and
(*Instructions for* **K** *and* **L** *on next page.*)

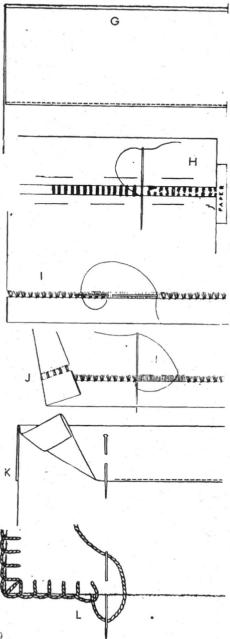

(*Continued from previous page.*)
needs to be replaced. Neatly packed blanket binding may be purchased at the haberdashery or ribbon counter of your local drapers. You may prefer to make your own binding of silk, rayon or sateen. New binding should have the same finished width as the old. For a 3 ins. finished binding, cut your strips 12 ins. wide. Fold the raw edges to meet in the centre. Bring the folded edges together and press.

Remove the old binding. Place the blanket edge into the new folded binding and pin, as in **K**. Baste, then stitch the binding on ¼ in. up from the folded edge, using a long stitch. Basting is necessary to insure your catching both edges of the binding with the one row of stitching.

An overcast blanket edge is practical if you do not wish to have the expense of new binding. Remove the old binding, and with mercerized crochet cotton or fingering yarn blanket-stitch the edge, as in **L**. Begin your stitches on the selvedge at old stitching line of the binding and work up to and round the corner.

Worn out wool blankets may be covered with cotton prints and used as the filling of a quilted bedspread. Quilt the thicknesses of material together by hand or machine.

Mend moth holes in a blanket by using a contrasting yarn and embroidering conventional designs, such as flowers or leaves, over the holes. If desirable, add several extra motifs of a similar design to give the whole a planned effect.

REPAIRING WINDOW CURTAINS

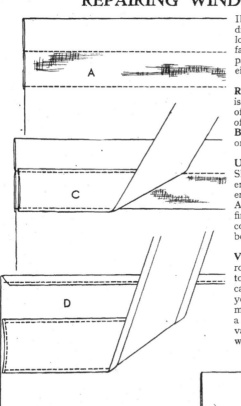

IF CURTAINS HAVE BECOME rotted and discoloured from exposure to the elements cut off lower part of curtains and use the best of the fabric. Split the cut-off section, removing worn parts. Make half-curtains which can be used either side of the top.

Repairing Torn Casing. If the casing of a curtain is worn as in **A**, replace it with an applied casing of similar fabric. Make a narrow tube, the width of the original casing, plus seam allowance, as in **B**. Turn the tube inside out and apply over original casing, as in **C**.

Using Remnants or Scraps of Curtain Material. Short lengths of fabric which do not provide enough for hems and casings can be made long enough by using other fabric in various ways. Apply a wide bias to form a casing, as in **D**, and finish the top with a narrow hem. A band of contrasting colour can be applied at the top or bottom if additional length for hems is needed.

Valances for Style or Necessity. Windows in some rooms require valances to give the correct finish to the top of the draperies. Very often a valance can be a veritable " curtain stretcher," as it helps you to extend short curtains by using another material at the top and covering this piecing with a valance of a harmonizing fabric — velvet valances with brocade curtains, or plain chintz with figured curtains, are attractive combinations.

REFURBISHING UPHOLSTERY

IF THE ARMS AND BACKS of a chair are worn or too badly soiled for cleaning, appliqué new fabric over the worn spots, as in **A**. Some people put strips of the upholstery fabric on a new chair at the points of greatest wear and remove them before the chair is cleaned the first time to prolong its freshness.

If a chair is stained or gets burnt or meets with other misfortunes, apply new fabric in a harmonizing print. Use this method for the cushion or for the entire front of the chair, as in **B**.

Household pets sometimes pull at upholstery, making necessary a whole new section, such as the back in **C**. Look for sturdy remnants or buy a fabric with an interesting weave or print.

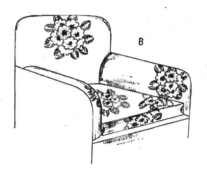

MENDING RUGS AND CARPETS

Mending Rugs. Mend thin spots or holes in rugs and carpets by sewing patches of heavy woollen material or canvas on the wrong side. Turn under the edges of the patch and whip it in place, see *Hemmed Patch,* page 55. Darn through the patch with yarn to match the rug if necessary.

When the patch is used on an oriental rug, hook in worsted to match the pattern as closely as possible and clip the hooked loops to correspond to the nap. For a rag rug or old hooked rug, patch with burlap and hook in yarn or rags. Clip the loops or leave them looped, according to the original work on rug you are mending. If a few strands are frayed out or laid bare, darn them with carpet wool. A piece of gummed carpet binding can be pressed underneath to reinforce the darned spot.

Frayed Edges. For badly frayed edges, ravel the threads to get a straight edge, then use gummed carpet binding, pressing it along the edge with a warm iron. On rugs that may not ravel smoothly, or that require a more sturdy finish, bind edges with regular carpet binding.

For a rug that is worn thin all over, so that mending might not be practical, use 2-in. adhesive tape on the wrong side to prolong its service.

Fibre Rug. The life of a fibre or grass rug may be lengthened by washing with soap and water. Mend the edges, if frayed, by pressing gummed binding over them. If there are large holes, cut the rug into two or more smaller ones and finish the edges with carpet binding.

Use a Backing. A hooked rug may be preserved by sewing on a backing of burlap or coarse canvas or denim. Cut it large enough to extend beyond the rug, turn it in and sew well around the edge. To make the lining lie flat, quilt it to the rug with diagonal basting-stitches on the wrong side.

RIPPING FOR REMAKING

WHEN IT COMES to ripping seams for making over garments, you'll find no invention of modern times is more valuable than the razor blade. A razor blade is almost as indispensable in a woman's work-basket as it is in a man's shaving case. It is really difficult to work without one. It is handy for snipping stitches, removing belts, buttons, snap fasteners and all the other things you need to remove.

There are several ways of ripping seams. The method you choose depends to some extent on the fabric. A razor blade will make an excellent seam ripper. When you use one of these, you usually pin one edge of the seam to a table or chair, then grip the other edge with your fingers, and very carefully run the blade, stitch by stitch, down the seam. Some women rip with the points of the scissors. Others pick and pull—pick up the end of a thread, draw it tight, break three or four stitches, and then pull the thread out, repeating this until the seam is entirely ripped. The pick-and-pull system is advisable for fabrics of nobbly or open weave, or very sheer materials. Some sturdy fabrics, especially those which have been made up for a considerable time, may be ripped by simply separating the seam with a little force and pulling it quickly, as you would tear a fabric. Remove the broken threads afterwards with the fingers or a whisk broom.

In ripping fabric, keep a tiny whisk broom in your work-basket and brush the seams as you rip. This will remove any surplus threads, lint or dust that has accumulated in the seams. It is surprising how much lint gathers in seams

In ripping garments, salvage all buttons, hooks and eyes, snap fasteners, slide fasteners and such findings, because they can all be used in the finishing of the remade garment, or other garments. A very convenient way to keep buttons, snap fasteners and hooks and eyes is to have small boxes neatly labelled so that you can locate what you need quickly, and find a needed article of exactly the right size and colour for the mending you have to do.

If you rip with scissors, use a small, sharp-pointed pair, and proceed slowly so that you cannot possibly snip the fabric and thus weaken it. Don't pull buttons off. Clip them carefully so as not to cut the fabric. Pull thread ends away. Use the razor blade to snip off hooks and eyes and snap fasteners. Cut the thread of the stitches and then pull them out either with your fingers or with tweezers.

Save the Wool from Old Hand-Knit Garments. Wash and dry the garment. Pull out a strand of yarn and wind it around a firm, flat surface. A strong suit box, drawing board, or the back of a chair will serve. Make a skein the size desired and tie the ends of yarn together. Before removing it from the board, tie the skein together in several places with strong thread. Make as many skeins as the garment provides, then wet each skein thoroughly in warm water. Squeeze out the moisture, using an old Turkish towel. Hang the skeins to dry, tying weights to the bottom of each skein (a cup will do). This will take out the kinks and make yarn ready to wind into balls.

LET'S CLEAN IT

MEND BEFORE YOU CLEAN, whenever possible. The mend will be less conspicuous if it is done before a garment goes to the laundry or cleaner, because when it is washed or cleaned along with the surrounding fabric, it will seem to belong to the garment instead of an addition.

When the hem is out of a skirt, or the stitches in a seam are broken, by all means replace these —repair the article entirely—before you send it to be cleaned. The pressing will help to make the mends invisible.

If you are going to remake a garment completely, it is better to rip, brush, clean and press it before recutting. Often it is best to use the wrong side of a garment that has been ripped up

for remaking, so that any faded parts will be less visible. Even though the texture may be slightly different, it should wear well. In fact, if the fabric is at all satisfactory on the wrong side, use it that way simply to give a newer look to your finished garment.

When you are cleaning fabric for recutting, decide what cleaning method is best to use. Look over the fabric for spots and stains, and clean or launder. Many fabrics can be washed and ironed satisfactorily, but don't wash and iron a fabric if this will make it look second-hand. Better have it cleaned, or dry-clean it yourself. This applies to woollens, velvets and brocades—all fabrics other than rayons, cottons, linens and silks.

Fabrics Having a Special Finish. Many fabrics undergo special treatment in the manufacture to achieve some particular quality. Examples are organdie, with a permanent crispness, non-crushable linen and velvet, and fabrics that are rain or windproof or that have been Sanforized, i.e. contracted in finishing to overcome shrinkage. Some of these finishes affect the methods of handling, particularly pressing, washing or cleaning. When you work with them, whether you are making, mending or refashioning, be sure that you treat them according to the manufacturer's directions on the label, which tells you what fibre the garment is made of and how it has been processed. As you take the label off the new fabric or garment make a note what it came on, and have a place to file all such labels for easy reference and thus save time and protect your fabric.

SPOT AND STAIN REMOVAL

General Instructions. The first thing is to know what caused the spot or stain, and to know the fibre of your fabric. Permanent damage may be prevented if you act quickly to remove the spot. Never press a stain before treating it, as some stains are sealed by heat. If the fabric can stand water, sponge the spot at once with a damp cloth. To do this, put the stain side down on an absorbent pad or blotter and work lightly from the edges to the centre of the spot. Before using any chemicals on the stain try them on a part of the garment that does not show to test the effect on the fabric. Stretch fabric over a bowl of steaming water and drop the chemical on the spot with a medicine dropper. Rinse after a moment by pouring water through or dipping into the bowl. Use clean cheesecloth on the fabric to absorb moisture, working from the outside towards the centre and keeping the edges of the wet spot irregular to avoid rings. Spraying around the area with the cleaning fluid is one way to prevent rings. If the treatment is too difficult or the stain too stubborn for home treatment, send the article to the dry cleaner with as much information as possible about the cause of the stain. In the chart below, specific suggestions for special stains are given. The materials for such emergencies should be kept in the home, with the cheesecloth, blotting paper, medicine dropper and bowl.

Cleaning and Bleaching Agents. Chlorine bleaches for laundering are sold under brand name and are used as specified by the manufacturer. Carbon tetrachloride, mentioned in many of the following treatments, is the main ingredient of many commercial cleaning fluids.

Stain	On Cotton or Linen	On Silk, Wool, or Rayon
Acid	1. Wash quickly to prevent acid destroying fibres. 2. Try ammonia solutions; if undesired colour reaction occurs, use diluted white vinegar or acetic acid. 3. Sprinkle baking soda on both sides. Moisten and let stand until effervescence stops. Rinse in water.	Hold over open bottle of strong ammonia so that the fumes penetrate the fabric.
Alkali (Washing soda, ammonia, etc.)	1. Wash quickly with cloth wet with water. Rub dry, doing this gently, using a clean dry cloth to absorb moisture. 2. Apply mild acid, such as lemon juice or vinegar. Rinse in water.	Fibres are easily destroyed by even diluted alkalis, so this may be a mending job.
Argyrol (or other medicinal stain)	Wash in warm suds with a few drops of ammonia added.	Sponge spot with lukewarm suds. Rinse; then press dry.
Blood	1. Soak in cold water. Then wash with soap and water. If discoloration remains, use chlorine bleach. 2. For old or stubborn stains, add 2 tablespoons of ammonia to 1 gallon of water to soak.	Sponge with cold or lukewarm water. Bleach with hydrogen peroxide if stain persists. May have to use appliqué patch to cover.

Stain	On Cotton or Linen	On Silk, Wool, or Rayon
	3. As a last resort on white goods try liquid bleach. 4. For thick fabrics, mix a paste of starch and cold water. Apply to stain. Brush away when dry. Repeat as needed.	
Blueing	1. Wash in boiling water. 2. For fresh stains, rinse thoroughly with cold water.	
Candle Wax	Scrape off wax. Put blotters over and under spot and apply hot iron. Remove colour with chlorine bleach.	Break up the wax and flick it off. Use iron over blotters as for cottons. Sponge with carbon tetrachloride. On a wool surface, break the wax into small pieces and flake off.
Chewing Gum	Scrape off with blunt knife. If hardened, use carbon tetrachloride, turpentine, kerosene, or egg white to soften. Then launder.	Scrape off excess. Sponge with carbon tetrachloride.
Chocolate or Cocoa	Launder. If brown stain persists, use chlorine bleach or wood alcohol.	Sponge with carbon tetrachloride and bleach with hydrogen peroxide.
Cod Liver Oil	Wash in warm suds and rinse. Use chlorine bleach for old stains.	Remove grease with carbon tetrachloride. Bleach with hydrogen peroxide.
Coffee	Launder. If stain persists, use chlorine bleach. As a last resort on white goods, use liquid bleach.	Sponge with lukewarm water. Bleach with hydrogen peroxide. If cream remains, dissolve with carbon tetrachloride.
Cream, Ice Cream, Milk, Butter	Soak in clear water. Launder. Bleach remaining stains with chlorine bleach.	Sponge with warm water. Sponge with carbon tetrachloride to remove grease.
Dye	For sunfast fabrics, soak several hours and expose to sun. For white goods, use liquid bleach.	Bleach with hydrogen peroxide.
Egg	Scrape off excess. Sponge with cold water. Then launder. Use hydrogen peroxide if stain remains.	Sponge with cold water. Sponge with carbon tetrachloride if grease spot shows. Bleach with hydrogen peroxide.
Fruit and Berries	Hold a kettle of boiling water two feet above stain. Pour scalding water through stain. Sponge spot dry. Bleach with lemon juice in sun or use chlorine bleach.	Sponge with warm water. If not removed, drop hydrogen peroxide on stain over bowl of steaming water. Sponge coloured fabric with 10 per cent solution of acetic acid.
Glue	1. Soak in warm water. 2. Sponge with diluted acetic acid or vinegar.	Sponge several times with diluted acetic acid or vinegar.
Grass	Launder. If stain persists, bleach with chlorine bleach.	Sponge with ether.
Grease and Oil	Scrape off excess. Rub lard into road oil or tar. Then launder.	Cover spot with french chalk or fuller's earth. Brush off when dry. Sponge with carbon tetrachloride. Use turpentine on road oil or tar. If spot is very stubborn, apply chloroform with clean cheesecloth, rub lightly, then rub gently all around area to prevent ring. Don't use on rayon without testing.

Stain	On Cotton or Linen	On Silk, Wool, or Rayon
Indelible Pencil	Soak in denatured alcohol. Then launder or boil in heavy suds. Bleach with chlorine bleach if stain persists.	Sponge with carbon tetrachloride
Ink	Different types require different treatments. 1. If spot is still moist, apply french chalk, fuller's earth or oatmeal. Brush off when dry. Repeat as needed. 2. Wash with hot suds. 3. Soak in milk one or two days. 4. Use commercial ink remover according to manufacturer's directions. 5. Use chlorine bleach, or apply lemon juice and expose to sunlight. 6. Alternate hydrogen peroxide and oxalic acid, exposing spot to steam from tea kettle.	Methods 1 or 6 under Cottons and Linens, but test first the effect of oxalic acid on fabric.
Iodine	Sponge with diluted ammonia. Then launder.	Subject to steam from tea kettle.
Iron Rust	1. Squeeze lemon juice on stain, holding it over a bowl of boiling water. 2. Sprinkle with salt, moisten with lemon juice and expose to sun. 3. Apply 3 per cent oxalic acid at intervals over bowl of steaming water. Rinse. 4. Boil with 4 tablespoons cream of tartar to 1 pt. water.	Almost impossible to remove from silk or wool. Cover with appliqué or embroidery.
Lipstick	Rub with kerosene or lard. Launder. Bleach with chlorine bleach or hydrogen peroxide.	Sponge with carbon tetrachloride. For heavy marks rub with kerosene or lard, then remove grease with carbon tetrachloride.
Mercurochrome	Launder, or boil in heavy suds. Bleach with chlorine bleach. Rinse with ammonia solution.	Almost impossible to remove satisfactorily. Try potassium permanganate alternating with oxalic acid on silk or wool; not on rayon.
Mildew	Fresh spots can be washed out. Sometimes soaking in sour milk and exposing to sun without rinsing will help. Otherwise, bleach with chlorine bleach. Rinse with ammonia. Deeply ingrained spots almost impossible to remove.	Alternate application of potassium permanganate and oxalic acid on silk or wool; not on rayon
Mud	Let dry and then brush. Launder. If grease or grass stains are mixed in, treat as for those stains.	Let them dry and then brush.
Nail Polish	Sponge with acetone or polish remover. Launder.	Sponge with acetone or polish remover. Test remover on hidden part of fabric before using; never use on acetate.
Paint	1. Fresh stains may be washed out with soap and water. 2. Sponge with or wash in turpentine. Then launder. 3. Moisten with ammonia; then sprinkle with turpentine. Launder. 4. For shellac, sponge with wood or denatured alcohol.	Sponge with carbon tetrachloride or turpentine.

135

Stain	On Cotton or Linen	On Silk, Wool, or Rayon
Perspiration	Wash in hot suds. Bleach yellow stain with hydrogen peroxide.	Sponge with clear water
Powder	Launder.	Rub with piece of rough crêpe to remove excess powder or lint. If powder is ingrained, use carbon tetrachloride or in an emergency, toilet water, which will evaporate and leave a pleasant fragrance.
Scorch	Deep scorch cannot be removed. Light scorch, wash in soap and water, bleach in sun.	Light scorch may be bleached with hydrogen peroxide.
Sugar, Syrups	Launder. If fruit or chocolate stains remain, treat as described for those stains.	Sponge with clear water. Treat for chocolate or fruit stains if they remain.

WASHING, IRONING, CLEANING, PRESSING

	COTTONS OR LINENS	WOOL
Washing	Soak *white* clothes in lukewarm water, fifteen minutes to four hours, depending on condition. For washing, use very hot water, 130° to 140°. Have a 2-in. standing suds. If the clothes are not soaked, use water 115°. Use bleach if necessary. Follow manufacturer's directions. Do not soak *coloured* clothes. Wash in water 100° to 110°. Replace soap and water as needed. Avoid "dead" suds. Use washing machine as directed. Rinse thoroughly at least twice, first warm, then lukewarm. For white clothes, use blueing in last rinse. Use tinting powders for other colours. Use thin, cooked starch for cottons and linens. To prevent white film on dark clothes, add colour to starch; strong tea for reds and browns, blueing for blue.	Shake well before washing to remove loose dust. Take measurements or make outlines of garments. Turn knit garments inside out. Wash gently and quickly in lukewarm water and have rich suds of mild soap. Use washing machine, or if washed by hand, use push-and-squeeze method to force suds through fabric. Do not rub or wring. Press water out. Rinse three times in lukewarm water.
Drying	Hang white cottons and linens in sun. Coloured clothes in shade. Lace dresses and tablecloths should be rolled and kneaded in soft towels to remove moisture. Dry loosely knitted garments on flat surface. Use clothes pegs sparingly. Hang all clothes straight with the lengthwise threads.	Squeeze gently to take out water. Roll in Turkish towel to remove additional moisture. Lay knitted articles on flat surface and stretch gently during drying to meet original measurements. Dry away from direct heat or sun. Hang firm woollen pieces and blankets well over line to distribute weight, and change position occasionally. Avoid clothes pegs. Slip waxpaper under double thicknesses of colours that may run.
Ironing or Pressing	Sprinkle lightly with warm water. Roll tightly. Iron on right side with lengthwise threads, using long, pushing strokes. Press fasteners, lace or embroidery into thick towels. Do not iron folds in bedding, and change fold lines in table linens at each washing. Do not iron Turkish towels. Fluff them.	Wool need not be bone dry to press. Lay on board so weave is straight. Use evenly dampened press cloth over fabric at all times. Work from wrong side with medium iron. Press down and lift, then repeat in new area. Do not move iron back and forth. Press blanket bindings only. Brush nap lightly. For mannish-type woollens, brush as you press.

Stain	On Cotton or Linen	On Silk, Wool, or Rayon
Tea	1. Launder. If stains persist, soak in borax solution and rinse in boiling water. 2. Apply lemon juice and expose to sun. 3. Apply potassium permanganate and oxalic acid alternately.	Sponge with clear water. If stain persists, use potassium permanganate, then lemon juice, but not on rayon.
Water Spots	Wash entire garment or sponge and press while damp.	Flick the edges of the spot with the edge of a serrated coin. Press under damp cloth. Shake garment in steam from briskly boiling kettle of water.
Wine	Treat as for fruit stains.	Treat as for fruit stains.

ESSENTIAL TO CLOTHES UPKEEP

SILK OR RAYON

Use soft, lukewarm water with lively suds of mild soap flakes well churned in. Turn satins inside out to prevent fuzzing surface. Squeeze suds gently but thoroughly through fabric. Do not rub or twist. Rinse at least twice in lukewarm water. Press water out between hands without wringing.

To roll and press garments in a towel is the preferred method for removing moisture. Do not dry quickly. Keep out of direct heat and sun. Large pieces, as nightgowns, however, may be hung over line for short time. Do not use clothes pegs. Shantung may be dried thoroughly. Handle rayon with care as fibres are weak when wet. Knitted rayons, as stockings, should have twenty-four hours to dry unless they are specially treated.

Generally, iron when partly dry on wrong side with medium iron, following the straight of the fabric. For finishing touches on right, protect fabric with dry cheesecloth. Press lace and embroidery trimming over Turkish towel to avoid flattening designs. For rayons, use iron slightly less hot than that used for silks. Iron acetate rayons while almost wet. Iron shantung dry.

MISCELLANEOUS

Elastic Goods. Make heavy lukewarm suds of mild soap. Use washing machine or squeeze suds through and through fabric. For very soiled spots use firm, soft brush. Rinse three times in lukewarm water. Press water out. Do not wring. Roll in towel to remove excess moisture. Dry in shade or indoors away from heat. Hang over line without clothes pegs. If garment does not open, stuff with tissue paper and lay on towels. Press fabric sections and straps with warm iron. Never touch elastic parts with iron.

Oil Silk or Rubberized Fabrics. Sponge off occasionally with clear cool water. If quite soiled, wash quickly on flat surface with sponge, mild suds and lukewarm water. Do not scrub. Sponge suds promptly with clear water to prevent cracking. Keep folds from touching while drying.

Glazed Chintz.. Go over surface quickly with sponge well squeezed out of warm suds. Do not get fabric soaking wet, as this removes glaze. Sponge again with clear water. Wipe off lightly with towel.

Lace. (Fine or fragile.) Enclose in bag of cheesecloth or open-mesh knitted bag and wash in mild, lukewarm suds. Rinse in bag three times with clear lukewarm water. One or two small pieces may be washed in a fruit jar with warm suds. Have jar only two-thirds full, including lace, and shake vigorously for a few minutes. Rinse in clear water the same way. Pat in towel to remove moisture. Dry flat on towel and iron on thick towel to bring out design. If very fragile, baste lace to muslin before washing.

Lacquered Fabrics. These generally have cotton-napped backing and are used for breakfast and luncheon cloths. Wash off with damp cloth. Do not immerse in water. Fold in original folds if kept in drawer.

Water Repellent Fabrics. Send to cleaner, as many of these fabrics must be refinished after each cleaning.

137

FRESHENING FABRICS

SOME CLEANING or freshening methods do not properly come under the heading either of laundering or of spot and stain removal. They are simply ways of rejuvenating fabrics which are still usable but shabby. Here are some suggestions for the rejuvenation of some types.

Velvet. Rip seams and pull and brush out old threads. Place the fabric pile down on a table, and whip it with a thin switch to remove dust. Brush the back before turning the fabric over; then brush the pile with a stiff brush. If there are streaks or soiled spots on the right side, make a mixture of oatmeal and benzine in a small bowl. Sprinkle this over a piece of the velvet on the nap side with a brush. Go over every part. Rub it in and then brush it out and shake. Do not touch the damp pile, as it will show the print of your fingers when the velvet is moist from the cleaning fluid. Steam it to make the pile stand up. Hang large pieces in the bathroom as you run a bath of steaming water. Hold small pieces nap side up above a hot iron wrapped in wet cloths, and brush the pile with a soft brush, or hold them over a kettle of boiling water. If pressing is necessary, it should be done on a velvet press board. This is a board or canvas with wire bristles. Lay the velvet pile side down on the bristles, lay a cloth over it, press through the cloth.

Ribbons. Velvet ribbons are treated as velvet fabrics. Satin and taffeta ribbons can be freshened by cleaning soiled spots with a cloth dipped in benzine, and then dipping the whole ribbon in benzine.

Serge and Other Hard, Firm Woollens. If the fabric is shiny in some sections, dip a rough, lintless cloth (a terry washcloth is good) in vinegar, ammonia or alcohol, and rub the surface briskly. If this does not lift the nap, or if the surface is too badly worn, brush gently with fine sandpaper, and then rub again with the vinegar, ammonia or alcohol.

Black Lace or Ribbon. Sponge with benzine and then press, from the wrong side, to restore freshness. Use a dry press cloth over the fabric, and over this a wet cloth, so as to steam, but not wet, the fabric.

Corduroy or Velveteen. Brush the nap and the back to remove loose dust; then launder. Hang such fabrics up, without wringing, and straighten on the line by shaking it. Catch corners with clothes pegs. Do not place fabric over the line, as this will mark it. Brush briskly when it is dry.

Felt and Velour. Sponge with benzine or cleaning fluid. When this is dry, go over the surface gently but thoroughly with fine sandpaper. Then rub all over with a piece of old velvet. If the colour is faded, consider turning the fabric wrong side out.

Straw. To restore straw hats: Brush carefully. If the straw has lost its gloss, it can be sprayed with diluted shellac. If the colour is faded, there are straw dyes sold at drug and haberdashery counters that will give a new colour. Follow the directions on the bottle. Stuff the crown and hold the brim in place so that, when the dye wets the straw, the shape will not be lost. If you wish to change the line of the brim, or cut it smaller, cut a pattern from paper, pin it to the brim and cut with a razor blade. In such a case it is necessary to bind the brim to conceal the raw edges. If the hat has a ribbon band, replace it with a new one or wash the old one with suds of mild soap flakes. To do this, hold the ribbon flat and brush the suds on with a brush. Rinse thoroughly by dipping the ribbon up and down in water. Do not squeeze. Pat out the water and press. A new lining or a few tucks and stitches to alter the shape of the crown may make the hat look and seem new.

Fibre Mats. Brush or sponge with hot suds. Rinse with clear water and then dry in shade on a flat surface.

The Coloured Linens. Don't try to remove spots with a local application of remover. Add two or three tablespoons of hydrogen peroxide to a gallon of hot suds and soak the articles in it. This may lighten the colour a little. Ecru tints may be renewed from time to time by dipping in warm tea or coffee. Other tints may be obtained by use of dyes.

Caution. In using benzine or a cleaning fluid, keep it away from fire, cigarettes, matches, etc. Place small pieces in a jar and shake to clean rather than rub with the hands. Small cleaner machines prove a real economy if there is much cleaning to be done. If your hands get in the fluid, wash them with lukewarm water and a bland soap. Then rub hand cream well into them.

MOTH PREVENTION

MOTHS ARE A NUISANCE to every person who has the responsibility of caring for clothes. Extreme care is the greatest safeguard. Precautions are given here that should prove helpful. The very best thing to do about moth havoc is not to let it happen! If it has happened—then reweaving or patching or appliqué are recovery possibilities.

About moths—the mamma moth that you see flying around is not the one who makes a meal of your sweaters, blankets, bathing suits, furs and so on. But she does lay eggs. She picks nice, dark places and cosy corners inside your bureau drawers and cupboards and along seams and in pockets of your garments, to lay her eggs. Unless you get rid of them in a hurry, in a few days out come a hungry horde of moth larvae (the worm stage) who love wool, fur, feathers, or hair, and who have nothing to do in life but to eat their heads off.

Your cottons, silks, rayons and linens are safe from moths unless there is a mixture of wool with them, or spots of food on them, but better be sure of your fabrics before trusting them too far. Of course, garments that are constantly in use don't give the moths much chance, either. The things you have to worry about are those that are stored for a season, or those that are used only occasionally and lie in drawers or boxes and hang in cupboards, inviting disaster.

Your chief protection is absolute cleanliness. Moths can't survive laundering or dry cleaning. Sunlight and airing also destroy moth eggs. So, if you are going to store clothing or blankets, wash them or have them washed or cleaned first. If they won't stand laundering or have not been used enough to be soiled, hang them out in the sun for several hours and let the air blow through them. Shake and brush them thoroughly to get moth eggs out of corners and folds. Things that are to remain in open cupboards or drawers should be taken out at least once a month and brushed, aired and sunned thoroughly as a preventive measure.

An excellent addition to the laundering process for blankets, sweaters, etc., is a mothproofing compound, used in the final rinse water. This, it is claimed, makes the fabric inedible for moths. It should be used with care.

When you put your woollens away, put the coats and suits in garment bags or boxes, and seal every crack and crevice in the bags with gummed paper or adhesive tape. This includes the side opening and the hole for the neck of the hanger. Blankets, sweaters, woollen scarves, caps, socks and gloves should be wrapped in heavy, dark paper with all openings sealed. Label the package so you won't open it to look for something that you put somewhere else.

Furs and fur coats are too valuable and too difficult to care for to be stored at home. If you possibly can, send them out for professional care and storage.

A cedar chest is satisfactory for storage only if it is tightly constructed of red heart-wood ¾ in. thick. Even so, it loses its effectiveness after a few years. To be on the safe side, use all the preventive measures you would if the chest were just a drawer.

Insect sprays will kill moths at any stage of development, but must hit the insect directly to be effective. Many are safe to use on fabrics, and it may also be worth while to use them on your rugs, upholstered furniture and draperies if you are going to close your house for any length of time. Use a hand spray or the power spray if fitted on your vacuum cleaner.

Mothproofing compounds, which prevent the larvae from eating fabric, may also be sprayed on. Such compounds must, however, be sprayed on every thread of the fabric, which means practically saturating the garment with it. Consider whether a garment will stand this before using it. The power spray does the most complete job for this mothproofing, but you may use a hand spray to go over the surface painstakingly inch by inch.

Moth flakes, crystals and other types of fumigants mean death to moths if they are used in a fairly warm, tightly closed space, but they are not worth using in open cupboards and drawers. These are made of paradichlorobenzene or naphthalene, which gives off fumes as they slowly evaporate. The discs which are sold to hang in cupboards work on this principle. They should be hung inside sealed garment bags for best results. Fumigants should be used plentifully, the rule being a pound for each hundred cubic feet of space. Arrange to put some at the top of the space in an open container, and sprinkle some on paper on the floor.

If you can spare a whole cupboard for storage, clean and pack the things as described, use the moth preventive method of your choice, and then seal up the cracks around the edge of the door. Don't open the cupboard until you take out things for the next season.

Never put away a garment that is not completely clean. Remove any spots or, better, send it for a thorough cleaning before storing away. Wrap everything in newspaper as moths don't like printer's ink. Store as quickly as possible after its return from the cleaners. Finally—the air-tight sealing of clean clothes is the best.

LET'S MAKE IT FIT

SOME RENOVATING PROBLEMS are only a matter of proper fitting. A dress may have become too large or too small. Or it may never have been fitted properly. Very often the neckline is the thing that does not fit correctly, as in **A**.

Neck Too Large. Put on the dress and pin it in at the back-neck if it is large. Rip the collar or other neck finish at the back and pin in the surplus properly, as in **A-1**.

This fulness may be distributed in several ways: Two or more darts may be stitched on the inside, as in **A-2**. Make them about ⅛ in. wide at the top, tapering to nothing 2 ins. to 3 ins. from the neckline.

In sheer materials, where darts may look too tailored, shirr the fulness, as in **A-3**. For wiry or heavy fabrics, run fine tucks from the top to the bottom, as shown in **A-4**, provided the width of the back permits.

When the neckline has been taken in, the collar or other neck finish will have to be adjusted. A flat collar should be split in the back to reduce it as in **B**. A roll collar will have to be cut and a seam taken in the back, as in **B-1**. If the collar is cut bias, it will be advisable to put on a new one, or remove the original, press, and refit it.

Neck Too Tight. In a tailored dress having a closely fitted collar, the neck may be too tight.

Remove the collar and clip the seam edges of both neck and collar, making the clips from ¼ in. to ¹⁄₁₆ in. deep and ½ in. to 2 ins. apart as required, as in **B-2**. Pin the collar on in a new seamline.

Sloping Shoulders. These may cause the dress to draw or wrinkle at the underarm towards the neckline, as in **C**. To eliminate these wrinkles, rip open the shoulder seams and rip 3 ins. to 6 ins. at the top of the sleeves, or remove the sleeves entirely. Put on the dress and get someone to gently smooth the wrinkles up, front and back, with hand flat against your shoulder, and pin, as in **C-1**. Even ½ in. taken up is important. Ease in the extra fulness of the sleeve when stitching it back into the armhole. Use a shoulder pad.

Square Shoulders. These make wrinkles form from the tip of the shoulder towards the centre-front, as in **D**. Adjust the shoulder by opening the shoulder seam at the neck. Have the front smoothed upward and take a deeper seam at the neck, as in **D-1**.

Short Shoulders. The shoulders may be too long, as in **E**. All the fulness may be needed over the bust, so a dart is taken up to retain it, as in **E-1**. The length in the back-shoulder should be taken up in a smaller dart, and the back-shoulder should be eased in slightly throughout the whole length.

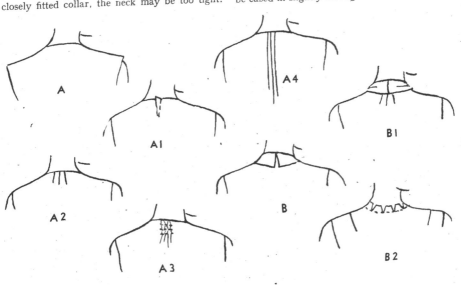

LET'S REFASHION IT

What Makes a Dress Smart. Fashions for people change as the seasons do — naturally and gradually. Even so, manufacturers work diligently to create fabrics appropriate to each season, and designers do their utmost to create clothes that make women look as attractive as possible. No woman should, or needs to, wear clothes that are definitely outmoded and consequently conspicuous.

Classic types of clothes stay in fashion- longer than do so-called high-fashion clothes. A well-tailored classic suit, for example, can be worn from five to ten years without being noticeably out of fashion, but there comes a day when even such a suit will look " different," or " dated." The sleeves may be too tight or too loose; the armholes may look wrong; the notch of the collar may be too high or too low; and the fulness or length of the skirt, or perhaps just the look of it, may present a real fashion problem.

Those who wish to dress well and yet keep within the bounds of a modest budget, should avoid clothes that are faddish and buy only the classic type—whether it is an evening dress, tailored suit or business dress. And because they want considerable wear out of a dress or suit, they should look for good material, good workmanship and simple cut.

When you are remaking a dress, the quality of your material has a definite bearing on what you do to refashion it. Ask yourself—is it worth while buying new material, possibly of a quality inferior to the original fabric but which would wear sufficiently well with it? Is the dress worth ripping and remaking in its entirety?

Often the colour of a dress that has hung in the cupboard for five years or so may be out of fashion; it may not be the fashionable shade of brown, red, blue or green. You can salvage such material sometimes by using a fashionable colour with it and, through the combination, make the whole dress smart. Again, there is the dye pot. You can have the fabric dyed, or dye it yourself so that it is right for fashion and, at the same time, becoming.

But remember that your dress must always be one of two things—classically right, or fashionably right. And in either case, it must also be right for the individual in order to be really smart.

Many people who do not know about designing do not understand what it is that makes a dress smart. A designer sees a silhouette in her mind's

eye and starts to work with fabric, pins and scissors, or sketch pad and pencil, to portray the lines she wants. She makes a basic figure with the bust, hips and waistline. Then come the neckline, the shoulders, the sleeveline and finally the hem. If you watch a good fashion artist drawing a picture, you will know how a dress is conceived. If, when you wish to refashion your dress, you think about it in this same order, you will be sure not to overlook the fashion essentials.

The suggestions we have given in this book are really ideas from which to work. You must study the fashion books, study the lines of the garment you are going to refashion, and see what you can take away from or add to your dress, suit or coat to make it right for you and as smart as possible.

Don't spend time and effort on refashioning a dress unless you can really make it practical and smart, and enjoy wearing it. If you know someone who can wear your clothes becomingly, feel dressed up in them, and continue to wear them after they have served you, then by all means give your things to her. But if you are thrifty and want to save, or if your clothes budget simply will not allow you to discard good fabric, then set about doing the refashioning with as much care as if you were making or choosing a new dress. Good fabric is always deserving of time and thought.

What to Do with What You Have. Look over the garments that you have and try each one on. Consider whether some new material or some real work in recutting the shoulders, refurbishing or readjusting the neckline, waistline or hem will do anything for the garment. And, in turn, consider whether the garment, if refashioned, can do anything for you. If the answer seems negative, then give the dress away or rip it up and make something completely different from it.

An old evening dress serves admirably when completely recut as a day-time dress. Often it can make a very special apron, or an afternoon frock. Sometimes the skirt of a dress can be salvaged to wear with different blouses, or it can make a good petticoat or, with a lace top, a good slip.

Consider the uses for your clothes fabrics, and scan through this book for ideas. Many of them should be helpful for your own particular clothes problems.

Choosing a Pattern. When you have decided what you can do with a dress, look through one of the pattern books. It is always interesting, especially to people who are not familiar with pattern fashions, to find that they keep closely abreast of good ready-to-wear. Invariably, you will find in such books the same smart styles that you see in fashionable shops. If you have seen a dress, a coat, housecoat or housejacket with a fashionable new feature displayed in a shop window or an advertisement, you are sure to find a similar fashion in the pattern books.

Choose your pattern carefully Usually you require the same size in a pattern as you do in ready-to-wear garments. Expensive ready-to-wear runs a little larger in size than the less expensive, and patterns generally conform in size to the more expensive. In other words, if you buy your ready-made clothes in a very good shop in bust size 32, then a pattern in bust size 32 should fit you; if you buy a bust size 34 in less expensive shops, a pattern in bust size 32 should be right.

Adjusting a Pattern. When you have your pattern, take from the envelope only the pieces you are going to need in recutting. Possibly it is a bolero you want, or a short collarless jacket. Then take the Cutting Guide from the envelope and notice how the pieces are laid on the material for cutting. Read this Guide so that you can pick up any construction tricks that will help you and save your time.

If you are recutting a dress and the pattern shows it a little wider than your material, remember, there are seam lines where you can always piece your material. If the difference is very slight and will not affect your garment, then fold back the pattern to avoid piecing. Adjust the pattern to your own measurements before you lay it on your material. Suggestions for doing this adjusting are invariably given with the pattern.

Piecing for Cutting. Often it is necessary, in refashioning a dress, to sew pieces of the fabric together to make it big enough to recut. Always try to place these piecings where they will have structural form in the garment. Let us suppose that you are going to put a new front in a dress, and use the old fronts to make a new back. It is possible to seam these front pieces together to make one piece for cutting the new back. If you must cut away worn parts under the sleeves, it is best to add the new material first, and then lay the new sleeve pattern on to cut the sleeve in correct size.

Always piece with the grain of the fabric, never contrary to it. It is a good idea to baste first when you piece so that your needle can help you to follow the warp and woof lines in both the top and under pieces. Basting also prevents the piecing seams from being drawn at any point.

Remember that you can use distinctive stitching, pleats, machine tucks—many decorative tricks—on seams to make them interesting when they appear at points where you feel they do not belong. If your trimming lines are even, your seams straight and well turned, they need never detract from the appearance of a finished garment.

Cutting Without Patterns. Some simple garments may be made without patterns, but it is not generally recommended to do this, for good pattern making requires equipment and experience beyond the home sewer's ken.

Commercial patterns are inexpensive, widely distributed, up to date in fashion, and as true to body measurements as is possible for home sewing.

In an emergency, a pattern may be made from an old garment. To prepare it, rip the garment, brush and press each section. Note the lengthwise thread in each, and mark it with chalk if necessary. Lay on the new material and cut. Watch the line of old stitching and provide ½ in. seam allowance beyond this, rather than follow the edge of the material, as seams may have frayed or been let out. Make notches if they are required to aid you in putting the garment together. Mark position of pockets and pleats with chalk or tailor's tacks.

★   ★   ★

"CUT YOUR COAT TO FIT YOUR CLOTH"

THERE IS on old, old adage that is often applied to living within one's means—" Cut your coat to fit your cloth.''

In refashioning your clothes, remember well this old adage and consider what you have. For example, if the fashion calls for a circular·skirt and your dress is little, slim and skimpy, then take the little skimpy dress and make a jacket or blouse to wear with a very full danseuse skirt. Buy for the skirt an inexpensive material such as rayon sheer, taffeta, lawn, organdie or chintz— whatever is appropriate to go with the material for your blouse or jacket.

If the fashion is for large-patterned materials and your fabric is plain, then buy some material and appliqué some designs on your plain fabric. Or take two dresses and combine them to make one that is smart. Rarely would you use two prints together, but a print and a plain fabric always complement each other.

Skirts. If you have a velvet skirt, remember you cannot turn the fabric round, because it has an up and down. You must plan to cut it with the grain running the same way as in the original skirt. But many a velvet skirt would make a beautiful blouse, especially with a lace yoke. Remake it into something lovely, don't discard a velvet skirt!

Gored skirts are a problem, because the widths of fabric are so narrow that you have little leeway in cutting apart and reseaming. However, an evening skirt can be made into a day-time skirt, a petticoat, a play skirt or a gay apron.

Gathered skirts are easy. Rip them up, clean the fabric, press it out and have it like new yardage to cut in any way you desire.

Pleated skirts are another problem. Pleating, if the job was well done originally, is very difficult to press out. If you must unpleat a skirt to refashion it as you want to, then try either to stitch pin tucks on the original pleating lines or to cut the garment so that the original pleating lines will not be too conspicuous. Sometimes a pleated skirt can be opened out, pressed and used with a sheer coat or dress.

If you must shorten a pleated skirt, try to do it at the top. It is a man-sized job to shorten·a pleated skirt when you must re-baste and re-press all the pleats and be sure they are even. If the pleated skirt has a good hemline, try to make any alteration or adjustment in fitting at the waistline.

Blouses. A fitted blouse is difficult to remodel because usually it fits snugly and can be changed only by using a different type of sleeve—substituting short sleeves for long, or making full sleeves if it had tight ones. Sometimes a fitted blouse can be cut short at the waistline to make a " bell-hop jacket.'' If the material is very good, perhaps it can be used to make a bag, pillows or novelty bedroom slippers. Usually a fitted blouse is made of firm and sturdy fabric, pieces of which can be salvaged to make other small articles.

Shirtwaists are often made of sturdy material of good quality and sometimes it pays to rip these up and recut them into little shirts or blouses to wear with a play suit or jerkin or jumper. Again, old shirts can be worn admirably as gilets (false blouse fronts). Business girls find that they can make very attractive gilets from their blouses.

The Balkan and raglan types of blouses are the most difficult because of the shoulders. If there is much material below the waistline, you can lift it up and recut the blouse to a new pattern. Very often this type of blouse can be pieced at a point about four inches above the waistline by adding the tail of the blouse and concealing the joining with a tuck, insertion or ribbon.

New Sleeves for Old. It was from royalty that we learned to use a different fabric for sleeves from that of the garment. To confirm this, you need but to look at the great portraits in the great museums. There you will see the fine dresses, buff coats, the contrasting colours of hanging sleeves, leg-o'-muttons, virago sleeves, to say nothing of the mancheron, dolman, angel and bishop sleeves.

Every fashion somehow manages to give us opportunity to use some kind of new fabric for sleeves or omit sleeves entirely so that, if we wish, we can refashion a dress from the sleeve standpoint. And, of course, there are always opportunities to drape, tailor or ornament a neckline to conform to the new style of the sleeve.

Evening Coats. Many an evening coat has been recut to make a housecoat, an evening jacket, or a very lovely skirt to wear with a soft, flattering blouse. An elaborate evening coat may go into boudoir cushions or be made up into evening bags. There is always a use for distinguished fabrics whether for dress or household decoration.

If the fabric of the coat is good and lovely, think of how it can be used in a practical manner. Do not take a large coat and make one small bag of it. But think of the way you can utilize the greatest amount of material in the most satisfactory way. One of the things to learn in remaking clothes is not to save the original stitching but rather to rip, clean, press and recut. When a garment is recut, it will have a new fashionable smartness. Too many times people try to save seams and by doing so they cheat themselves of the fashion-rightness of the garment

Capes. Capes represent a problem for cutting. A large circular cape, if the material is very good, should be put away and kept, because in the cycle of fashion it will come in again and again.

One of the loveliest capes I have ever seen was thirty-five years old and the owner said it cost so much originally that it has been carefully preserved and worn by three generations of the family.

So, if the cape costs a great deal, is a thing of beauty in the beginning and simple enough to be a classic, then keep it, for fashion will favour it again. If it is not of a material or workmanship that warrants such protection, then plan to recut the cape into a circular skirt, a shorter cape, or a short jacket. Lay the cape out and look it over. See how much will come on the bias in recutting. Measure its length and see if it is long enough for a skirt. Determine whether you can get enough good pieces out of it to make an appropriate garment.

Capes of cloth or brocade are easier to cut than velvet because velvet has a nap and must all be cut one way. Sometimes it is difficult to place the new pieces economically on an old velvet cape

Embroidered Apparel. If you have a beautiful piece of embroidery, salvage it if you can by recutting it into a garment that is appropriate and smart. If you cannot, consider having it dyed all one colour. The texture usually will be very interesting.

Don't try to remove embroidery from a fabric, because holes made by the needle and yarn or thread will show so much that you cannot remove the embroidery without having the fabric look shabby. It would be better to dye or cut the embroidered part away. Sometimes it can be made into work bags, shopping bags, cushions— a number of things.

Beaded Articles. Occasionally one has a dress with beading. Beading, like embroidery, is difficult to remove without leaving marks on the fabric. So try to use what you have in an attractive way and if you cannot do this, then put the garment away and keep it as an heirloom.

Robes. Housecoats and robes can often be made out of old evening coats, old beach robes—many things. Choose a smart pattern and be sure there is enough material from the original article to make a fashionable silhouette in a housecoat. Very often it is possible to recut a man's flannel robe for a woman or a boy or girl, cutting away all the worn parts and completely remaking the fabric into an entirely new practical garment. For example, a flannel robe that has shrunk in the cleaning, is snug in the sleeves, and no longer fresh at the edges, can be ripped up, washed in soapsuds, carefully pressed, recut and made very attractive at little cost. Perhaps binding the edges in a gay colour will give it the desired brand-new look.

Plus Fours. Many an old trunk or attic cupboard holds pairs of plus fours, once so fashionable on our golf courses. In these, sometimes, there is very good material that will make a pair of trousers for a small boy or a pair of play shorts or a bell-hop jacket for a girl or young woman. It all depends on how long the trousers were in the beginning—how big the man who wore them— and the condition in which you find them. But usually material of especially good quality was used in these garments and it is well worth salvaging, provided someone does not treasure them beyond their use to you.

Riding Habits. Old riding habits have so many seams that they are usually difficult to refashion, but very often they can be cut down and completely remade over for someone of smaller size, by making new seams, changing the length of the coat. Dyeing will make them a fashionable colour, fresher and thus more becoming.

★   ★   ★

"WAS TOM'S—NOW JUDY'S"

BLOUSES AND GILETS can be made from men's discarded shirts, and aprons and little pinafores from shirts too badly worn even to serve as blouses.

Entire outfits may be made, for little boys and girls, from trousers, robes or old plaid flannel shirts.

Unused or outgrown clothes, idling in cupboards or trunks, give new scope to the fabric-conscious females who are determined to be well dressed even if they have to cut up Tom's double-breasted or Dad's old grey tweed suit in order to manage it.

Good woollens are always deserving of conservation. But—first, don't cut up a suit if any person you know can get good wear out of it. If the suit is really shabby, out-of-fashion, or too small for its owner, get permission (and this is important) to cut it up. Don't think you can whip up a pair of slacks or a dress in twenty-five minutes. You will need six hours, at least—one for ripping and pressing; one for cutting; one, possibly two, for basting; half an hour for fitting; half an hour for adjustments after fitting; one for stitching; half an hour for buttons and buttonholes; half an hour for a complete pressing. These proportions of time mean concentrated work—working quickly and making every stroke count.

Choose a pattern from your favourite pattern catalogue—one that is simple in line and calls for small pieces of fabric. Follow the pattern instruction chart for the actual laying out of the pieces, the cutting out, making and finishing of the suit.

In making a suit of this kind, use matching thread-and set your machine for a longer stitch than on a silk dress, because the thickness of the wool will make the stitch shorter. Use buttonhole twist for the buttonholes. If you are not expert in this, take the coat to the local tailor and pay him to make the buttonholes for you, or take it to your local sewing-machine shop and let them make them for a small fee. A zipper ripped from an old dress may be used in the placket opening. If you haven't a zipper, use the trouser buttons for the placket. Make the same number of buttonholes as the original coat had buttons. For a professional look, use the sleeve buttons for your sleeves with simulated buttonholes. The original collar stand and sleeve padding will help to give your suit that well-tailored look that you always envy and covet.

If you can, recut the coat lining to make a lining for your jacket, otherwise, overcast all seams. In such tailoring as this, remember the essentials of good tailoring. Press each seam before it joins another. Clip seams on curves to make them flat.

SAVE THAT COAT

IF YOU HAVE A CHESTERFIELD that has become shabby in the buttonholes or worn at the top of the pockets and at the bottom of the sleeves, cut away the bad part of the coat, and add a band of grosgrain ribbon, velveteen or flannel, on each side of the front, as in **A**. Cut away the worn places at the bottom of the sleeves and add a band there. Band the top of the pockets, too, making the band deep enough to come over the worn part. If the collar is frayed, new material can be used to cover that. Careful planning, basting, stitching and pressing should bring such a coat through with enough vitality to last for many a day.

B. If you habitually hold your bag up close to your waistline, you may wear your coat out on that side more quickly than elsewhere. Repair this by inserting a section of harmonizing fabric through the centre, as shown. Make new cuffs and a new inside neck facing of this material and, presto, you will have a coat that seems like new. Do the same thing if you want to lengthen your coat or make it different. If the fashion requires more change, recut the skirt and sleeves and shoulders.

C. Perhaps you have one of those loose swagger or smock coats that no longer appeals to you. Rip up such a coat, clean the fabric, and recut it entirely, using a new facing up the front, around the neck and for the bottoms of the sleeves. Use the same fabric for the lining or perhaps a harmonizing checked fabric. A very good warm topcoat can be refashioned from your old outmoded coat if you have the will to style your coat smartly and finish it to perfection.

D. In many a cupboard there hangs a double-breasted tweed coat still good for many a day's wear, but so outmoded that it makes one look like the forgotten woman. Usually it needs ripping, washing or cleaning and a complete recutting. A single-breasted version can usually be made from a double-breasted coat. Velveteen can be used attractively to top the pockets, cuff the sleeves and collar the neckline. A tweed coat may be made into a topcoat, as in **C**, or perhaps a fitted style, as in **D**.

B. Wrap-round coats are usually made of soft fabric that drapes nicely and compliments the waistline. Such coats usually grow shabby where they tie and at the neckline. Try cutting down such a coat to make it just come together at the centre-front. Take 1¾ ins. grosgrain ribbon, shir both edges and hand-sew it all round the front and neck edges of your coat. Take a piece of cord, gather some ribbon on this cord and make figure-eight loops for the front closing. Four buttons, made from the scraps cut away from the coat, will finish such a coat in a very nice way. If the sleeves are worn, face them back with the ribbon. If necessary, use a new lining throughout the coat to make it really like new.

Relining Coats. Remove the old lining, smooth it out, and cut the new lining by it. Stitch underarm seams and seams in the back section if it is fitted. If more width is needed at the bottom, add gores at the sides. Crease or baste along the centre-back line. Turn the coat to the wrong side and put it on a dress form, or if you haven't one of these, lay it on a table. Mark the centre-back line of the coat and pin the centre-back of the lining to it. Smooth the lining up against the shoulders and pin. Pin the side seams of the lining to the coat side seams, with pins across the seam, as at **F**.

Turn under the front seam edge of the lining and pin this along the facing, with the pin points facing away from the edge, as at **G**, pinning up and down from the waistline. Pin the shoulder line with the back of the lining over the front facing. Slip-stitch the lining along the front facing. Fell the lining in position along shoulder seam and across the back of the neckline.

Stitch the sleeve seams. Turn under the raw edges at the wrists Pin and whip these edges in place. Slip the top of the sleeve lining under the edges of the armhole and overcast it to the seam. Turn in the edge of the body lining and pin it round the armhole, as at **H**.

Then whip it in place. Turn the bottom edge of the lining and either hem it or slip-stitch it, according to the way it was finished originally. If the bottom of the lining is turned up and hangs free from hem of the coat, it is tacked in place at the side seams.

Have the coat pressed, or press it carefully yourself, working from the right side.

Sometimes all that is needed is a half lining in the shoulder section. New sleeve linings may be put in without changing the rest of the lining.

If shoulder padding is needed, it should be attached to the armhole under the lining.

Frayed Sleeve Lining. When the bottom edge of a sleeve lining is frayed, as in **I**, a piece of grosgrain ribbon can be pinned over it and whipped in place. Turn the end of the ribbon under and finish off, as at **J** keeping it in line with the seam of the sleeve.

This same repair can be applied to frayed lining edges along the bottom of a coat.

If a coat lining is worn only at the neckline, use a piece of similar fabric to patch it, as in **K**. Cut the patch piece to fit along the seams at this section, turn the edges under and whip in place as shown.

Underarm Shield. Cut two pieces in shield or half-moon shape, as in **L**, making one end of the moon higher than the other, as at **M**. This end goes toward the front of the armhole. Seam the pieces together along the outer curve, as shown, and turn to the right side Clip along the inner curve, as at **N**. Rip the sleeve lining at the underarm and insert the shield. Sew it in place with running-stitches, as at **O**. Then whip the sleeve lining back into its proper place, as at **P**

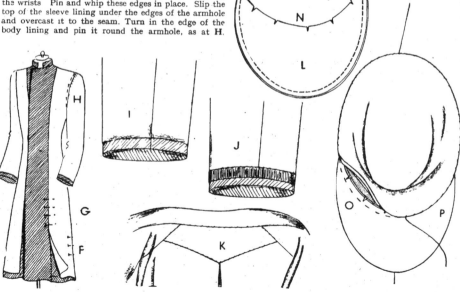

ONE YARD OF FABRIC—TO MAKE A DRESS

"I want a piece of calico
To make my doll a dress
It doesn't take a big piece
A yard will do, I guess."

THIS VERY OLD little jingle is here to inspire your imagination to work with remnants and scraps of material and to realize that much can be accomplished even with one yard more or less of fabric.

Fabric can extend itself to your requirements if you plan wisely. Never discard a good piece of fabric. Re-use old garments; rip, clean, press, re-cut and re-sew with enthusiasm and skill to insure smartness. There are many ways to use even small pieces of fabric—as yokes, cuffs, inserts in sleeves, collars and trimming pieces. Look at your worn dresses; see what is needed to make them serviceable and fashion-right again. Then choose the suggestions given here that are appropriate to your own dresses, and replace the old fabric with new—smartly and easily.

You will notice that short sleeves are shown in many of the remodelled ensembles suggested in this book. This is done to effect economy in material. If fashion insists upon long sleeves, remember that you can make them of new fabric, or make deep cuffs of new fabric to add to the sleeves. You can also insert new parts in sleeve sections so that your sleeves may be made whatever length you desire.

A. This old dress, shabby in front and at the neck—was made like new with a yard of new material If you have such a dress, buy a yard of velveteen, crepe, flannel—any fabric that goes with the dress fabric. If the dress is worn and out of fashion, rip, clean and re-cut it. Make a new front and collar. Use the old front parts and the old sleeves to make two-piece sleeves; or, if the sleeves are good and the back is worn, cut a new back from the old front, and retain the original sleeves.

B. Here is a dress that had its lower blouse section completely remade. Many business girls wear their dresses out first around the waist. In such a case, cut away the worn part and add a new section. Usually ⅔ yd. of 40-in. fabric is enough to give a whole new middle part to a dress, and sometimes this seems to make a drab dress new and gay Freshen up all the old parts to make

a new yoke or collar, or perhaps to piece the sleeves if they need renewing.

C. If the skirt of your old dress is good, cut away all the worn blouse parts and add new material. In the illustration, a new front and new back were added, and the good parts of the original back and front were used for new sleeves.

D. Often a collar is the first part of a dress to lose its fashion-rightness. In such a case, don't hesitate to cut away the out-of-fashion collar and apply one that is more appropriate or style-right. In this dress, the collar and front needed refurbishing, so a new collar and a vest portion were added. You could easily place a similar centre panel down the back if it were needed, extending it to the same depth as the front, or making it a little shorter, or continuing it all the way to the waistline

E. This shows a new two-piece costume with a simulated vest, made from an old dress having a worn blouse front. The vest part was fashioned of new material and stitched in place to make the waistline completely new.

F. If you want to rejuvenate a dress of a light colour—possibly too light for general wear—buy some dark material that is right in texture for your dress. Add a section of the dark colour to the top of the skirt, make a new belt, and add new fabric to the sleeves—and thus treat yourself to a new dress that you can wear all the year round. If the front opening in your old dress is good keep it as it is, but make a new one if it will make the dress seem newer to you. You can do this by adding a front facing of the new fabric, or by inserting an entirely new front with a pleat or a zipper fastening.

G. Here is another way of refurbishing a dress. This soft gilet is usually flattering and is very easy to make. If you buy half a yard of lace for re-styling a dress in this manner, you can cut the original sleeves either short or three-quarter length or make new loose sleeves as desired.

H and I. These illustrate a happy way to

rejuvenate the top of a dress or blouse. It is particularly appropriate for frocks of velveteen or jerseys. Use rayon or wool to cut a new yoke and new sleeves. Have buttons covered with the new fabric, or use any fashionable, appropriate type of button or a zipper for the front closing. Make a smart, new collar. Cut your sleeves so that they are "comfy."

J. This is a very practical and satisfactory dress, remodelled from an old button-down-the-front frock. If you have such a dress, a wool dress, especially, with sagging buttonholes and missing buttons, buy a yard of fabric and cut a new front that goes from neck to hemline. Do your piecing with a seam at the waistline and use a smart belt to cover it. Line the upper part of the front panel and sew snap fasteners along the edges. Add cuffs of the new fabric to finish the sleeves or make entirely new sleeves. This is a convenient way to refurbish when fashion allows and makes an especially practical garment for a young mother, though it is not exclusively a maternity style. If a new collar is to be made, cut it from the old material that was removed from the front, and, if you wish, cover it with the new.

Remember always that the purpose of these pages is to give you an idea. The silhouette of your garment may be different but the idea applicable to your needs. Study these pictures and see in what way you can add to what you have to eliminate the worn, shabby or out-of-fashion part without a patched or overdone appearance.

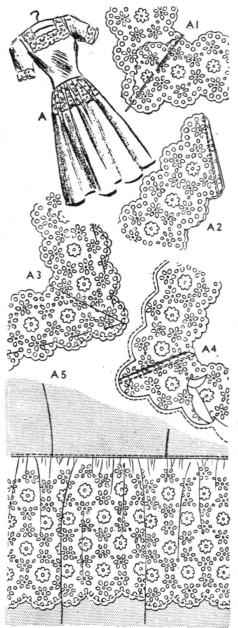

SEE WHAT EYELET

IF YOU HAVE a crepe frock that has lost all its pep, rejuvenate it with eyelet embroidery. You will be delighted to find how new and crisp a garment can look after it has had such treatment. A few examples are shown on this page. Perhaps your dress is different in cut, your material different from those mentioned here. Even so, eyelet embroidery can work wonders if you will apply your ingenuity to the dress you have, and let this comparatively inexpensive yardage help you in its own smart way. Consider your dress in connection with the use of embroidery insertion, embroidery flouncing, or all-over embroidery. See whether your dress can be remodelled, and let these suggestions help you to determine the best way.

Eyelet embroidery is, as you realize, a summer fabric, and is more practical for wash materials than any other; but white embroidery on black or navy-blue crepe is often very chic, especially when worn with white accessories.

A. for example, represents a dress that was shabby at the neck and waistline, with worn-out sleeves—no " oomph " at all. The old neck was cut away and the good part of the neck section used to restore the sleeves at the under-arms. The top of the skirt was measured to determine how much 9-in. embroidery to buy. Usually 1½ yds. is sufficient. Two-thirds yard of 2-in. insertion was also required for the sleeves, and 1¼ yds. of 3-in. for the square neckline. The use of eyelet embroidery in this instance allows you to lengthen the skirt, take out badly worn parts, and make a new waistline—an admirable way to revive a garment that can continue to do service after the right rejuvenation.

It is a simple matter to apply eyelet embroidery to a dress such as the one shown in **A**. Before cutting the old neck away, fold the embroidery for the neck widthwise in the centre. Pin this centre-line to the centre-front line of the dress, placing it for a becoming neckline. Bring the trimming piece out to the sides, turn it at each corner and pin bias mitres, as shown in **A-1**. Bring the pieces over the shoulders and make mitres at the back. (These back mitres should be higher than those in front.) Pin the four corners securely. Provide for hems or a zipper at the centre-back.

Put the blouse part on, making sure that it fits. Adjust any pins necessary to make the yoke

EMBROIDERY CAN DO

smooth and flattering, and mark with basting thread where the lower edge of the yoke line comes. Then remove the yoke and stitch the mitred corners, as in **A-2**, stitching the seams twice. Trim them to within $\frac{1}{4}$ in. of the outside stitching line, as shown, and overcast the raw edges. **A-3** shows how to pin, then baste, the yoke in position on the blouse; also how the line of stitching is put in all round the scalloped edge. **A-4** shows the yoke from the wrong side and how the fabric is cut away under the yoke to within $\frac{3}{8}$ in. of the stitching line. **A-5** shows how the skirt yoke is stitched to the fabric and how the waistline of the blouse part is brought over the gathered top edge and stitched.

Apply embroidery bands to the bottom of the sleeves and complete the dress throughout, simply, and without too much work. A dress can be remodelled in this way in a few hours' time and give much practical service.

B. Here again you cut away all the jaded parts of a dress—the sleeves, yoke, old collar line. Dress up the skirt with big pockets; insert a belt to lengthen the skirt, if necessary. Eyelet embroidery (broderie anglaise) can be bought by the yard. Three-fourths of a yard is needed to rejuvenate this type of dress.

B-1 shows how the skirt and blouse parts are gathered for joining to the inserted belt. **B-2** shows how the embroidery yoke and belt are stitched down on the right side over the gathers of the blouse and the skirt. This extra stitching gives strength and allows you to trim the seams on the wrong side close to the stitching line. Overcast raw edges if the material frays easily. **B-3** shows how a binding is applied to a bow piece to finish the centre-front of the bias-bound neckline. **B-4** shows a strip of fabric over the gathered centre of the trimming piece. **B-5** shows how the hem is made at the top of the pockets. **B-6** shows the hem complete, with the raw edges trimmed, ready for applying to the dress. **B-7** shows how the pockets look when stitched in place.

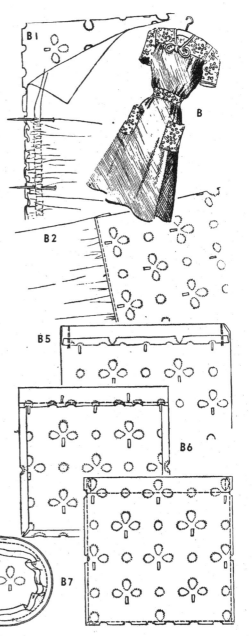

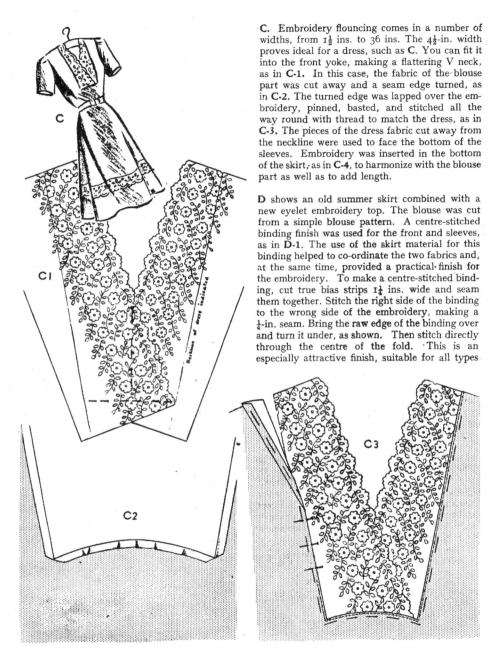

C. Embroidery flouncing comes in a number of widths, from $1\frac{1}{2}$ ins. to 36 ins. The $4\frac{1}{2}$-in. width proves ideal for a dress, such as **C**. You can fit it into the front yoke, making a flattering V neck, as in **C-1**. In this case, the fabric of the blouse part was cut away and a seam edge turned, as in **C-2**. The turned edge was lapped over the embroidery, pinned, basted, and stitched all the way round with thread to match the dress, as in **C-3**. The pieces of the dress fabric cut away from the neckline were used to face the bottom of the sleeves. Embroidery was inserted in the bottom of the skirt, as in **C-4**, to harmonize with the blouse part as well as to add length.

D shows an old summer skirt combined with a new eyelet embroidery top. The blouse was cut from a simple blouse pattern. A centre-stitched binding finish was used for the front and sleeves, as in **D-1**. The use of the skirt material for this binding helped to co-ordinate the two fabrics and, at the same time, provided a practical·finish for the embroidery. To make a centre-stitched binding, cut true bias strips $1\frac{1}{4}$ ins. wide and seam them together. Stitch the right side of the binding to the wrong side of the embroidery, making a $\frac{1}{4}$-in. seam. Bring the raw edge of the binding over and turn it under, as shown. Then stitch directly through the centre of the fold. ·This is an especially attractive finish, suitable for all types of fabric. A word of caution about eyelet embroidery: it shrinks. The fabric, being tightened by the embroidery, shrinks more than most cotton fabrics. So never fit a skirt, or a blouse, or a sleeve of this fabric tightly, for it is likely to be too tight after washing. Fit the garment comfortably—almost loosely—so that you will not meet with disappointment.

E. If you have a linen blouse or, for that matter, an old linen or "sharkskin" skirt that you would like to remake into a blouse, buy all-over eyelet embroidery for the skirt and combine the two to make a new dress, as shown.
E-1 shows how the sleeves are banded with the fabric of the blouse. **E-2** shows how the hem is finished—with a row of gathering run round the bottom edge first, to control the fulness and insure smoothness.
To finish seams in eyelet embroidery, use a double-stitched seam; i.e. stitch on the seam line all the way down, and add a second row of stitching $\frac{1}{4}$ in. outside the seam line. Then trim the fabric to within a scant $\frac{1}{8}$ in. of the outside row of stitching. If the embroidery pattern is very open, even a third row of stitching may be desirable, to make certain that it cannot fray. Remember also, in working on eyelet embroidery, to stitch over paper so that the stitching will not tighten at any point.

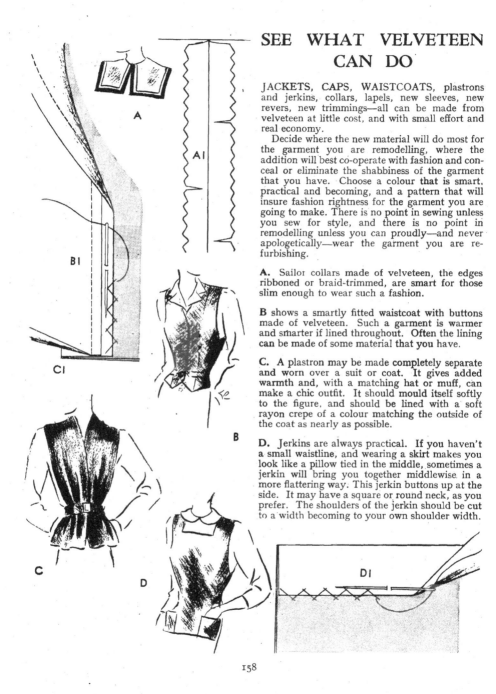

SEE WHAT VELVETEEN CAN DO

JACKETS, CAPS, WAISTCOATS, plastrons and jerkins, collars, lapels, new sleeves, new revers, new trimmings—all can be made from velveteen at little cost, and with small effort and real economy.

Decide where the new material will do most for the garment you are remodelling, where the addition will best co-operate with fashion and conceal or eliminate the shabbiness of the garment that you have. Choose a colour that is smart, practical and becoming, and a pattern that will insure fashion rightness for the garment you are going to make. There is no point in sewing unless you sew for style, and there is no point in remodelling unless you can proudly—and never apologetically—wear the garment you are refurbishing.

A. Sailor collars made of velveteen, the edges ribboned or braid-trimmed, are smart for those slim enough to wear such a fashion.

B shows a smartly fitted waistcoat with buttons made of velveteen. Such a garment is warmer and smarter if lined throughout. Often the lining can be made of some material that you have.

C. A plastron may be made completely separate and worn over a suit or coat. It gives added warmth and, with a matching hat or muff, can make a chic outfit. It should mould itself softly to the figure, and should be lined with a soft rayon crepe of a colour matching the outside of the coat as nearly as possible.

D. Jerkins are always practical. If you haven't a small waistline, and wearing a skirt makes you look like a pillow tied in the middle, sometimes a jerkin will bring you together middlewise in a more flattering way. This jerkin buttons up at the side. It may have a square or round neck, as you prefer. The shoulders of the jerkin should be cut to a width becoming to your own shoulder width.

E. Many an old cloth coat can be turned wrong-side out, re-seamed, and made like new again with a new collar, sleeves, buttons and bound buttonholes of velveteen. This makes it especially smart to wear over a matching velveteen dress.

F. Lamb's wool or " teddy-bear " coats that wear out at the pockets and buttonholes and get shabby at the collar, can be rejuvenated beautifully with bands of velveteen. Here again, entire sleeves or deep cuffs can be used if the sleeves are worn.

G. Use velveteen or wide-wale corduroy to refurbish a dress or blouse with a new yoke or sleeves.

H shows revers and collar, made to be tacked into the neckline of a collarless coat, thus making it seem completely different. Velveteen cuffs may be added and any shabbiness of the pockets covered with a strip of the velveteen cut to match the grain of the coat fabric.

I shows a circular collar made from $\frac{3}{8}$ yd. of velveteen, lined with matching taffeta or crepe.

Details. When sewing velveteen there are a few precautions to observe. Because it is a napped fabric, baste or pin the seams very carefully to prevent the top fabric from slipping under the presser foot and making the under fabric more full in the seam than it should be.

A-1 shows how a pinked seam in velveteen should be clipped to insure its steaming flat. Velveteen must have all its seams and edges steamed just the same as velvet.

B-1 shows how a lining is stitched to a velveteen edge—then how velveteen is herring-bone stitched to itself; this is done to hold the lining in place to get a flat edge at **C-1**, rather than a round one.

D-1 shows how a velveteen edge is herring-bone stitched down in garments that are unlined. **E-1** shows how a lining is applied over such an edge.

F-1 shows how the fulness of a curved edge, as on a collar, should be gathered first and even hemming-stitches put in to distribute the fulness evenly. These stitches, like the herring-bone stitch, should barely catch the velveteen.

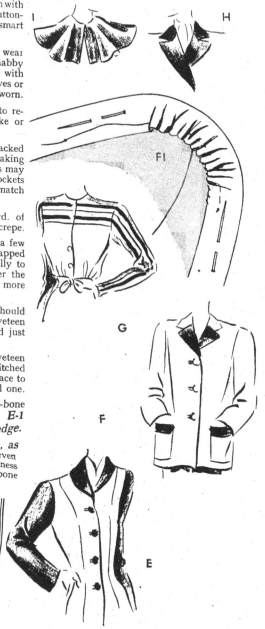

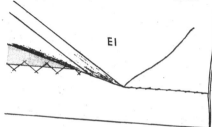

SEE WHAT TAFFETA CAN DO

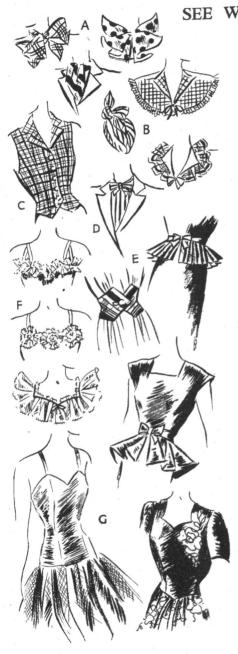

PERHAPS NO RAYON FABRICS are lovelier than the taffetas. They are colourful, crisp, easy to handle and inexpensive to buy. Taffeta should be worn with a dash. Use taffeta for remodelling, for freshening, for colour and for attractiveness.

A. Taffeta can be used for under-the-chin bows or ascots. Both should be cut on the bias and the edges should be hand-rolled or finished with a narrow machine hem or picoting. Never cut a bias bow too narrow. The hemmed edges help to avoid stringiness.

B. Large collars with pleated ruffles and draped turbans are effective in taffeta.

C. Waistcoats or jackets of taffeta should be lined with light-weight muslin or georgette to give them a little more body and to prevent strained seams. Any taffeta garment that is fitted closely should have a fitted lining so that the strain will come on the lining. For example, in a close-fitting taffeta skirt, always have a yoke of a light-weight lining material that will come down well over the hips.

D. Gilets may be made of taffeta ribbon and may be checked, striped or plaid for a gay touch.

E. Taffeta peplums and belts provide a practical way to apply colour to a dress. The peplum should have a hemmed edge and may be pleated or gathered. The band itself should form the bow. The belt should have a firm interlining.

F. Pinked taffeta is an old-time, ever-fashionable favourite for evening wear. This can be used as double ruffles, single ruffles or as rosettes to relieve the plainness of a dress or to make it more becoming. Choose your colour and decide on the effect you want, and then pink and gather according to your plan.

G. Three types of bodices are shown in this group. Choose the one that meets your need best, but be sure to line your taffeta. The close-fitting bodice will fit and wear better if cut on the bias. At the upper right is the peplum type. If made with a zip fastener down the back, this is easy to get into and out of and is ideal to wear with tailored evening skirts. The form-fitting evening bodice at the left is a grand style to use in remaking an old net or lace frock. It allows you to cut away the worn parts and make it good as new. At the lower right is shown a printed frock with a new taffeta blouse. A design from the print has been appliquéd to the bodice. This is very easy to do with taffeta, because of its smoothness. Lay your design in the position you want, pin, baste and carefully stitch in place.

A LOT FROM A LITTLE

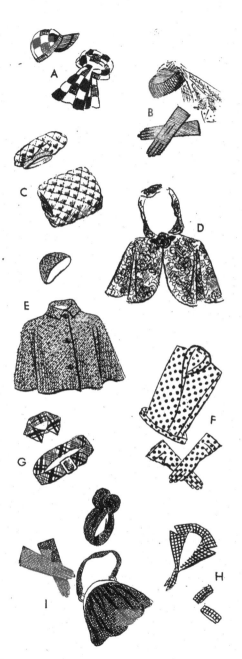

A. Scraps of yarn or scraps of beautiful fabric or ribbon can be put together to make a sports cap and scarf. The yarn should be wound round paper, stitched across the ends and sewn together. Groups of these windings can make a piece of fabric for the top of a cap or scarf. Ribbon can be interlaced for the effect you desire. Squares of fabric can be seamed together to make the most interesting effects imaginable.

B. A turban can be made of scraps of material from a dress you make. When well put together, with an attractive veil, it can often finish a wardrobe and give it dash. Fabric gloves and fabric mittens are very practical. They, too, can match your hat or scarf or both.

C. Quilting has a variety of uses. It can make collars, revers, hats, berets, muffs—so many things. Quilted fabric can be bought by the yard in many colours, or you can quilt it yourself if you can't find the colour you want in the ready-quilted materials. The quilted beret and muff were made to match a suit.

D. Lace from an old dress or scarf can often be used to make a little head-dress or a cape and head-dress. Re-styling it is up to you. A picot edge is usually best for the finishing of lace. Have this done at a shop that does hem-stitching

E. A cape or a skirt may be used to make a short cape and skull cap or any kind of hat that is smart or flattering for you.

F. Gilets with gloves to match are always attractive and, when fashionable, are usually expensive to buy. You can easily make them of sateen, taffeta or chamois-leather.

G. Matching collars and belts can be made of even small scraps of plaid wool or taffeta or ribbon.

H. Tailored collars and cuff bands are ideal for wearing with tailored suits. They can be tacked, buttoned or snapped into position and give the effect of a blouse One-quarter to one-third yard will usually make a beautiful set. This should be made double, of course.

I. A turban, gloves and bag to match are grand things to have, especially for those who travel, because they are easy to pack and give a completeness to the ensemble that is desirable. Jersey or any soft, pliable material like velvet, velveteen, duveteen or chamois-leather is ideal for the articles shown.

It is well worth while to buy a good pattern for any of the articles shown here so that your accessories are smart and professional-looking.

161

THE BASIC DRESS

WOMEN WHO HAVE the assured reputation of dressing well, know the importance of having as the backbone of their wardrobe, each season, a basic dress—one that is excellent in fabric, flattering in line, becoming in colour and practical to wear throughout a day.

The chief characteristic of a good basic dress and the secret of its success is its extreme simplicity. Its silhouette is flattering and smart but very simple. No trimming or fussiness obscures its classic line. Its colour is generally plain and dark or neutral. Because of simplicity and good design, the basic dress has as many lives as a cat. It offers an endless variety of changes with the simple addition of gilets, collars, jabots, jackets, boleros, redingotes, belts, jewellery and other accessories, so that it looks completely different with each wearing. You have your choice of all your favourite colours to wear with it in turbans, gloves and belts. You can make it dainty and feminine with lace or embroidered neckwear, trim and tailored with jackets and dickies, or sparkling and sophisticated for dinner and date with a jewelled clip or necklace. A little ingenuity can make it your magic all-in-one wardrobe.

It is rumoured that a famous actress went on a tour across the country with one basic dress and three dickies. For travelling or for business, when one must always look smart and chic, the variety of costume afforded by that one basic dress is a point worth considering.

If you have a basic dress in your wardrobe, consider how you can refurbish it, refashion it, and renew it with just a change of accessories. You will be surprised how ingenuity and clever fingers can revitalize a basic dress.

It is essential to keep your basic dress fitting perfectly. Fabrics do shrink and figures too often bulge. Hence, lines sag or shrink. Special attention should always be given to the hemline, because much smartness is measured there.

In providing accessories for a basic dress, always make them so that they appear to be a part of the dress. Snap jabots and collars securely in place; a belt should be placed so that it will look as if it really belonged to the dress.

If you have an individual colour and prefer it generally, then your scrap bag or cupboard should provide many possibilities for smart accessories for wear with a basic dress. Remember, good-quality fabric, charming in design or texture, is always deserving of a second, even third using. The sketches here should give you several ideas of things to make for wear with your basic dress.

piece is a bright colour and is put on the wrong side of the garment. The pocket opening is so cut that the added pocket colour shows through. The bow at the top of the pocket matches the pocket colour.

H. A felt or velveteen belt of a gay colour can make an old fabric young-looking. The one here is fitted and laced at the front.

I. Even a recut tennis coat can gain distinction with pockets of felt, to which motifs of another colour of felt can be stitched or glued. Or an interesting fabric design can be cut and used in this way on coats of washable materials.

J. An old blouse and an old dress can often be combined to make one good dress. This shows the blouse recut into a bolero top.

K. Jerkins of flannel, corduroy, wool, gingham, denim—all are practical and often very becoming. They are particularly useful to wear with tailored suits and blouses or with slacks. A remnant of left-over piece of suit or dress or an old skirt can be cut up to make such a garment.

L, M and **N** show what ribbon and flowers can do to rejuvenate a dress with colour. You can use one bow or several. Drape your ribbon on, pin it and tack it with a minimum number of tacks to get the effect that you want. Use artificial flowers for rejuvenation, for colour and to be young and gay. You can arrange them on the bodice, on your skirt, in your hair.

Tassels. Make tassels of floss, thread or yarn of a colour to contrast with or match the fabric.

Decide on the appropriate size for the tassels. Cut a piece of cardboard as long as the tassel is to be and wide enough to make a tassel of sufficient bulk. Take three strands of the floss, secure them to the cardboard with a paper clip, as at **A**, and wind them evenly around the cardboard until you have enough bulk. Thread a needle with double thread, run it under the winding, as at **B**, and tie a secure knot. Cut the bottom loops to make the tassel fringe. Then, with the thread you used to tie the top, wind several turns around the tassel a little down from the top, as in **C**. Finish by taking the needle in under this binding and out through the top and using this thread to sew the tassel in position

Fringe. Narrow fringe can be made with the machine craft guide, pages 41 and 42. For wide fringe, wind the thread on cardboard, as for a tassel. Cut the cardboard $\frac{1}{4}$ in. wider than the desired depth of the fringe. When the strands are wound, stitch across them $\frac{1}{4}$ in. down from the top of the cardboard, as at **D**. Cut the bottom loops and remove the cardboard. The strip at the top can be pulled after the fringe is stitched to the fabric edge.

Pompons. Wind a long narrow strip of cardboard with thread or yarn, as in **E**. Slip the yarn off and tie it at regular intervals, as at **F**. Cut the yarn apart between ties, as at **G**, and at the ends, as at **H**. Draw the tie threads very tight, knot them securely and fluff out the yarn ends to complete a pompon, as in **I**. One winding thus makes several pompons. To make them perfectly round, it may be necessary to trim the thread.

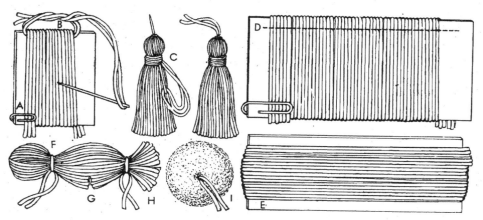

LACE, ROMANTIC

IF FABRICS COULD TALK, lace perhaps would tell more love stories than any other, and more stories of great emotional occasions, since it is the fabric of the Church, of brides, of grand old ladies and of all who would be alluringly feminine. Collars, gilets, pill-box hats, Juliet caps, bows for combs, bows for dresses, bows for necklines—lace answers for all. With the right colour and texture, be it sturdy or gossamer, the right effect can be achieved if you know what you want and really work with care to achieve it.

Many an old dress has been enlivened with a new collar or top of lace. A beautifully cut real silk dress is deserving, indeed, of a whole new top and sleeves of lace.

Bands of lace can be inserted in an old chiffon or georgette dress to make it seem new. Bands of lace in dresses or lingerie can give the garment new life and help it to fit better.

An old lace dress can always be rejuvenated with a new velvet, satin or taffeta bodice. Even one of sheer wool is not amiss, because lace enhances practically every fabric.

In the lace examples shown here, we have tried merely to suggest where you can use lace effectively. Use lace that you have or buy new lace to rejuvenate garments which are worth saving.

The old saying, "A lady might as well be off the earth as out of style," is one to remember when you have clothes which are too good to throw or give away and yet do nothing whatever for your appearance. Get out your old dresses and a good fashion book. Consider what you can do to rejuvenate them with lace; consider the type of lace most suitable. If you find a lace in a flattering colour, have the fabric of the old dress dyed to go with the lace. Most lace, like net, is finished with a sizing and, therefore, should not be dyed.

If you lay a fabric and lace, or two thicknesses of lace over paper and stitch it that way, you can stitch just as perfectly as if you had two pieces of even-weave fabric and get very satisfactory results. Lace in remodelling should be used for effect, and hand appliqué, therefore, is not generally recommended as it requires more work than is necessary.

A shows two ways to rejuvenate an old dress— one with shoulders and sleeves of lace, the other with new shoulder straps and a lace bolero.

AND LOVELY

B shows how to use a peplum of lace with a tiny wire stitched in the hem to make it stick out. If you do not wish to use a wire, then buy starched lace. Simply cut the peplum and sew it to a piece of ribbon which has been cut long enough to provide an ample bow for the front.

C. If you have a dress that is too short, put in bands of lace to make it longer and use the same lace to trim the neck and sleeves, so that it looks as though you trimmed on purpose rather than from the necessity to conceal piecing.

D. If you want to look different, yet wear the same dress, try making a belt of lace and a matching lace flower for your hair. You certainly will be able to fool some of your friends at least with this little trick of camouflage.

E. If you want to turn a formal dress into a dinner dress, try making a new top of lace. It is a simple thing to do and very practical. Lace jackets and boleros are easy to make and are very effective for giving variety to a basic formal dress.

F. If your evening dress is badly worn and you need more than just a top, then make a whole princess bodice of the lace, having it come well down over the skirt in a becoming line over the hips. Use a square, V or sweetheart neckline for this. Just be certain that the neckline as well as the bodice length is becoming to you.

G. Lace jackets are a delight to have. If you come home from work in a suit, it is very easy to put on a little lace jacket and feel dressed up. Again, such a jacket made with long or short sleeves is grand for informal dinners. One long skirt can be worn with any one of several lace blouses or jackets and seems new and different each time you put it on.

Lace mitts with matching scarf are always festive for evening. These in bright colour can rejuvenate a tired drab dress. Net should be included in any consideration of lace because it, too, has such a great variety of uses.

Lace will do your bidding, and lace is romantic and lovely. Choose it carefully, sew it with pride and it will reward you many times over.

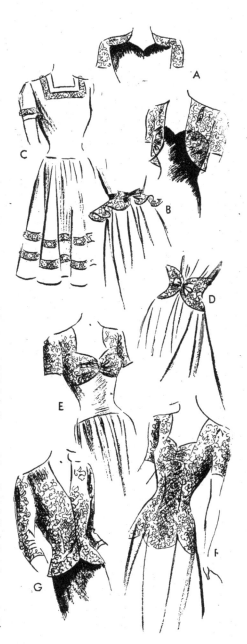

WHEN YOU LIKE THE FABRIC OF YOUR OLD DRESS

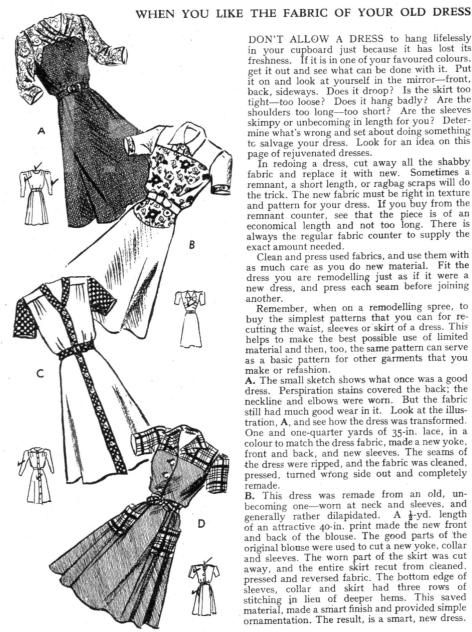

DON'T ALLOW A DRESS to hang lifelessly in your cupboard just because it has lost its freshness. If it is in one of your favoured colours, get it out and see what can be done with it. Put it on and look at yourself in the mirror—front, back, sideways. Does it droop? Is the skirt too tight—too loose? Does it hang badly? Are the shoulders too long—too short? Are the sleeves skimpy or unbecoming in length for you? Determine what's wrong and set about doing something to salvage your dress. Look for an idea on this page of rejuvenated dresses.

In redoing a dress, cut away all the shabby fabric and replace it with new. Sometimes a remnant, a short length, or ragbag scraps will do the trick. The new fabric must be right in texture and pattern for your dress. If you buy from the remnant counter, see that the piece is of an economical length and not too long. There is always the regular fabric counter to supply the exact amount needed.

Clean and press used fabrics, and use them with as much care as you do new material. Fit the dress you are remodelling just as if it were a new dress, and press each seam before joining another.

Remember, when on a remodelling spree, to buy the simplest patterns that you can for recutting the waist, sleeves or skirt of a dress. This helps to make the best possible use of limited material and then, too, the same pattern can serve as a basic pattern for other garments that you make or refashion.

A. The small sketch shows what once was a good dress. Perspiration stains covered the back; the neckline and elbows were worn. But the fabric still had much good wear in it. Look at the illustration, **A**, and see how the dress was transformed. One and one-quarter yards of 35-in. lace, in a colour to match the dress fabric, made a new yoke, front and back, and new sleeves. The seams of the dress were ripped, and the fabric was cleaned, pressed, turned wrong side out and completely remade.

B. This dress was remade from an old, unbecoming one—worn at neck and sleeves, and generally rather dilapidated. A ½-yd. length of an attractive 40-in. print made the new front and back of the blouse. The good parts of the original blouse were used to cut a new yoke, collar and sleeves. The worn part of the skirt was cut away, and the entire skirt recut from cleaned, pressed and reversed fabric. The bottom edge of sleeves, collar and skirt had three rows of stitching in lieu of deeper hems. This saved material, made a smart finish and provided simple ornamentation. The result, is a smart, new dress.

C. Too often dresses that button all the way down become shabby in front. Sometimes the buttonholes droop and become shapeless. If you have a dress like the one in the small sketch at **C.** it is desirable and easy to refurbish it as shown. Use a piece of new fabric to add a facing band on both sides of the front opening, extending it around the neck. Make new sleeves and belt.

D. This dress was remodelled from an old linen one of still good fabric. If you have a good flannel or linen dress, salvage it with a new yoke and sleeves and patch pockets of plaid, checked, striped. or flowered fabric.

E. This circular-skirt dress was made over from the one in the little sketch. Flared or circular skirts have plenty of material. Often their hems become uneven and they need refashioning. Rip the seams of such a skirt, recut it from a new pattern and get a new and smart hemline. Sometimes you can buy an inexpensive blouse ready-made and use it with the re-made skirt, or you can trim an inexpensive blouse with the fabric of the skirt to make it seem like a one-piece ensemble, as shown.

F. Many small and medium-sized girls and young women wear jumper dresses with a real flair. If you are one of these, by all means, whenever fashion favours jumper styles, remodel your worn dresses of suitable material in this way. **F** shows a charming jumper dress made from an old wool frock of excellent fabric. If you have a wool dress that is too bulky and is worn in places, make a jumper dress from it. Cut away the neck, cut big armholes, and make the shoulders of a width becoming to your height and size. Face the neck and armholes with a matching colour of bias binding, and turn a new hem in the skirt. If you wish, finish the hem, neck and armholes with three rows of stitching. Wear the jumper over any smart blouse or sweater of a colour that contrasts or harmonizes with the dress material.

G. This shows a summer play frock made from an old party dress. If you have a party frock that has ceased to give you a thrill, or that you have worn too many times with the same people, salvage its good material and make a play-suit or garden dress of it. Make a snappy new skirt, a brief top and a plain little jacket. If the original dress had a jacket, by all means use that. **G-1** shows a brief top that was recut from an outmoded dress.

H. Here is a good-looking afternoon or day-time dress made over from an old evening dress. Cut off the bottom to make the dress a becoming street length. Use the cut-away skirt part to add to your blouse part and make short sleeves. You may have to cut the sleeves on the bias, but even so, if the fabric is good and you plan your dress carefully, it can look just as good as new!

TOO GOOD TO THROW AWAY

IF THE FABRIC of a garment is good and its design, colour and texture appeal to you though the usefulness of the garment has gone, make the fabric into something that you will enjoy wearing.

A. The small sketch next to **A** shows a dilapidated housecoat with torn sleeves and frayed collar. The material of this housecoat was entirely recut and made into an over-all apron. Good-sized pockets were added, and the armholes were made large for ease in working. The original zipper on the front of the housecoat was retained for the front opening. All the worn part of the original garment was cut away in making this new garment which gave many months of service.

B shows an organdie party frock that was once gay and perky, but it hung in the cupboard for so long that it was droopy and forlorn-looking and no longer had that crisp, new feeling that looks good in organdie. So it was made into a charming Sunday-night-supper or special party apron. Possibly in an organdie dress that you have there is enough material to make two such gay, colourful aprons. And you can probably count on having just as grand a time in your new apron as you had in your original party frock, with twice as much use from the fabric, see **A** on page 154 for mitreing a square yoke; look at page 155 for instructions on applying a patch pocket.

C. If there is a rubberized silk bathroom curtain in your home that has served too long as a curtain, why not make it into an apron? It will protect your frocks, gain a new lease of life, and give you a plus value. Rubberized silk is easy to sew. Hem it by machine just as you would any other fabric. Choose any pattern that allows you to cut the apron from your curtain and that will give you a style of apron that you like.

D. House dresses and out-of-fashion sports dresses hang in cupboards for weeks, or even months, without being worn, or they get pushed around in the clothes basket and are not ironed, simply because they have lost their appeal. If you have some garments like this, why not make them into over-all aprons? Cut out the worn collar line, cut away the sleeves and bind or face the openings neatly, using the material you have cut away. If the dress was open all the way down the front, the chances are that the front opening is worn and the buttonholes are pulled out. In that case, add a strip of embroidery insertion, or a strip of cotton plaid—something to dress it up and allow you to cut away all the buttonhole and button sections. Big patch pockets—hold-alls for your housekeeping " handies "—are desirable.

E. Summer linen slacks have been very popular in the past, and when they become worn or lose their shape they can be turned very easily into smart attractive aprons. Open the legs of such slacks and smoooth them out. Place your pattern so as to cut the apron on the bias. You should have easily enough fabric to make an apron with a bib and shoulder straps, and a big pocket.

F. From an old loose-cover that has seen better days, but still is not completely worn out, cut out a practical, distinctive apron. If the fabric is too faded and drab, a little dye will give it new colour to go with the colour scheme of your kitchen or your basic house dresses. The durability of such fabric will well repay you for the care in making a smartly tailored, well-put-together apron.

G shows an apron made of a large-patterned fabric. This, of course, can be made from any print, but if you have a short length of fabric with an attractive motif, then use it to make an apron.

If you have had some charming chintz or cretonne on a window, and part of it has faded, or you have decided to change your room furnishings and your fabric does not fit in with your colour scheme, why not use that fabric for short, gay aprons—the kind you can put on and take off quickly? Cretonne and chintz usually wear well and are easy to handle. If you were foresighted in the beginning, you chose your favourite colours for the curtain and, therefore, can continue to enjoy them in your apron.

H. Here we have a short smock cut from an old curtain. Usually the bottom part of the curtain is worn, being exposed to the weather when the window is up, but the top part is good. Cut your smock from the top part.

I. Note this dirndl apron made from an old dress. Such an apron can be made by cutting away the worn parts and making new seams. It is often possible to make such an apron from the bottom part of an old housecoat, and very little alteration is involved.

Plain-coloured percale is nice to use for bands, pockets and collars or remade fabrics. Percale costs very little by the yard, and half a yard will go a long way in remaking a garment.

Ready-made binding is also practical for finishing such garments and sometimes will simplify the making considerably. It is very attractive too.

The materials mentioned here are simply to give you suggestions as to what you can do with garments and other articles that have lost their original usefulness. These same ideas are applicable to remnants, or in re-using whatever fabrics you have that could be put to practical use for the types of garments shown.

The fashion pattern books always illustrate patterns for attractive aprons that conform to the fashionable dress silhouette. Choose one that will serve as a basic apron pattern from which you may derive several that would be smart and practical. It can't fail to be economical when you use fabrics you have on hand and need to buy only the ever-essential matching thread for the stitching.

Many women have made suits out of upholstery fabric, play suits from old curtains and bedspreads, table linens from old linen skirts and from draperies, women's slacks from men's old corduroy trousers. Every wearable type of fabric, if good enough for ripping and remaking, can find its place in a garment. Many women, having bought a new pattern for play clothes or house dresses, cut and make the garment first out of old material to make sure that the new fabric may be cut advantageously and to fit the garment correctly and becomingly.

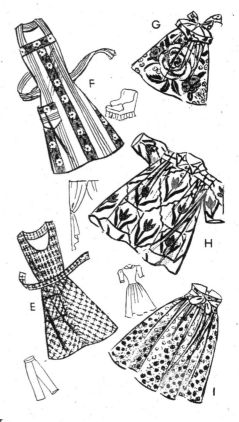

171

CAN YOU TOP THIS?

EACH ILLUSTRATION HERE shows a new top added to a garment to make it look entirely new. Each garment tries to outdo the next in both economy and wearability.

A. At the upper right, see a refashioned dress. The tiny sketch shows the original dress, which had a self yoke and short, skimpy sleeves, and looked lifeless and dilapidated. Five-eighths yard of 40-in. plaid rayon, a little time and sewing skill made it as good as new. The worn parts were cut away and a new yoke, sleeves and collar put in, the yoke extending straight across the back. A new hemline on the skirt was possible because the dress needed to be a little shorter than formerly. The old sleeves were used to make a new belt by piecing at the centre-front and centre-back, and buttons were used for trimming. The slide fastener at the left side seam was removed and replaced in a newly made placket, see page 36. It is important to re-do a placket when a dress has been cleaned and pressed many times, because sometimes the placket gets out of shape, as well as shabby. Make a new seam and put the slide fastener in again for better fit and a smarter body line.

B Here 1½ yds. of piqué make a bolero and a new sash belt. This bolero allows one to take the sleeves out of an old dress, cut a new neckline, and thus make an underdress that is quite satisfactory. Face the armholes and neckline with bias strips cut from the sleeves, see page 33 for instructions for doing this. If necessary, turn a new hemline on the skirt. If the skirt is skimpy, lift it up at the waistline, refit it there, let out the hem, and stitch or face the edge. In this way it will look like new. Boleros are easy to make. They may have round or square corners in the front, long or short sleeves. They may be made with or without a collar and be trimmed in many ways with braid, ribbon, organdie ruffling. The essential is to have them fit nicely on the shoulders and to be in their entirety appropriate for the dress.

C. One yard of 40-in. material makes a yoke front and back, a collar and long sleeves. Any plain blouse pattern that has a smart collar and the type of sleeves you like is satisfactory for cutting such a dress. Stitch around the yoke line, as shown, so that you take away the plainness from the front of the blouse. The irregular line helps to blend the yoke and the body part of

the blouse. If the underarms of the blouse are worn, take some of the material from the top of the old sleeves and insert a panel along the underarm, removing all the worn parts.

D. A shabby jacket and an old dress are put together here to make one good dress. Remake the skirt of the dress, use the blouse part for new sleeves, and make the body part of the blouse from the best parts of the old jacket. A bargain remnant of just enough material to make the body part of the blouse may be used together with an old dress in the same way. You may be able to buy a generous skirt length and have enough fabric left from cutting the skirt to make two-piece sleeves. Combine this with a remnant that is just enough to make the bodice part of the top. Be sure always that you use colours that go together, make a smart ensemble, and are fashionable and flattering to you; also, that your textures harmonize in weight and wearability. Work for smartness. Never let your dresses look made over. Strive to have them look as though you planned them and made them from new materials.

E Here is an excellent example of what to do with an out-of-date print dress. Plain rayons are very inexpensive; you can buy them for only a few shillings a yard. Such a sheer fabric makes a practical coat to wear over a print dress whose sleeves long ago ceased to be good. Use the sleeve tops to restore the blouse part where it is worn. Cut away the old neckline and face the armholes and neckline as you did in B. Make the over-all coat softly full. Apply a continuous band 1 in. wide round the front, neck edge and bottom edge; also on the sleeve edges, see page 35. Make a tie sash 1¼ ins. wide. If you wish, top-stitch this on, when finished, to hold the waistline fulness nicely and to insure an even hemline. You can wear such a coat with several different dresses, even dresses that have sleeves. Some like this type of wrap made sleeveless with a circular cape that comes slightly above the waistline. Sometimes the cape is stitched on and turned back to serve as a finish for the neckline. Such a cape should be bound on the edges with an imitation French fold.

F. If you have a print that you adore, refashion the skirt; refit it around the waist; turn a new hemline; make a new placket. Cut up the worn

172

part of the blouse of the dress into true bias strips 2¼ ins. wide, see page 9. Seam these together to make about 5 yds. of bias. Fold the strip and stitch the two raw edges together to make a double ruffle, which is then used to trim a blouse of plain fabric, as shown. Your finished result is a smart outfit. The fabric for the blouse can be any firm rayon crepe, " sharkskin," piqué—anything that will harmonize with the fabric of your print skirt and not be too heavy to go smartly with it.

G. Every girl who likes to wear slacks or to rough it in the country, or who enjoys wearing her coat in school, will like a jacket like this. It is made from an old wool skirt and a ¾-yd. remnant of 54-in. wool fabric. The old skirt makes the lining for the jacket, the sleeves, and the collar, and the new length makes the body of the coat and the big generous pockets. Use any plain, short coat pattern to cut this.

H. If you have a very good, substantial skirt that is out of fashion, or is too short or too snug around the hips, or is for any reason unwearable —recut it into a shoulder cape. Make it as long as fashion and your skirt length allow. Use bright-coloured velveteen, flannel, or printed cotton to line it. Work for effect, and you should have a smart cape at very little cost. The fashion periodicals always show one or more attractive cape patterns. Use one as a cutting guide, and tailor your cape according to the instructions that come with the pattern. Capes go out of fashion less quickly than almost any other article of wear. Therefore, when making or buying a cape, choose a conservative style and be able to wear it at intervals over a decade. Do not casually recut your cape into another garment unless you can make a good salvage.

173

LET'S MAKE IT FOR JUDY OR JACK

CHILDREN'S GARMENTS may be made successfully, and at a saving, from old clothing. Before undertaking to make over for children, consider the following:

TIME SAVER QUIZ

1. Is the fabric worthy of my time?
2. Is it easy to wash and keep in repair?
3. Is it worth the expense of needed new material?
4. Is it in suitable colour and weave for a child?
5. Is it right for the child who is to wear it?

If satisfied that results will be worth while, then:

1. Wash, or clean the garment.
2. Rip it apart, or, if the garment is large enough, cut it apart at the seams.
3. Mark each piece with chalk or basting stitches to indicate the lengthwise thread and the right side, if necessary.
4. Tint or dye the material, if desired.
5. Draw a chalk line or baste around parts that show too much wear.
6. Decide whether wrong side may be better for the "new" garment.

Select the Pattern. A good pattern is so important in making any garment, but particularly so when making over an old garment. Choose a pattern having a number of small pieces, as the old material may be quite cut up, or piece your fabric before laying the pattern on it. Select the style with an eye to combining another material with the original to eke out a garment, or to give old material a fresh look.

Choose a pattern that has a simple closing. A "remake" usually requires extra piecing lines, and inconspicuous or back closings are best. Consider the child's personality. The athletic child may be hampered and unhappy in a sheer, frilly frock that would bring pride and confidence to the shy child.

Examine the pattern to know how to piece the garment sections successfully. Piecings may be introduced to add new lines to a garment or they may be concealed on inside facing pieces, belts, collar linings and at similar points.

Sewing Without Patterns. Some simple garments for children may be made without patterns. Accurate measurements and sewing experience are required when cutting directly on the material, however, and unless one has a special interest in this type of work, it is not recommended. Small,

simple patterns, as collars, aprons and sunsuits, however, may often be cut successfully from paper by following the lines of an old garment.

To Let Down or Let Out. To extend dresses for growing girls, let out hems and seams, insert bands, belts, yokes and pleats. Take out sleeves or rip off the waists to make jumper and suspender dresses.

Drop the Hem. If the entire hem width is required to get the length, the dress must be faced. When adding a hem facing, use material like the dress, or similar in weight and colour, or use a bright contrasting colour with rickrack or binding put on over the joining.

If a dress has faded, and the underside of the hem is brighter, or if the old hem turn is worn thin from laundering, the method for lengthening shown in **A** is suggested, see *Drooping Hem Lines*, page 105. This plan tends to make the difference in the material less noticeable and hides the worn hem edge. It does take up some of the length, however. When the full length is required, try covering the old hem line with a strip of rickrack, or any similar trimming that fashion suggests.

When More Than the Hem is Needed. If a hem is not enough, you may add a false hem, insert a band, or put a new top on the skirt, see **B**, **C**, **D** and **E**. If the blouse section is short also, supply a girdle, as in **F**. There are always current style

features that can be used to camouflage the lengthening and make it seem planned.

To Trim or Not to Trim. A made-over garment is too often regarded as a make-shift, but if it is worth making over at all, it should be worth the few extra stitches needed to make it look like a completely new dress.

Often, in addition to making it look brand-new, a touch of hand embroidery may be used to cover defects in made-over materials. Look over the suggestions for amusing and decorative patches, page 63, and try out some of the embroidery stitches on pages 16 and 17.

Ready-made trimmings are also practical and effective. Bias binding, rickrack, embroidered bands and lace edgings are helpful.

Tucks may be used for trimming only, or to cover piecing lines that may be necessary in remaking for children, see page 28 for ways to use tucks.

Appliquéd designs cut in the shapes of flowers or animals and applied to a not-too-faded dress may be used to give a dress a lift or to cover a darn or a tell-tale ink spot that won't wash out.

Collars and cuffs of fresh piqué, organdie, lace, plaid or checked silks or ribbon provide simple ways to dress up Judy's limp frock. The sections on lace, taffeta and eyelet embroidery, pages 166, 160 and 154, may give some inspirations for children's clothes as well as for your own.

A new tie, belt and buttons will enhance Jack's well-worn suit. New varicoloured ribbon bands and bows make an important change for a dress. Belts of ribbon are always in favour with young folks.

Tie Closings. Use tie fasteners of narrow tape or ribbon, as in **A,** or wider ties of material for first garments, and tot's dresses, as in **B.** Tie fasteners are not easy for a child to handle, and should be avoided on garments for children who are learning to dress themselves.

OUT-OF-FASHION
HOUSECOATS—ROBES

THESE GARMENTS too often go out of style before they are worn out, but they can be used to make sturdy and attractive little housecoats, robes, pyjamas, nightgowns or play suits. Some robes will provide corduroy for overalls and jackets, trousers and caps. Flannel robes can make winter play suits, skirts, tams or small bath robes and slippers.

As a rule, such garments should be completely ripped, cleaned and refashioned to make smart, becoming clothes. If the lining of a housecoat is worn, buy a new brighter coloured one. Work for effect, and consider the child and his pleasure as you reconstruct new garments for him. The garments illustrated may suggest an idea for you. Most of these things for satisfactory results should be cut from good patterns. Consult the pattern books and magazines for styles appropriate for your child.

A is a nightie made from a cotton hostess gown. B is a negligé from one of taffeta. C is a boy's bathrobe made from a man's. D is a pair of pyjamas made from an adult's pair that had shrunk. E and F show possibilities for a girl's or boy's suit from an old corduroy bathrobe. G is a pair of overalls made from a flannel shirt, with an appliquéd motif on the bib part; H, overalls from a corduroy robe. I shows a charming little dress and cap made from a flannel skirt and gaily embroidered, and J a play suit with matching cap from a flannel robe.

The last few items are wool embroidered. The big easy stitches are so quick to do and provide so much colour and help in banishing drabness that they often are well worth any effort necessary in their making.

PLAY CLOTHES FROM HOME FURNISHINGS

MATERIALS IN THE HOME, other than from clothing, can be made into children's clothes. Cotton and lightweight velveteen draperies may be made into play suits; cretonnes will make sunsuits and pinafores.

Drapery fabrics are usually sturdy enough to be practical for play clothes for children. Use bold or gay designs to make attractive and colourful garments, choose styles for comfort and freedom. Scraps of left-over oilcloth, too, will provide bibs, aprons, soles for bedroom slippers and washable toys.

Hats and Tams. Hats and tams may be made from scraps left over from jackets, coats or dresses. Old garments, including knitted sweaters, will also provide material. For trimming use ribbon bands, bows, wool yarn, embroidery, tassels or buttons.

Make winter caps for small children from the legs of old wool socks, especially colourful sports socks. Cut the foot off, leaving 10 ins. or 12 ins. Gather the top tightly and finish it with a button that has been covered with a scrap of the sock.

Mittens and Gloves. Knit mittens and gloves from reclaimed yarn and embroider the backs of the " dress-up " pair. Make play-time mittens on the sewing machine from old machine-knit sweaters or heavy socks. Cut a pattern about ¾ in. larger all round than the child's hand and wrist. Seam the mitten, overcast the seams and wrist end, and make snug with a little elastic at the back. Mittens may also be made from velvet or soft wool cloth.

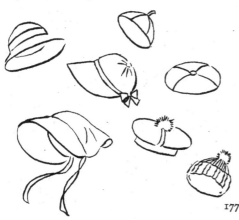

INDEX

INDEX

INDEX

INDEX

INDEX